introduction to early childhood education

introduction to early childhood education

Ruth H. Nixon and Clifford L. Nixon
Pembroke State University

Random House  New York

Copyright © 1970, 1971 by Ruth H. Nixon and Clifford L. Nixon.
All rights reserved under International and Pan-American Copyright Conventions.
Published in the United States by Random House, Inc., New York, and simultaneously
in Canada by Random House of Canada Limited, Toronto.

ISBN: 0-394-31020-9

Library of Congress Catalog Card Number: 72–125500

Manufactured in the United States of America. Composed by Cherry Hill
Composition, Pennsauken, New Jersey. Printed and bound by Halliday Lithograph
Corp., West Hanover, Mass.

Cover Design and Typography by Karin Batten

First Edition

9876543

The list of recommended equipment and supplies in Chapter 18 is reprinted from the
Association for Childhood Education International's Bulletin 39, *Equipment and Supplies*.
Reprinted by permission of the Association for Childhood Education International,
3615 Wisconsin Avenue, N.W., Washington, D.C. Copyright © 1968, by the Association.

We wish to thank Mr. B. O. Wilson, former Superintendent of Schools in Contra Costa
County, California, for permission to quote from Bulletin 102, *On Relaxation*, published by
Contra Costa County.

Photo credits: *Part I:* from *Following Through with Young Children*, written and
photographed by Elizabeth T. Kellogg with Dorothy M. Hill. Reprinted with permission from
Following Through with Young Children. Copyright © 1969, National Association for the
Education of Young Children. *Part II:* The Merrill-Palmer Institute, by Donna J. Harris.
Reprinted with permission from *Young Children*, Vol. XXIV, No. 3, January 1969. Copyright
© 1969, National Association for the Education of Young Children. *Part III and Cover:*
The Merrill-Palmer Institute, by Donna J. Harris. *Part IV:* Anne Zane Shanks and Comco, Inc.
Part V: The Merrill-Palmer Institute, by Donna J. Harris. *Part VI:* from *Following Through
with Young Children*, written and photographed by Elizabeth T. Kellogg with Dorothy
M. Hill. Reprinted with permission from *Following Through with Young Children*. Copyright
© 1969, National Association for the Education of Young Children.

Dedicated to L. L. Murray, without whose
encouragement and support this would neither
have been begun nor completed.

Preface

Writing a book about the art of educating young children is a delightful assignment because it deals with one of the most important and interesting subjects possible. Each child is unique. The task of helping children learn is complex but highly rewarding.

There are other valuable, interesting books in the field. In the course of our discussion we recommend many of them. The natural question is, "Why then this particular book?" The answer is that it has its own unique purposes.

The first and most obvious purpose is to more adequately cover the age range, three through eight. Educators are coming to consider this age range as a logical unit of study. A statement of purpose by The National Association for the Education of Young Children reads in part:

Today's concept of early childhood education now includes the nursery, kindergarten, and primary years as a psychological entity requiring consistence in the child's development of concepts, relationships, and positive attitudes toward himself and his achievements. This is essential preparation for the more organized school life to follow.

Although this view is finding increasing acceptance, as yet it is not adequately reflected in current texts. The acceptance is being formalized by agencies authorizing credentials and by official college courses. The lack of adequate texts can be verified by examining the best books on the market. They deal with the nursery and/or the kindergarten—perhaps with passing reference to the primary years—or with the elementary grades with little or no discussion of the earlier years. This text recognizes that there are no hard-and-fast cut-off lines in the education of the individual. However, it specifically aims at the period that is generally considered as belonging to the field of early childhood education.

The second reason for this volume is more complex. It differs in its approach to the problem of early childhood education. It attempts to present certain general and potentially unifying concepts and their practical application. None of the ideas discussed are in themselves unique. Many of the observations made must still be tentative. In the very nature of the attempt some will be oversimplifications. We hope, however, that the ideas and the applications as presented and illustrated contain elements of originality and creativity that are stimulating.

A final purpose is to offer the possibility of reconciliation with reference to some of the divergent tendencies within the field of early childhood education. Probably the most exciting aspects of such education are some of the interesting learning experiments being conducted that raise questions about present theory. Few of the findings are conclusive. However, they are suggestive and thought provoking. In this text we hope to present the basic concepts of early childhood education but so expanded as to incorporate current research and conclusions dealing with effective learning by young children.

In this endeavor the authors have considered their primary audience to be teachers and prospective teachers. We see a special value in the book as one of the texts for teachers updating their credentials. This is pertinent because so little opportunity was offered in years past for the teacher to obtain a comprehensive view of the total field of early childhood education. This text can provide stimulation to the experienced teacher. It should be equally helpful to the prospective teacher.

In writing the authors have also kept in mind the interested lay person, particularly, the parent. The public faces many problems and decisions in the field of education. Such individuals should be both concerned and knowledgeable.

The authors have a deep concern for the relationship between both parent and child and parent and teacher, and throughout the text we have stressed these relationships. The entire book is intended to present concepts as potentially useful to the concerned parent as to the competent teacher.

Acknowledgments

We wish to express our appreciation to Dr. Daniel E. Todd, Jr., for assistance in reading the manuscript, and checking the content with reference to the accuracy of the statements about public education. Mrs. Shirley Pennington carried the chief burden of manuscript preparation. A host of people directly and indirectly have contributed ideas and assistance. These include fellow professors and college students (graduate and undergraduate) who have contributed from their experiences and observations. They include a host of children—taught, counseled, or known through the work of others.

Contents

introduction to early childhood education

Introduction

This is a book about the education of young children in the United States as we enter the 1970s. It centers on the six-year period in the life of the child from the age of three through age eight and it covers an educational continuum from nursery school through what is usually called the third grade.

No absolute boundaries can be applied to either the age or educational range of early childhood. As a matter of fact, this text will sometimes wander beyond the suggested limits. Both learning and growth for children are basically a continuum. Growth begins with conception, and that event is, itself, a link in a chain that reaches back through the ages. Learning for the individual goes back at least to birth, if not beyond. In a social and historical sense all learning is rooted in the totality of human experience of all kinds.

One may categorically set the age of three as the minimum entrance age into nursery school—and three is the most commonly accepted limit. However, there are schools that accept two year olds. The National Education Association (NEA) has recognized that the three-year old standard is frequently not honored and the future norm for "organized" groups for toddlers is being lowered. In a supplement to its journal it discussed the concept of small neighborhood groups for two year olds.[1] Some programs today even make provisions for infants and toddlers.

[1] Harold G. Shane and June Grant Shane, "Forecast for the 70's," *Today's Education*, LVIII (January 1969), 9.

1

This text begins with the three year old because currently three is the usual minimum age for the nursery school child. In addition, there seems to be a consensus developing among educators and psychologists that the period from three through eight forms a logical and psychological unit in the life of the child.

There is, of course, no definite cut-off point at the age of eight (grade three). Children differ greatly at birth, and as they move on through life, their differences become even more pronounced. A few children at the age of eight still need what is sometimes called a transitional kindergarten-first-grade experience. Other children at eight have moved far beyond the usual third-grade curriculum. In the development of most children there is generally no striking change in the third and the fourth grades. The fourth grader is older; he is also moving toward closer identification with his own sex. But basically he is the same child, only chronologically one year older. In many states there is a tendency toward a shift in the curriculum structure at these graded levels from broad education with special emphasis on the skills to a study of specific subjects. If primary schools for ages 3 to 8 should become one of the common patterns in America, as is implied by the acceptance of this six-year "block," the authors' main concern is that the transition to the next level be made as happy an experience as possible. Whether the shift comes between what is now known as the third and fourth grades or between the fourth and fifth matters little—what is of the utmost importance is that teachers of young children be as fully prepared as possible for the important work of teaching the age group with which they will work.

There are several factors which enhance the probability of an increased emphasis on the education of children in the age range discussed in this text. Among these factors is the current expansion of nursery school education.

As an overall movement, it is probably growing even more rapidly than the opposite extreme—college education. Concern for such education as to the quality of nursery and then kindergarten education and the adaptation of primary education to cope successfully with the needs of all children are matters of increasing discussion and research. Before we examine the type of education needed, we shall briefly review the development of early childhood education.

Historical Perspectives on Early Childhood Education

Probably every great educational thinker in history has had something to say that has bearing, either directly or indirectly, on the field of early childhood education. Plato had a plan that would appeal to modern educators, and while his overall plan was greatly affected by the then recent disastrous war with Sparta, Plato's reactions to this defeat were somewhat different than that of many Americans to the Russian launching of Sputnik. Perhaps that is chiefly because the threat was different.

Sparta won, not because the Spartans were better educated, but because they were tougher and better trained for war. Thus Plato would stress physical education in his program, teach stories and songs to lay a foundation for heroism, and reform the literary program to omit the stories of sexual misconduct of the gods. Even though there are some underlying objectional elements in his program, Plato's envisioned early childhood program might have been more fun than some primary programs that can be observed today.[2]

Jesus said many things that could be applied to education and to the education of the young child—specifically, "Let the children come to me, and do not hinder them; for to such belongs the kingdom of heaven."[3] These words have other applications, but they do emphasize the importance of the young child more graphically than anything John Dewey said. They are in harmony with one of the few concepts that almost all people believe about the education of young children. There may be disagreement as to "where we go from here," but all educators recognize the child's need for welcome, acceptance, and concern.

Comenius, the seventeenth-century Moravian educational reformer, was concerned with phases of early childhood education as school experience as well as with the training of mothers.[4] Rousseau recognized childhood as a distinct and important period in the education of individuals.[5] Pestalozzi was involved with the training of children in the home as witnessed by his series of "Gertrude" books.[6] He was also concerned with the education of young children and, particularly, the socially disadvantaged. He did much of his teaching by providing concrete experiences. This was undergirded with an intense concern and love. If space permitted, one could show a relationship to the education of the very young from the work of many others, including the Swiss psychologist J. Piaget, whose concepts of stages of intellectual development are pertinent and influential in early childhood education. Much that Dewey said is pertinent and valuable though sadly, it may be easier to put over an idea as a successful Russian innovation than to sell the theories attributed to this great American philosopher and benefactor of American children.

In the current scene there are many whose work is relevant and whose contributions have made lasting marks on preschool education.

Jerome Bruner, for example, places great emphasis on making education meaningful at all levels. It is Bruner who has done the most to gain acceptance of the fact that a wide range of academic subject matter is adaptable to kindergarten investigation.[7] He contends—and we agree—that the important

[2] See Plato, *Republic,* from *Dialogues of Plato* (New York: Pocket, 1951), pp. 253–255.

[3] *Revised Standard Version of the Bible* (Camden, N.J.: Thomas Nelson, 1953), Matt. 19:14.

[4] S. J. Curtis and M. E. A. Boultwood, *A Short History of Educational Ideas* (London: University Tutorial Press, 1953), pp. 195–201.

[5] Robert Ulich, *History of Educational Thought* (New York: American Book, 1950), p. 219.

[6] H. G. Good, *A History of Western Education* (New York: Macmillan, 1949), pp. 231–247.

[7] Jerome S. Bruner, *The Process of Education* (New York: Vintage Books, 1960), Chapter 2.

element of learning is the basic structure of the subject, that that basic structure tends to be simple, and that it can be presented in some meaningful and intellectually honest way at any level.

The work of B. F. Skinner[8] should be recognized as pertinent to early childhood education. Carl Bereiter, for example, in his model for teaching the disadvantaged child, makes use of the concepts of operant conditioning,[9] concepts most closely identified with the work of Skinner. The present authors belong to a different school of psychology. They would put teaching in terms of conditioning as a last resort. But regardless of this, there is abundant evidence that the young child when frustrated by the complexities of a task may need patient help in moving by small steps toward the desired goal.

In the field of early childhood education there is no one outstanding name associated with the full age range of the interest of this book. Many have been involved, including those early Puritans of Massachusetts who more than a century before the founding of this federal republic declared that public education must be provided for the children of that colony.

Frederick Froebel[10] is usually considered the "father" of the kindergarten. In the early 1840s in Germany he established a school for young children, named it a Kindergarten, and developed a program. That program laid great emphasis on educational "play" materials. Most modern educators would be amused by his feeling that these materials had deep spiritual significance. But the most generally accepted model of the American kindergarten and of the nursery school and combinations of the two is clearly related to Froebel's concept of the use of materials, which, in the context of his time, combined the elements of play and educational discovery.

One regrets that Maria Montessori cannot honestly be called the "mother" of the day-care center. The denial to her of this title certainly is not meant to reflect on her importance or on her teaching. Even before she became the director of what we would call a day-care center in Rome, she had accomplished much. She had the distinction of being the first woman physician in Italy. Early in her medical career she was appointed assistant doctor at the Psychiatric Clinic in the University of Rome. Part of her duty was to visit "asylums for the insane" in Rome. In the course of her duties she became intensely interested in the plight of the children of the inmates who were confined in the same institutions and were known as "idiot" children. In one institution she came across a number of children herded together in a prison-like room. The room had no toys or materials of any kind. Montessori was instrumental in the establishment of a special school to which these and other retarded children were brought. E. M. Standing writes of the resulting achievement:

[8] B. F. Skinner, *Science and Human Behavior* (New York: Free Press, 1953), Chapters 5 and 6.
[9] Carl Bereiter and Siegfried Engelmann, *Teaching Disadvantaged Children in the Preschool* (Englewood Cliffs, N.J.: Prentice-Hall, 1966).
[10] Clarice Dechent Wills and Lucille Lindberg, *Kindergarten for Today's Children* (Chicago: Follett, 1967), p. 52.

Such indeed was her success that a number of idiot children from the asylums learned to read and write so well that they were able to present themselves with success at a public examination taken together with normal children.[11]

In accomplishing this seeming miracle Dr. Montessori and her associates developed and employed a variety of educational play equipment. She, herself, was careful not to attribute the entire success of the venture to the materials used. Her statement concerning this experience reads in part:

I . . . believed that not the didactic material, but my voice which called to them, awakened the children, and encouraged them to use the didactic material, and through it, to educate themselves. I was guided in my work by the deep respect which I felt for their misfortune, and by the love which these unhappy children know how to awaken in those who are near them.[12]

This passage embodies one of the problems of educational research. To what extent is change brought about by technology and to what extent does it represent differences in the communication of those who employ the methods. Froebel and Montessori disagree in part on these points. But both agreed on, and practiced love and respect for children and childhood.

The day-care experimental program that Montessori set up was really established as an economic expedient, not as an altruistic venture. In Rome a large apartment complex was deteriorating because the working parents were away. Their children below school age were left unsupervised and naturally did much damage. The owners decided that it might be cheaper to provide some kind of care for the children than to constantly repair their property. Maria Montessori was asked to undertake the job of supervising the sixty children from ages three to six. Her helpers were two untrained women. For the sponsors the program was a dollar-and-cents proposition, not an educational endeavor.

Although she could only devote part of her time to the project, through the months Maria Montessori put into practice theories that she had already developed. In addition, she tested others that she learned from her observation and work with the children. She observed that some children worked long and hard repeating manipulative tasks. Many have since confirmed this. John Holt points out that no one experience is sufficient to convince a young child of the rightness of any conclusion.[13] Montessori also concluded that the child was the best judge of what he was ready to attempt. She observed that through sensory perception—feeling sandpaper letters, and so forth— children could learn to write and then to read. Her ideas, these and many others, deserve careful consideration.

---

[11] E. M. Standing, *Maria Montessori: Her Life and Work* (New York: New American Library, 1962), p. 30.

[12] Maria Montessori, *The Montessori Method* (New York: Stokes, 1912), p. 37.

[13] John Holt, *How Children Learn* (New York: Pitman, 1967), pp. 24–26.

Almost from the time of Dr. Montessori's day care experiment, her work and theories had been admired by many in the United States and other parts of the world. During the first years of World War I she considered making her headquarters in the United States and was offered substantial backing toward the establishment of a training center. She lectured in this country in 1915 and was well received, but declined all offers to continue her work here. There have been Montessori schools, and to some extent Montessori concepts have influenced education, in subsequent years. The past decade, however, has witnessed a marked increase in both. Montessori schools now flourish in many parts of the country, though, ironically, they generally serve the affluent. They are usually well staffed, superbly equipped, and expensive. Only a few seem to be making efforts to provide for the kind of disadvantaged children the original project served. Educational devices similar to those Montessori developed are in use in many nurseries, day care centers, public and private kindergartens and primary classrooms. Unfortunately, perhaps, not all of those who make use of such materials are aware of either Dr. Montessori's contribution to their development or the educational context in which she intended their use.

The Current Situation

Of the whole range of early childhood education programs, the most recent and most complex development has been at the nursery level. Child care itself is as old as human existence. Present trends are concerned with the increasing need for care outside the home and the increasing recognition of the educational possibilities inherent in nursery school programs.

Each society in which mothers have worked has found some means of caring for young children. These may have no definite connection with organized programs of education, or they may be fully integrated into such programs. One can easily illustrate the concept of care with relatively little concern for education either from current practices in the United States or from more primitive cultures. Without a doubt, the reader would have little difficulty in citing an example from his own experience. The authors, for instance, have a friend who had supplemented her income by serving as an assistant in a private day care nursery for working mothers. This was her only training in child care—apart from raising several children of her own. She eventually decided that it would be more profitable to take care of children in her own home and yard. The state did not even require she have a license. Her "sitter" service has been a successful operation for several years. The children are kept safe and happy, and there are undoubtedly aspects of education in that small hill-top nursery. But the chief idea is simply to provide a safe place to leave children while the mothers are working.

In primitive societies it was commonplace for young children to be cared for by others while the mothers attended to the duties demanded from them by their society. The eminent anthropologist Margaret Mead points out in *Coming of Age in Samoa* that all small children were turned over at a very early age to the care of only slightly older female siblings or other close and young female relatives—young children caring for even younger children.[14] (It should be noted that both programs are in harmony with the social standards of their respective societies.)

It would be simpler to describe the programs for the care of young children of certain foreign nations than the current scene in America. Several of these programs, particularly those in communistic countries provide child care almost from birth on. Frequently there is a specific program for the age range of four through seven. One program in a noncommunist nation involves the traditionally socialistic Kibbutzim (communal farming communities) of modern Israel. The Kibbutz children, representing less than 5 percent of the total child population of Israel, are cared for in the Kibbutz programs from the first weeks of life through high school. These children have been of great interest to educators and others.[15] Educators have been particularly interested in the practice of placing children from about the age of four through seven in a nonpressuring learning situation that leads them gradually and successfully to "academic readiness."

The Nursery School

In the United States provisions for public nursery schools are practically non-existent. Only a small number of communities—generally large cities—sponsor such facilities. In the past some provision had been made for the care of those few children whose mothers had to work, but almost the only organized nurseries were those sponsored by universities and colleges. These were provided primarily to serve the training needs of the schools rather than to care for any large number of children. The increasing entrance of women into occupations was given a tremendous boost by the exigencies of World War II. A natural consequence was the need for child care. Many child-care centers were formed, some run cooperatively, some conducted for a fee, some drawing federal emergency funds. The emphasis was on care, not education. Immediately after this there was a major decrease in the demand for this kind of care.

The overall change in the decade of the 1960s seems to stem from three major forces—(1) the increased employment of mothers, (2) educational results stemming from Sputnik, and (3) the war on poverty.

1. *Increased Employment of Mothers.* Although the employment of women declined at the end of World War II, it has been increasing ever since 1950.

[14] Margaret Mead, *Coming of Age in Samoa* (New York: Mentor, 1928) pp. 24–26.

[15] Urie Bronfenbrenner, "The Dream of the Kibbutz," *Saturday Review,* LII (September 20, 1969), 72–73, 83–85; Aliza Brandwine, "Upbringing of Children in Kibbutzim of Israel," *Young Children,* XXIV (May 1969), 265–272; and Leslie Y. and Karen Rabkin, "Children of the Kibbutz," *Psychology Today,* III (September 1969), 40–46.

If such women have small children, they must find some means of providing for their care. This care for the woman from the middle class in America has increasingly taken the form of enrollment in nursery school. These schools are mostly private, though there may be community, church, or service organization sponsorship. At first such care emphasized the safety and health of the child—any educational benefits were incidental. Today the emphasis is shifting.

2. *Educational Results Stemming from Sputnik.* The discovery that Russia was ahead of this country in space exploration came as a shock. For better or for worse, this led to an emphasis on learning more and learning it faster at all levels, including nursery schools.

There was a perceptible and deciding change in the total emphasis of nursery school education. Many credit Sputnik with the acceptance of the long rejected Montessori school. Whether Montessori, or otherwise oriented, the most exclusive of the nursery schools came to be geared to the competitive drive of the upper-middle-class American. And attendance at nursery school became a status symbol as well. At every level of the educational system—regardless of the region of the country—pressure was applied to achieve. The ultimate goal for the middle-class child was acceptance in an Ivy League college. This even permeated down to the nursery school level where the rumor was that the road to an Ivy League school began with acceptance in a supposed Ivy League nursery school. We shall not discuss here the pressures felt by the children nor the disastrous results for many—even in the elementary grades. It is to be hoped that this kind of pressure will not move down to the nursery school.

Most good nursery schools have no difficulty in fulfilling their promise to further the educational advancement of the students without resorting to pressure. The trained personnel are not adherents of high-pressure programs —be they Montessori trained or graduates of home economics departments of universities.

Another important development since Sputnik has been the realization that the ages from three to five are actually very important educationally. Montessori asserted this many years ago, but few heeded her. Now a host of psychological researchers and educational observers are confirming her finding.

3. *War on Poverty.* The final factor to be discussed is the attempted federal War on Poverty, which has included a number of provisions related to early childhood. Many have reason to believe that it was not a well-planned or adequately executed war even as related to early childhood education. But even with its many faults early childhood education may well have been the most effective aspect of the total program.

At the level of the three or four year old, the aid from the War on Poverty came in the form of Day Care Centers. This care is becoming more inclusive, and the term Child Development Center is being used more frequently. Such centers are designed primarily to meet the needs of the poor. They frequently operate in inadequate housing, but they do provide overall care that has included food, protection, recreational and enrichment experiences, educational experiences, supervision, and consultation. Generally, the staff includes some trained personnel plus supplementary personnel, trained or not. Where no public school kindergarten exists, the educational aspects of the program cover nursery and kindergarten. Where public school kindergartens are available, the program is on the nursery school level. The establishment of such programs in a community has depended on the existence of proven need, the presence of a local sponsoring organization, and the availability of funds.

Kindergarten

In some states the day care centers have been providing the equivalent of kindergarten programs for disadvantaged five-year-old children. There have been other federally sponsored programs that have had some effect on the kindergarten situation. One of these has been the summer Head Start program, a six- or eight-week program. There have been questions raised as to the effectiveness of Head Start. Perhaps the amazing thing is that it has been effective at all. Six or eight weeks is a very short time. Primary school teachers are not automatically good kindergarten teachers, and they have generally been employed as the teachers. Many programs have had difficulty getting underway because government funds have sometimes not been forwarded until after programs were expected to be operating. In fairness it should be noted that the operation of the program has improved. It should also be mentioned that much of the apparent failure of the Head Start program may be due more to the failure of first-grade teachers in the regular elementary school to adjust their programs to provide continued support and a program in which disadvantaged children could find continued success. William Glasser speaks grimly of Head Start programs as "similar to preparing a soldier for combat by sending him on a vacation to the Riviera."[16] He is not criticizing the Head Start program.

If any one date is of specific significance in the attempt to provide what is not too appropriately called "preschool" experience for the disadvantaged child, it would probably be 1965. It was then that the Congress of the United States passed the original Elementary and Secondary Education Act. This act has since been amended and expanded. It is under these amendments that some kindergarten programs have been established in certain school districts. Help provided for this purpose, as with other types of "preschool" programs assisted by federal funds, has been dependent on proven need and the approval of plans submitted by local authorities.

More than half of the five year olds in the United States are now attending state-supported public kindergartens. In 1966 only fifteen states provided kindergarten education on a statewide basis. These, however, included most

[16] William Glasser, *Schools Without Failure* (New York: Harper & Row, 1969), pp. 28–29.

of the largest and richest states, though not Texas or Alaska. The state of New York reported slightly more children in kindergarten, 287,700, than in first grade, 273,000. California had slightly fewer in kindergarten than first grade, 373,624 as opposed to 376,536. In some cases large cities had as many children in kindergarten as in first grade, whereas this was far from true for the state as a whole.[17] In all, approximately 66 percent of all five year olds were in some form of kindergarten in the fall of 1969.[18] This estimate includes all forms of kindergarten—state-supported, federally financed, parochial, and private. Obviously, millions of children are not attending any form of kindergarten. Even more children have no opportunity to attend either a state or federally supported program.

The gaps in the provision made by state and federal programs are partly made up by private and parochial schools. Almost all of these must charge at least a modest fee, a fee beyond the means or inclination of many families. The trend is clearly toward full state support for kindergartens. However, there will always be a need for private and parochial kindergartens, even in states that provide full public support. There is value in an alternative to public education.

Most states that do not have public kindergartens are moving in this direction. Sometimes the pace seems agonizingly slow. One of the authors served in 1967-68 on a subcommittee of the Governor's Commission on the study of education in the state of North Carolina. During one meeting it was pointed out that committees had been urging at regular intervals for decades the establishment of kindergartens and that nothing had happened yet. Something did happen, however, in the next session of the state legislature in Raleigh. Money was appropriated for state-supported pilot kindergarten programs. In further illustration of a general trend, it may be noted that South Carolina took somewhat similar action in the same legislative year. Virginia state law now provides for statewide, tax-supported kindergartens, but the state even in 1970 had not been able to implement the law completely. One problem was the lack of trained personnel.

The Primary Years

Traditionally American schools have been graded. A number of patterns have been tried. The most traditional pattern is grades one through eight and nine through twelve. Probably the second most commonly used organization has been grouping of grades one through six, seven through nine, and ten through twelve. Other combinations are possible and have been tried. There is a trend toward implementation of the concept of primary school, middle school, and high school. The authors envision an overall plan for young

---

[17] North Carolina State Department of Public Instruction, *Kindergarten Curriculum Guide*. preliminary draft for discussion purposes only. (Raleigh: State Department of Public Instruction, 1967), pp. 42–44.

[18] *U. S. News and World Report*, LXVII (September 8, 1969), 38.

children—nursery through primary—covering the six-year span, to include children from three years of age through approximately eight years of age, or what is usually called third grade.

More interesting and important than grade and age ranges have been attempts to formulate plans that will improve the learning experience. Project Follow Through,[19] for example, involves federally funded programs that attempt to lead the child on without disruptive changes in method from the beginnings made in Head Start programs. This is a "new" concept only in its application to disadvantaged children. Some schools have attempted this kind of transition from kindergarten to primary school for many years. What is significant is that educators now recognize that all schools need to implement what has been known for many years. Children differ and each one can only be taken on from *his* present level of achievement—not from one prescribed by a state department of education.

Included in the demand for change is the concept that no child should be labeled a failure before the age of eight. (We hope that this will be carrried through to all levels of education, but here we can only discuss early childhood education.) To achieve this goal, the best procedure appears to be a broad and ungraded approach in the primary school. Children do not learn at the same rate. Why should any school be bound by the tradition that a child either learns all of a certain subject range in a particular time period or repeats the entire "grade"? The concept of taking the child from where he is to as far as he can go without undue pressure makes sense. So does an increased emphasis on relevance to life and social situations, acceptance of cultural differences and honoring the abilities the child already possesses.

Such a program may well include the breaking down of units of learning into smaller sections to be mastered at the child's own speed. It may include the use of teaching devices and teaching assistants. It probably must include intensive study and special help for a small minority of children who are "blocked out" from phases of learning. Vital to all change is the attitude that every child is important and every child can be taught. A logical extension of the upgraded approach would be to discard the premise that preschool experience is distinct from school experience.

Nongrading the Antithesis to Social Promotion

The nongraded approach is *not* social promotion. The general public and many prospective teachers confuse the two ideas. Social promotion moves the child who has made little progress after spending one or more years in a grade on to the next. He may even be moved into high school without ever having learned to read. The authors have even been associated with classes for "functional illiterates" that contained high school graduates. The nongraded approach neither promotes the nonlearner nor holds back the learner.

[19] *Young Children,* XXIV (March 1969), 194.

It moves the child ahead as he learns. It is flexible. It labels no one a failure. Neither does it make necessary the pretense that any learning has been mastered when, in fact, it has not.

The authors are convinced that team teaching is a necessary adjunct to a nongraded program. A team of teachers, particularly when aided by capable assistants, can develop a program that provides both depth and flexibility. Like other educational innovations it can work only when people make it work. For it to be effective, teachers must be able to work together and be willing to try new approaches. Team teaching is being tried in various school systems throughout the United States. Sometimes it has been tied to experiments with nongrading but more frequently it has been done within the framework of the traditional grade setup. The results have varied, but when optimal conditions have existed, they have been most gratifying.

Purposes of the Book

This book could have been organized in various ways. It would have been relatively simple to have written first about the nursery school, then the kindergarten, and finally the primary age range. However, it was decided that a more meaningful organization would be to emphasize certain essential concepts as they relate to levels of early childhood education.

The text has been divided into six Parts. In Parts One through Four the theme is discussed in broad terms and then separate chapters are devoted to the application in the nursery, the kindergarten, and the primary levels. The chapters in the final two sections discuss themes related to the full range of early childhood education.

It is intended that *all* of the text be of value to persons concerned with the education of young children. The individual involved, for example, with primary children would be helped by the chapters on nursery and kindergarten education. Concepts examined in the chapters dealing with the education of the youngest children are not necessarily discussed in subsequent chapters, even when the first concepts might be useful to teachers of older children. Nevertheless, the reader interested in a specific level of early childhood education will have no difficulty in selecting the relevant chapters.

The underlying philosophy of the text is not outlined in technical terms. Instead, the authors in their presentation have aimed at conveying a particular point of view for the reader's consideration—that the education of young children is, to some extent, out of balance. The whole range of early childhood education needs to be brought into focus—a focus as free from distortion as possible.

The Introduction in each of the six sections explains more fully one phase of the basic premise. The chapters that complete the part illustrate the point and examine its application. The reader may judge for himself whether or not the situations under consideration need correction and if the remedies suggested are reasonable.

The themes of the six divisions of the text consist of paired concepts.

1. Choice and Responsibility
2. Problem Solving and Knowledge
3. Structure and Creativity
4. Skills and Insight
5. Goals and Perspectives
6. Materials and Resources

To some, except for the last part, they may appear to be conflicting ideas, but on examination the reader will discover that they are really dependent upon each other. The authors have attempted a balanced presentation of the concepts. However, there is a discernible emphasis that varies in degree in each Part. This reflects not so much a feeling as to what is true or important as it does a feeling as to what is more often neglected.

Choice

For example, the authors acknowledge that their discussion is weighted in preference of choice, even though choice can be hard to achieve. This is not because choice is more important; little meaningful choice is possible under conditions in which there is no responsible conduct. It is because choice seems in danger of being squeezed out of the school curriculum.

In the authors' opinion there is a need in education today for an emphasis on choice that leads to problem solving and permits creativity. These are basic elements of both skill and insight.

Problem Solving

Problem solving does not stand in contrast to knowledge as a goal in education. The two concepts are both interrelated and overlapping—knowledge can be so defined as to include the process and results of problem solving. The emphasis in the section devoted to problem solving and knowledge is placed on problem solving because of the danger of equating information and memory with knowledge. Both are a part of knowledge, but all teachers need to be constantly reminded that the active inquiring mind learns more and remembers longer. Furthermore, information that helps in the solution of problems—the problems of the learner—is more meaningful. It is more likely to become part of a body of knowledge that is being shaped and reshaped into an organized whole. The whole purpose of education is to assist people to develop the ability to face and solve personal problems and to show concern and contribute to the solution of the broader problems of society.

Creativity

Among highly creative artists, structure is the servant of creativity. Even for the normally creative adult creativity and structure may work in full harmony. For that matter some structure is present on every level. In all of early childhood education, however, the evident need is for greater freedom to express emotion and thought. Structure will come but the danger is chiefly on the side of too much, too soon.

Insight

It is with greater hesitancy that an emphasis is placed on insight rather than skills. Even on the nursery school level the authors see no conflict between the two. What they have witnessed on all levels is an overemphasis not so much on skill as on drill. Drill has a place if used appropriately. Skills are essential, but they interrelate with insight. Ultimately, the purpose of skills is to secure and communicate meaning.

Perspectives

The text is intended to express goals that seem in harmony with the main stream of historical, educational thought in Western culture. There is no intended controversy as to major values, even the so-called middle-class values. There is evidence that having goals unexamined and unrelated to reality will no longer do. Values deserve reexamination for clarification and for effective application within the framework of American education.

Summary

The attempt has been made to point out some of the major influences—historical, philosophical, psychological, and sociological—that have made early childhood education what it is today in the United States. The present situation is varied and dynamic. There are many flaws. There is much that is good. The increasing attention now being given to this age range gives reason to hope for a brighter future.

The further purpose has been: (1) to explain the organization of the text, and (2) to indicate major concerns of the authors. The emphasis is on the "why" rather than the "what" of the organization of the text.

choice and responsibility

I am my choices.
Jean-Paul Sartre

1 2 3
4 5 6

Do not
Touch
Max

Choice and Responsibility as Major Goals of Life and Education

Many students and teachers—not to mention the general public—seem to see choice and responsibility in terms of extremes. When some speak of freedom, they think "chaos." When the word "limits" or even "planning" is mentioned, others think of complete adult domination. Both extreme interpretations of choice and responsibility are ridiculous and harmful as applied to all education, and particularly as related to early childhood education. The authors do not agree with those who hold that all that the human being does is decided by heredity and environment and that, therefore, there can be neither choice nor responsibility. They do acknowledge that there is no such thing as absolute free choice. What they seek in education (and all of life) is as much choice as is reasonably possible within the limits of a given situation and behavior that is appropriately responsible. This is a very practical concern for all educators. Freedom always exists within boundaries. Choice is always limited to possibilities. Responsibility is also limited to the possibilities of choice. Throughout history there has been a need for individuals who are capable of choice and responsibility in conduct. The school should be in the forefront in developing such individuals. They are not the only institutions involved in this endeavor, but they are in a position to contribute to or to undermine the attainment of self and social competence. It is evident that the goals involved are only partially and gradually achieved. Choice, responsibility, competence are values recognized by almost all people as applied to the adult level. Society values the individual who can face tough problems and take responsible action. Most people are probably willing to go at least one step further and concede that unless these goals have been substantially achieved by adulthood, anything else a person has learned is of questionable value. Thus, it seems clearly evident that the development of ability to make reasonable choices and to accept responsibility for these choices are twin and major goals for life and education.

In practice education has tended to ignore one or the other or both goals, or if not to ignore them, to work toward them in impractical ways. In most schools much of the actual classroom situation is too structured, allowing little opportunity for choice. Responsibility cannot be developed where freedom is absent. This is not a call for unlimited freedom in the classroom. Limits are a necessity. (Many years ago a magazine published a cartoon of a chaotic classroom of young children with one child standing by the teacher's desk asking, "Isn't there anything we can't do?")

Inevitably some will misinterpret the concept of choice. A consultant is reported as having instructed a group of workers in federally sponsored programs to let the children do anything they pleased. He is quoted as saying, "If the children want to hang from the chandeliers, let them." One doesn't see many chandeliers in schools so the specific advice was safe enough. Further, if the consultant gave the reported advice, he was probably trying to make a point by overstating it. If so, he is hardly to be blamed—something like 99.9 percent of the danger among the group to which he was speaking lies on the side of overcontrol.

Or, again, it has been reported that in one experimental program visitors were told that if a child should attempt to kick them, to let him do it. We assume that this direction, if actually given, was an overstatement attempting to emphasize freedom. Even as overstatements though, such advice is not rational. There is no place or time in education or life when "anything goes."

The concept with which this book is concerned is very different. In early childhood education there are many rightful limits, but the concept of gradually expanding freedom of choice and a gradual assumption of responsibility for choice is basic. A child does not learn either of these in the midst of unlimited chaos, nor does he learn them unless the possibility of real choices exists. Such choices will not exist unless the teacher wishes them to, unless she plans her program to provide for the possibility of choice, or unless her teaching procedures permit such elements of freedom as are possible and practical.

It has been stated that choice and responsibility are rightfully the major goals of any school. In reality, they are *essentials of a meaningful life*. This could be demonstrated in countless ways. For example, there would be no democracy without them. Choice and responsibility are what democracy is all about. Democracy does not mean and has never meant the right of anyone to do as he pleased. (It does not mean that children run schools.) It does involve a group of people free to and capable of arriving at, accepting, and carrying through its decisions. This is the responsibility of a democratic society. Unfortunately, large segments of the adult population have refused to accept the responsibility. One reason may be the failure to give people the practical experience they need in making real choices within necessary limits and accepting responsibility for these choices.

Leading psychiatrists and psychologists are now telling us that a basic problem in the life of "civilized" man today is a lack of meaning and purpose in life, a lack of involvement. To whatever extent this is true, the schools of America must accept part of the blame. It would seem logical to assume that the basic failure of many schools to involve their students in real and meaningful choices may have something to do with irresponsible actions of both youths and adults.[1]

In spite of many years of emphasis on individual differences among school children, most schools still give only lip service to treating children as individuals. This is not a blanket indictment of schools. Many innovations are being tried in order to draw out the individual child. But it is true that far too many schools and teachers still attempt to teach children as though they were all alike. The results have been tragic. Children have left the schools in droves. In North Carolina there is still almost a 50 percent loss between first grade and high school graduation. For the nation as a whole the loss is said to be about 40 percent.

Much more than the matter of choice is involved here. Perhaps if there had been more elements of freedom of choice applied to the curriculum these pupils might have been able to demonstrate where they were and what they needed. No teacher can take a child on from a point he has not yet reached. Margaret Anderson, in her delightful book, *Children of the South*,[2] tells of the little girl asked by a teacher to count from twenty-one to one hundred. According to the story, the little girl's lips were moving to form one, two, three, four, and etc. The teacher stopped her and said, "No. Start with twenty-one." To which the quoted reply is, "Tarnation! I got to git thar fust!" There are other ways than freedom of choice to discover something about where the children are in their abilities and interests—but probably there is no other way to show as easily and clearly both the strengths and interest of the child.

Even more important in the overall picture of education in America is the fact that it is all too often dull, overdirected, and irrelevant. William Glasser in *Schools Without Failure*[3] points out that no child comes to school considering himself unsuccessful. However, many of them are labeled failures by

---

[1] Rollo May, *Man's Search for Himself*, 2nd ed. (New York: Signet, 1967).

[2] Margaret Anderson, *The Children of the South* (New York: Delta, 1958), p. 129.

[3] William Glasser, *Schools Without Failure* (New York: Harper & Row, 1969), Chapters 7 and 8.

the school, and eventually the child himself is convinced that he is a failure. The attempt to impose the same curriculum on all has much to do with this.

Education in America suffers from an emphasis on "grades." Those who appear to be the most successful students learn very early that one of the most important goals in school is the grade received. Teachers on the college level meet students who have made a sincere commitment to learning, but too many are like the young woman overheard last spring when she noted that she had received an "A." Her first statement was, "My parents will be so happy." It is hoped her parents were, but there is also a question about this student's personal commitment. Was she at college to get grades or to learn? The pages that follow express the hope that emphasis on grades can be at least postponed. Young children should have the experience of enjoying learning for the sake of learning. Part of the answer is to let them choose among learning experiences for the sake of what they can learn for themselves.

Summary

This chapter has attempted to state the general viewpoint which will be applied to Nursery School, Kindergarten, and the Primary age range in the next three chapters. This viewpoint includes the concepts that freedom of choice is always within limits. It is also related to responsible conduct. Both the ability to choose and the *character* to accept responsibility are major goals in themselves. They are also basic to effective teaching.

CHAPTER ONE

Choice and Responsibility in the Nursery School

For weeks a mother had been trying to get her youngest child, about two years old, to stay with other children for a brief Sunday school class period. The little boy would have none of it. His invariable reaction was a highly vocal expression of his fear and sorrow. And so, for several weeks the mother remained with the child in the class. Then one Sunday morning, apparently "quite out of the blue," the little boy turned to his mother with what seemed like a command, "Mama! Why don't you go to your class?"

The illustration, whatever its implications may be, supports the idea that, given some minimal security and understanding, *rather young children are capable of making important decisions and accepting responsibility for their decisions.* This Duane did, and he carried through with his decision. It was not an absolutely free decision. His parents had taken him to Sunday school. His mother had insisted that he stay in a special room and with a special group—with or without her. One would need to be equally cautious if any attempt were made to describe the ingredients of the decision made. The fact is that Duane, a little over two years of age, did make a choice within the framework of his situation. It is possible that this choice had important bearing on his future and, particularly, on his continued ability to make meaningful decisions and to act on them in a responsible way.

The purpose of this chapter is to discuss the nature of choice and responsibility as it applies to the three- and four-year-old and to suggest ways that both may be increased. The chapter could have been entitled discipline, as could both of the chapters that follow. Discipline is involved in all that will be said. It has already been noted that the authors are in no sense committed to a view of absolute freedom. They are concerned that methods in discipline be directed toward ultimate self-discipline and that they avoid giving the child a grim view of life. (One can be disciplined, even self-disciplined, and still be rather grim about life.) Hopefully, for the threes and fours, even more than for the rest of us, the emphasis can be on a happy freedom within limits.

The last sentence uses the word "freedom." The two words, choice and freedom, are not synonymous, but neither is possible without the other. Choice and decision are more nearly synonymous and will sometimes be used interchangeably.

The Nature of Choice for Three- and Four-year-olds

One reason to emphasize the need to provide as much latitude as possible for three- and four-year-olds in nursery school is that under all circumstances their choice is limited. This is even more true of the three-year-old than the four-year-old. But in both cases there are a great many things the child is not able to do. He wants to do a great many things he cannot do, or does too slowly, or too poorly to meet adult standards. He wants to do many other things that would be too dangerous for him to try. His world is full of "noes" and "don'ts." He is directed and overdirected, protected and overprotected. A father and mother with time, means, and patience can greatly simplify his world, but not many parents have the time, nor the means, nor the patience. A nursery school can with comparative ease offer choice in larger doses within a more protected environment. Ideally, it is built to provide for maximum choice with minimum risks.

Limits to Choice in a Nursery School

Even though the effort is to maintain freedom, there are a variety of limitations within the nursery school experience.[1]

Entrance Requirements

Apart from the limits of various kinds of schools imposed by the nature of the institution, such schools catering to upper-income children or federally financed schools for the underprivileged, there are usually limits concerned

[1] Katherine H. Read, *The Nursery School: A Human Relations Laboratory* (Philadelphia: Saunders, 1966), Chapter 9.

with health and maturity. Children cannot attend with contagious diseases. Generally, children are not admitted who are not toilet trained—though accidents are expected and taken in stride in the very best regulated of nursery schools. Children must also be able to get along without their mothers. This may require a gradual period of adjustment and involve short visits by the mother, a mother staying for the first day, and so forth.

Limits in the Schedule

There are many limits to choice within a nursery school—even when the aim is to provide as much freedom as possible. Not only is due concern taken that no child hurts another child literally or psychologically, but there is a place for certain types of activities and some restrictions on what may be done in those activities. Even when the restrictions are exercised by positive direction, there are still limits. There is also some kind of time schedule. Children come at a certain time, remain until time to go, eat pretty much on schedule, generally rest at a set time, and return to their homes at a particular time.

Limits in the Materials

Further limits may be set by the purposes and circumstances of the school. Materials that have not been provided or made available cannot be used. Certain standards may have been set in the securing of materials. Hopefully they will have been chosen, at least in part, for their possible instructional value. Some materials may be of a self-correcting nature so that there is a specific way to use them. Some schools may have brief periods set aside for small groups of children or for one child to develop more specific concepts and skills by the use of certain materials.

Purposeful Limits

The nursery school may deliberately set limits. One demonstration nursery school discovered that it was creating too much of a gap between home and school in what a child was permitted to do. At the school the children could do almost anything. The environment was arranged for that purpose. The difficulty was that "home" was different. There were many limits, and the children were having trouble making the adjustment. The staff deliberately set up a small group of shelves with some attractive inexpensive vases. They then set limits. The children could look at the vases but not handle them. This rule was enforced, not harshly, but definitely. One of the authors of this text taught a similar lesson in kindergarten. She never had time to sit behind her desk, but she did insist that this one item of furniture not be used by the children. Very early in life the concept must begin to form that choice does not necessarily include everything in sight. There are always other rights to be considered.

No one can prescribe the exact mix of limitations and control and freedom and choice in nursery school. Most are very sure that there should be wide latitude of choice. In setting limits one must be certain that they are reasonable boundaries for the particular situation—reasonable both for the person setting the standards and for the person expected to respect them.

Choice in the Nursery School

There are rules and regulations in nursery schools, but far fewer than any place else.[2] As long as they are not interfering with other children or injuring themselves, children usually can work with any media that are available. Their choice is wide and varied. They can dig in sand, pour water, build or paint, or draw, dress up, look at books, and engage in all the forms of dramatic play of which they are capable. At the age of three few children are ready to play cooperatively with other children, but still they may want to be near another child and to do the same thing. Children like to imitate each other and adults. They are eager to discover and learn. They are learning by doing, by observing, by manipulating, by experimenting. At four they are full of questions. By four they may be more ready for small-group activities, and cooperative play may begin to develop.

Amount and Kinds of Choice

Nursery schools serve a variety of purposes and a variety of clientele. A school attended by children for only a few hours a day because their parents hope to improve their later academic achievement is limited both by purpose and by time. A school whose basic purpose is to provide a safe environment for children while their parents are working a full eight-hour shift may be able to provide many more options. A federally financed day care center that hopes to make up for deficiencies in the environment of children will find itself with a still different frame of reference. Even within the latter groups the goals of education will depend in part on the needs of children relative to life, including expected future learning experiences. These matters and many others will influence the kinds of freedom and choices possible.

A conclusion that follows is that there is no one "model" of a good nursery school. In the very nature of things there cannot be. If it were possible to describe the kinds of children involved and the basic purposes of the specific nursery school, one could come closer to developing a "model." However, some principles do have some validity for all nursery schools. Many of these belong primarily in future chapters and will be

[2] Anne Shaaker Schulman, *Absorbed in Living: Children Learn* (Washington, D. C.: National Association for the Education of Young Children, 1967).

discussed in greater detail there. Those discussed in this chapter have bearing on the kinds and amounts of freedom. Freedom in any school, from nursery to graduate school, is freedom for specific purposes.

Principles Basic to Choice

Freedom to Learn

It is a contention of this book that unless there has been some drastic lack or mishap in the background of the three- and four-year-old, *given the chance, the child will choose to learn with little or no pressure from anyone.* Children of nursery school age are the world's most eager and successful learners. They learn because they want to learn; they want to know; they want to grow up. With the vast majority of children it is not a question of forcing them to learn, but of finding the best ways to help them learn.[3] We have noted that nursery schools are established to answer different needs. But even day care centers whose main purpose for being is custodial service are coming to recognize that their obligation is more than to simply provide a safe environment. They must also provide an environment in which learning can take place.

An Atmosphere Conducive to Learning

The general tone of the activities in the nursery school must be appropriate. It should carry in it stimulation and excitement in learning—not dull suppression. This excitement, though, needs to be the excitement of discovery, not the excitement of rebellious frustration. Nor can it be the excitement of any other kind of uncontrolled emotion. The teacher in the nursery school maintains the proper atmosphere by her own interested calm, her careful control of the stimulation, her ability to provide learning experiences appropriate to the needs of her children.

Appropriate Equipment

The nursery school offers a "world" suited to children's needs, and the equipment available for the children is scaled to these needs. The school that selects equipment with the sole criterion of enjoyment neglects to fulfill its function as a place for learning. Equipment used in nursery schools is to be enjoyed, but it also should be designed to help a child learn specific skills and concepts. Simple equipment that is well made with these qualifications best serves the nursery school child. Too complex equipment will only frustrate a child—and this is particularly true in the first weeks of school. During this period the kinds of things to do should be relatively

---

[3] John Holt, *The Underachieving School* (New York: Pitman, 1969), p. 17.

simple and the number to choose from restricted. Choice and material can both become more complex as children grow in experience and ability.

Interaction With Equipment and People

For some children, interaction with other children may be the most important part of the learning process. Children learn to choose companions and eventually partners. When they do so, they learn that certain responsibilities are involved in companionship. Few learnings in all of life are more important. The child has little choice, usually, as to the teachers and other adults in his nursery school world. These adults, though, can give the child some choice as to when and how he enters into a relationship with them. It is a good rule for both teachers and other adults not to be overwhelming in their attention to children, particularly strange children. A teacher can be courteous and attentive, but she should let the children make the advances.

The Teacher as the Key

One of the recurring themes in this text is the importance of the teacher in every phase of early childhood education. This theme will be restated in a variety of ways. The work of the teacher of young children is tremendously important—probably more important than that of any other teacher. This is true because of the important foundational learnings that are taking place and because the teacher is a more important figure to the child than any teacher is likely to be again. It is a further reasonable assumption that of all those who teach outside the home, the nursery school teacher is the most important.

In the light of this, the nursery school teacher is the key to the extent and kinds of freedom of choice possible. Involved in this statement is the concept that the teacher, herself, must value the growing independence of her children and look with satisfaction on their increasing ability to make decisions and accept responsibility for them. If she is to be able to do this, she must be a self-accepting person and one who does not feel consciously or unconsciously any compulsion to keep children dependent on her. She must also be a capable, well trained person who can understand the children's present readiness for responsible choice and can provide settings in which their abilities to make decisions can develop normally.

Exceptional Circumstances

Are there ever any exceptions to the suggested principles? Certainly! The child from a very privileged home may have already enjoyed freedom of choice experiences ordinarily available in the nursery school. He may have more and better educational play equipment than the nursery school owns.

Such a child may need a more structured experience. This experience, however, should be adapted to his interests and abilities. Either Montessori-type self-correcting materials, interesting formal instruction, or more extensive exploratory materials, or any combination of these may be appropriate. There will be more meaningful choice in such a program for such a child than would be possible otherwise.

The child from the underprivileged home may also need a very different type of experience. No one generalization is true of any social class of children. The teacher needs to be aware, however, that both the freedom and the limits some children have known are different from those discussed in this chapter. For some any freedom granted may have to come gradually. Some children have had little experience with choice, and to such children aggression may not be abnormal. It should not be startling to the teacher; she has to adapt her methods to this situation. Or consider another example: In Head Start programs for children about to enter first grade, some teachers made the mistake of overwhelming the children with a wealth of materials such as they had never known. The children were both overstimulated and bewildered. Much more limited choices would have been more realistic. Thus there may be factors of such overriding importance that some basic principles of freedom and responsibility must be temporarily infringed upon. They should never be discarded. They will not be abandoned if teachers maintain their respect for the individual. Even when there must be temporary compromises, some elements of freedom of choice and some emphasis on the development of a personal sense of responsibility can be maintained. In our present imperfect world the application will be modified to a greater or lesser degree dependent on the children and the situation.

Summary

The interrelationship between choice and responsibility begins earlier for most children than even the earliest of nursery school experiences. In training children to make choices and accept responsibility the nursery school has some advantages over the home. Both can be provided for in the setting, equipment, and planning. Both can be regulated to conform to the present maturity of the child. There is probably no one ideal ratio to be maintained between the two. Purposes in the nursery school, the kinds of freedom offered, and the responsibilities assumed must depend on the type of children enrolled and the maturity and needs of the children. The importance of a gentle guidance of children into the ability to make responsible choices within the limits of their circumstances cannot be overstressed.

CHAPTER TWO

Choice and Responsibility in the Kindergarten

It was well along in the kindergarten year when the following incident occurred. The teacher had read and told many stories to the children; they had their favorites and knew many of them word for word. For months they had been given a choice as to which story the teacher would relate. At times they dramatized some of the stories and nursery rhymes.

One morning the teacher asked if anyone would like to tell a story. She hardly expected a response from anyone—certainly not from the little boy who did volunteer. Phillip was a "good" boy in the traditional sense. He had not made any difficulty; neither had he been particularly outstanding in any way. Up to this time he might have been regarded as a slow learner. That he volunteered at all surprised the teacher.

What followed astonished her. Where Phillip picked up the idea for his presentation is still not known. Perhaps someone in his home told stories in this way. Since he was a middle child in a large family, he may have been accustomed to entertaining the younger children. For whatever reason, he told the story of *The Three Bears* in quite an unusual way. Phillip did a little stage setting on his own—arranging table, chairs, and various other props— before he began. Then he came to the front of the group and narrated the first part of the story. That told, he hurried over to the proper place on his "stage" and dramatized. Back and forth he hurried: narration, dramatization; more narration, more dramatization.

The class was amused at first, then entranced. They reacted with laughter as the little actor interpreted the story with his own brand of humor, and a "star was born." For the balance of that school year the teacher lost part of her job; from then on the children frequently asked if Phillip could tell a story.

For the balance of the year one small boy found his place in the sun. He needed that success, and some of it rubbed off in his other endeavors. This is one reason for relating the incident. A more important reason is that while the event was unplanned and unexpected, it could not have happened if Phillip had not been given the opportunity to show what he could do.

Choice and responsibility belong on every level of education. They fit the kindergarten like the "proverbial glove." The emphasis in this chapter is on choice, but choice, as always, within normal limits and with resulting responsibility. Such choice contributes to making kindergarten a pleasant place. It makes it easier for the children to show what they can do; it, also, helps the teacher understand her children and so know how to plan their learning experiences.

Choice is only possible if the teacher has confidence enough in herself and the children to make choice possible. If she does, then, in a variety of ways, choice enters into everything that happens in the kindergarten day. The following discussion centers on this day. With appropriate adaptations the suggestions can be applied in the nursery school and primary-age range level—especially, during the beginning of the first grade.

Building Choice Into the Schedule

Many of the choices that arise in the kindergarten flow naturally out of a relaxed relationship and flexible schedule. In other words, there is no formal plan for children to make specific choices on a certain day and at a particular moment. The teacher, however, does plan in such a way that choices are possible all through the day. Although for the kindergarten teacher there is no typical day, there are principles to be considered in looking forward to any day. Much of the planning involves the selection of materials and the possible use of resources, but that topic will be considered later. For the moment the subject is the overall course of a day's activities. In kindergarten the teacher's day begins when the first child arrives.

Before the Clock Strikes Nine

Planning for choice includes planning for the period "before school."[1] In all good schools part of this before school is routine. Kindergarten children can

[1] Eleanor Burts, Joan Kennedy, and Jean Lutz, "Self-Selection and Self-Direction" *Toward Better Kindergartens* (Washington, D. C.: Association for Childhood Education International, 1965), p. 47.

usually hang up their coats once they have been trained in the where and how. What follows is almost habit. The children will know that certain activities are permissible while waiting for the other children to arrive. Puzzles can be worked, simple games played, books looked through. Choices will differ with the circumstances, but they may be fairly limited. Two points for this preschool time are: (1) the children do something, and (2) they are given at least limited choices as to what they do.

Limits and responsibility are both inherent in the before-school situation. The children have choices, but these may be within rather narrow limits. There is a sense in which recognizing limits is essential to responsible behavior. More than limits are involved. Routines, too, are concerned with acting responsibly. Many aspects of behavior are a matter of habit. The habit of taking care of one's personal belongings is responsible behavior in this sense. There is, also, the underlying assumption that if any equipment is used in this informal period, the child who uses it will accept responsibility for it. Another factor is harder to explain. Children behave responsibly when they are expected to. The teacher should be warm and personally interested in her relationships with her pupils but also expectant and respectful. She knows that the children are capable of responsible behavior, and she expects this of them. She may mention it briefly from time to time, but the mere mention of responsibility will not bring about such behavior. Children sense attitudes, and the teacher who expects responsible behavior is more likely to get it.

Large Group Activities

How the kindergarten day begins officially will depend on circumstances and the preferences of the teacher.[2] There will be in most kindergartens a time or times, early or late, when all or almost all of the children will assemble in one group. Time spent in these periods should be short. There is a negative correlation between the length of the large group assembly and the number of choices open to children. This is not to say, however, that no choice is possible in the large group activities. Sometimes, there can be an option as to whether individual children join in the group activity. The teacher might say, "This is story time; all of you who want to hear the story, come to the front of the room." If she puts the matter this way, all the children may come, or some may want to finish a project on which they are working. Although these boys and girls appear to be left out of the total group activity, they may be listening to the story while working with their hands. But they did have a choice, and in making their choice they made life easier for the class, teacher, and themselves.

Even when there is little real choice, there can be recognition of the dignity of the individual and the importance of his feelings. One new

[2] Ruth H. Nixon and Clifford L. Nixon, *The Art of Kindergarten Instruction* (Pembroke, N. C.: Pembroke State College, 1969), Chapter 3.

kindergarten child came to school unwillingly and for quite some time chose to do nothing except to sit as close to the door as possible. The teacher made no issue of this, but each day moved the chair in which he sat a little closer to an activity that was nearby. The day came when chair and boy were in the midst of activities. All the boy had to do was to drop on the floor and be part of a group. Choice had been made easy. The teacher had manipulated the situation, but an element of choice was still available to the boy, and respect for his feelings had been preserved.

Choice can be built into activities intended for the entire group of children. (Part of this choice is so subtle that it is never stated to the children in terms of a choice.) Children, as individuals and as groups, show by their behavior what they are interested in, what they can do, what they are ready to attempt. A large part of the art of kindergarten instruction is sensing this readiness. The teacher who is sensitive to the wishes of her class will schedule activities that the children want even though they have not specifically requested them.

There is an equally unspoken element of choice when the teacher feels that a given activity may be helpful at a certain stage in kindergarten and tries it out. The teacher who does not know whether or not something will work out, will not force it on the children, nor will she plan to devote a definite period of time to it. The trial may last for only a few seconds. If the venture catches on, it can be given more time. If it does not, the teacher changes to an alternative activity. Later, as she thinks about the experiment, she reaches a tentative conclusion. This may be to discard the particular activity. It may not be appropriate to her group of children. Or it may be appropriate a little later when the children are slightly more mature and experienced. It could also be, however, that the children are ready and the activity appropriate, but the technique wrong. Perhaps the children need a gradual introduction to the new experience. This can come by introducing it to the group a little at a time over several days. Or the introduction could come through working with a small group or even one individual from whom other children can learn. Thus the teacher recognizes the importance of her pupils as individuals, respects them as they are, and adapts her program accordingly. There will be countless other ways in which she can do this.

Even in large group "assemblages" there is room for individual and group choice. Children who are used to both freedom and cooperation can sometimes be granted a choice as to areas of activity—music or literature, for example. Even when the teacher chooses the major activity, choices can be left to the children—which record, what story. They may even be individual choices. "You pick out the animal you want to be and make the kind of sound he would make when we come to that part of the story (or song)."

Such choice can be carried even further. In a music period, for instance, when the teacher is skilled and the children are creative, the children can decide on the rhythm, the movement, or any number of possible varieties of activities. The teacher at the piano can play in time and mood, adapting to the activity, movement, or mood that the children have selected. The limits of choice are determined by the total situation, but, ideally, they are very wide limits.

Meeting with the whole class can serve other purposes. Two of these are probably more important to the possibility of real choice than anything said so far. If a teacher has, for example, a short meeting with the class at the beginning of the day, whatever else it does, this meeting should create *an atmosphere in which realistic choice is possible.* Children may come to school happy and excited, which is good, but a few minutes of calming down may avoid a possible explosion. Children sometimes become angry and hurt. They need a little time to heal. For any of us, feelings and choice are related, but feelings that are too strong make reasonable choice impossible. The attitude of the teacher, the few words spoken, the brief activities, can set a tone that makes freedom more possible. The second purpose (relative to individual choice) that can be served by the meeting of the whole group has to do with classroom management. Choice with a group of individuals requires not only the right tone but also the right planning for choice. Children can decide before leaving the group what work they wish to engage in. Where conflicts exist, these can be resolved. The necessity for such group planning is illustrated by the following incident. A prospective kindergarten teacher observed a good example of what *not* to do. A kindergarten teacher failed to create the right atmosphere and did not prepare her children for orderly choice. She dismissed the entire group at the same time to work on whatever they wanted. All twenty-five kindergartners rushed for the playhouse. The result was a free-for-all, a small riot. There was punching, kicking, and screaming, and in the end no one got to do what he wanted. It may be added that the teacher did not kick or scream, but she certainly had not used her head—and not surprisingly, she lost it.

Individual and Small-group Activities

The most important part of the kindergarten day consists of a large block of time devoted to individual and small-group activities.[3] This work period, as we shall call it, should be relatively long because it offers the most fruitful opportunities for learning. It is not a play period, even though it may seem so to an outsider. (Those kindergarten teachers who use this time to step outside to visit with other teachers, a parent, or sit at their desks resting or planning, are not good kindergarten teachers.)

It is during the work period that most of the decisions by the child are made. He normally has a choice, limited by the possibilities and situation, as to what he will do. He should have even more complete freedom as to what he does with the materials that he has chosen. This freedom, too, has its limits—not the fussy limits of a "prissy" adult, but the necessary limits of

[3] Synva Nicol, "A Good Day for the Fives," *Portfolio for Kindergarten Teachers* (Washington, D.C.: Association for Childhood Education International, 1960).

social obligations, property rights, and safety.[4] No child has freedom to spoil another child's picture; the teacher may need to explain this. Alternate activities may be suggested, or there may be some other way that the child can make a picture. As he thinks things over, there may be something else that he would rather do. Any other activity will involve limits too. Neither clay nor blocks are for throwing. Clay can be pounded, molded, stretched, and shaped. Many things can be done with it. The effective teacher emphasizes the positive choices.

Choice may be very simple but important to the child. Some children are so hesitant that even after they have chosen crayons and paper, they can not decide what to do next. The teacher may offer a little help, which may be as elementary as making marks on the paper with three or four colors and then asking which the child likes best. Some kindergarten children will then take over and simply color. They may color the whole paper with one color and then cover that with another color. Another child may indicate that he actually wants to draw something but does not know how to start. The teacher can suggest two or three possibilities or even suggest an alternative activity. Yes, she is helping in the process of choice, but the child decides. And his choice could be to let the crayons alone today and seek a job as a laborer in the construction gang that is building a superhighway across one end of the kindergarten.

Some children need time to make up their minds. This troubles many teachers. One teacher insisted that the parents refer their kindergarten child to a psychiatrist because of his supposed inability to make a decision. In the work time the boy spent about half an hour going from one group to another, never interfering, but just looking. Finally, he would decide which group to join. He then entered in with very worthwhile suggestions and contributions. Observation indicated that the child was very bright. The possibility is that early in life he seems to have learned something about choice that few kindergarten children consider—the weighing of possibilities before making a decision. It seemed that he learned much from his period of watching and observing.

The topic of choice during the work period will be covered more fully in the final section of this chapter.

Choice in Other Segments of the Program

In most kindergartens there are periods that for another age group would be designated as "recess." In the kindergarten such periods may be called *"play time," "outdoor time,"* or whatever serves the purpose best. Whatever the name, there will be times when the whole group of children change locations and move outside. Several kinds of choice may be involved. Should there be a game for the entire group? This will depend on the maturity of the children and the time of the year. If it is toward the end of the kindergarten year, some group games might be tried. The teacher should be aware of the children's abilities and interests in making her decisions. Whatever they do should be enjoyable to them. Much of the play time will be the kind of free play in which the child chooses his own activity. But some children may be ready for group games and would enjoy them more. Thus, some would prefer the choice of play equipment, and some may prefer the choice of a group game. The sensitive kindergarten teacher will be aware of this and adapt to the choices.

All good kindergartens have *rest periods*. The choice is chiefly that of the teacher as to the time and the type of rest. Generally, the rest period will be about the same time each day, but there need be no rigid rule about this. The teacher will vary the time if she thinks the children would benefit from an earlier period or if she thinks it would be better to continue an activity into the time slot normally allocated to rest. Children can be permitted either to sleep or simply relax. The sensitive teacher will know what helps her class relax and what stimulates them. If she is sensitive, the children will be choosing the music or the setting and atmosphere that is most conducive to rest for them, even though no choice is expressed in words.

Practically every kindergarten has a snack time. Choice may be limited and more subtle than for other periods. If the children do not respond to tomato juice but do to orange juice, why not adjust the snack—keeping within limits of what are basically good health practices. And here is one hint for both health and choice. If the child does not want to eat or drink something— go along with his decision; it may be important from a health standpoint. Milk is not good for all children; some may be allergic to orange juice. Snack time is important nutritionally for many children, but for some middle-class children it may be more important as a change of pace. A child may need encouragement to try something which for him is wholly unfamiliar. Even so, elements of choice can be worked into the procedure.

There is also a "clean-up" time in good kindergartens. The most important element here may not be choice, but responsibility. A child is usually responsible for the materials with which he is working when clean-up time approaches. Certain children, however, like to take care of particular general chores. Frequently a division of labor can be worked out that lets children do the things they like to do, and these they tend to do well.

During the day some time usually is devoted to evaluation or sharing. This may be a large-group activity in which the children think back over the day as to what they enjoyed, what they learned, what went wrong, what they want to find out at home, how they would like to continue major projects. It may be a much more informal activity with a small group of children or with just one child. Choice, reflection, problem solving, and acceptance of responsibility are all involved.

Making Choice Possible Through Materials and Resources

The topics of materials and resources are of an importance second only to the teacher's attitude and creativity. In reality, the teacher's attitude and creative ability are directly related to materials and resources. So, too, are the teacher's knowledge of children and sensitivity to individual needs and differences. Even though proper materials and resources depend in part on the financial resources and concern of the community, the right selection and use are within the providence of the teacher.

Predicting the Materials Needed

In providing materials and resources for choice, the teacher is dependent on her ability to predict—especially before the school term begins and during the first weeks of the year. A teacher never knows exactly the kind of children that she will have. She, however, should know the community and something about the range of cultural backgrounds of her children. Consequently, she should have general expectations concerning the probable interests and abilities of the five-year-olds who will be her pupils. Hopefully, sufficient money will be provided for most of the simple, rugged, and flexible materials essential for an effective functioning kindergarten. It is important that the teacher be able to make a satisfactory prediction as to which of these materials can be used profitably during the opening days of school. Kindergarten children in particular should not be presented with an overwhelming variety of materials from which to choose—and especially not during opening days of the school year.

In the continued use of materials, the teacher adjusts and upgrades her predictions. Fortunate indeed is the teacher who has a relationship with the school authorities that makes possible two simple arrangements. One is to have everything needed for the opening weeks of kindergarten on hand well in advance of opening day. Head Start and similar programs have been known to begin in bare rooms with scarcely any equipment of any kind and with none at all for the use of the children. This is a crime in the nature of a felony, whether the fault lies with the teacher, the school officials, or the federal bureaucracy. One would classify as a misdemeanor the opposite condition. Some schools have been flooded with materials never used—either because they were inappropriate or because of the inertia of the teacher.

The other arrangement necessary to effective functioning is that funds be reserved for use when more accurate predictions can be made as to amounts and types of supplies required. Some school systems do operate on this basis, but, unfortunately, most seem to request a list of all supplies needed in the next nine months to be presented the day before yesterday. In this case, the teacher does her best, and then improvises.

The teacher is the principal resource person for any class. If necessary, the good kindergarten teacher can find, save, and make many of the materials her class will use. She should be creative enough to do so. Money for materials used in kindergarten service are tax deductible—a fact many are not aware of. Of course, amassing materials is time-consuming, but the results of such efforts are very rewarding. (However, the kindergarten teacher needs all her energy to do the actual job of teaching. It is a demanding job, and even expensive tools are cheaper than teachers.)

Parents and friends are a further resource. Even in poor communities, there are parents who can make or repair some of the equipment. They may be glad to help and proud to have a part.

Setting the Stage for Choice

The chief point in what has been said thus far is that by using what is provided and whatever else that can be gathered as needed and appropriate, the teacher is engaged in setting the stage for choice. In doing so the teacher will be primarily concerned with the maturity of the children—a necessary concern for almost all teaching goals, and not only for providing choice. One may in the interest of good relationships with the community accept almost any materials for kindergarten use that are donated. And there is some use for almost anything, sometime in the school year and in some situation with some children. But the setting of the stage is determined more by the situational needs of the children than by the gifts of interested people. The teacher's chief concern is materials suitable to the children's present needs.

Certain materials are basic for kindergarten. The essentials include an assortment of various shapes and sizes of blocks, clay, painting, and drawing materials, equipment to play house and store, a few easels, a few well-built toys such as a wagon that will hold a five-year-old, and cars and trucks that are durable. Materials like these are adaptable for many uses. Some means is needed to provide music—a record player, a piano, if possible, and hopefully, a tape recorder. Books are another must. Only passing mention is made of them here because they are evaluated more thoroughly later in the text. What has been noted are general tools of learning. The list can go on and on, and, again, there will be a more extensive discussion in other sections.

What the teacher must never lose sight of is that the best materials provide choices within choices. Commercial kits of many kinds supposedly contain all the materials required for kindergarten. These vary from very useful to potentially damaging materials. In using the prepared kits the possibility exists that the teacher will disregard their actual appropriateness to her children and their situation. These specific tools, particularly those involving presumably organized programs, are not the first items to buy as equipment.

The number and range of choices of materials can be increased as the children mature and as they grow accustomed to freedom within limits and the pleasures of responsible action. Over the school year it is as important that materials that challenge the capacity of the most gifted be as readily available as materials that fit the needs of the less gifted or less mature. *No child should be held back from any learning experience that he is ready for.* By his choices the child is showing what he can and wants to do next. Setting the stage includes setting it for the most mature and the least mature and all he children in-between.

Developing Choice Through Activities

The child in kindergarten has the widest range for choice during the work periods, which are comparatively long. For most kindergartens they are the most important part of the day. Such periods should be enjoyed by everyone involved. They may look like play, but to the child work and play are essentially the same. During the work periods children learn language skills, arithmetical and scientific concepts, and understandings pertaining to the social sciences. They are also learning not only to choose, but how to make good choices within the limitations of the situation.

The Role of the Teacher

The teacher is an active participant in the work period. The period is not the time for the teacher to rest or to visit at length with anyone. Fellow teachers, principals, and supervisors should be welcome to visit and observe the children. Conferences about a child are important to both the teacher and the parent, and above all to the child, but these should not be scheduled during the work period. However, parents should be welcome during a work period and if possible put to work. If they do participate, they should be helped to understand the purposes and methods of the kindergarten in advance.

This is a work time for the teacher too. She is in the midst of the action. She is not directing (unless this becomes necessary), nor is she doing the children's work. What she does may not look much more like work than what the children are doing, but those periods that look so much like fun are very hard work for the effective kindergarten teacher.

The teacher helps in choice in the work period by the kind of person she is.[5] The good kindergarten teacher is a successful person in that she has made a choice and is doing what she likes to do. She is working with.

[5] Margery Baumgartner, "Epilogue: The Place of Love in Education," in Anne Shaaker Schulman, *Absorbed in Living: Children Learn* (Washington, D. C.: National Association for the Education of Young Children, 1967), pp. 197–199.

children she loves and respects. She is deeply concerned without wanting to dominate. And she herself is not afraid of choice. She makes the decisions she must make and permits and encourages decision by others.

The teacher helps in choice during the work period by what she says. Teaching on any level involves more than merely talking. Lectures have no place in the kindergarten; neither do lengthy demonstrations. The kindergarten teacher keeps her remarks to the whole group brief. When talking with small groups and individuals, she does the same. In fact, *she talks very little;* but when she does, she says just what is needed and no more. Some child may need help in evaluating the choices available; another may need an introduction to children working on a project that he would like to join. The teacher seems to always be right there when needed. Her conversations are brief. This is teaching as it should be with five-year-olds, and an important part of this teaching is concerned with the improvement of choice.

Observing, Listening, and Sensing

The teacher helps in choice by how she observes. The latter statement does not imply that the teacher is on the lookout for trouble, although she is aware of possibilities of trouble. Some of the talking mentioned above may consist of explanation as to what is not done. More important than this is the positive observation of what the children are doing—what they seem to like to do, what they do well, and how they are reacting and interacting while working.

The teacher is also listening. Frequently the five-year-old is a fluent talker. Some kindergarteners are delighted to have a listener, especially if it is the teacher. Other children do not find it so easy to express themselves through talking. But both kinds of children in all their variations are likely to tell you more when they are not talking directly to you or to the point. They will talk to each other and to themselves as they work. The teacher should listen to them. She is not eavesdropping; the children know she is there. It is just easier to talk when one is not trying too hard to talk. It is easier to talk when the listener is not asking questions and interrupting. The teacher can learn a great deal about her pupils when they are simply being themselves. The relationship of this to choice becomes clearer if stated in a different way.

The teacher helps with choice by what she senses. The teacher is listening, observing, and *feeling* with the children. Their actions and reactions let her know whether they are doing the right kind of work and whether her predictions have been accurate. She is learning what modifications she needs to make in her plans. She is picking up ideas for and from the children.

The teacher helps with choice by what she does about the insights gained. This may be as simple as making certain that there is fresh, bright paint available for the next work period or ordering a new item of equipment that some children are now ready for. It may involve planning a field trip. One teacher discovered by listening that the boys playing with toy airplanes all thought that real airplanes were small—bigger than toys, but not much bigger. The teacher arranged for a trip to the local airfield. It was a carefully supervised trip in cooperation with all the authorities involved. She used the resources available—the school bus and driver, some of the parents, and the airport personnel. The children not only saw the exteriors of several large airplanes, but they were permitted to go inside one of them. They saw its size and its facilities. No doubt every child learned something new to him that day, but all learned that the specks they saw passing over them in the sky were sometimes immense airplanes. The teacher did something because she sensed both an interest and a need in her children.

This chapter does not really end: choice is involved in all that remains to be said in the balance of the text. The final word for the present is that what has been discussed thus far does work. A college student visited a kindergarten for underprivileged children conducted by a teacher who believes in the basic ideas presented in this chapter. The children were working individually and in groups in a variety of projects. There was no deathly silence, but neither was there any objectionable noise or behavior. What astonished the visitor most was the fact that the children as they finished one project moved to something else on their own and without disturbing anyone. After one child finished a picture, she took it down and placed it where it could dry. Then she took off her smock and hung it up. Another child got a smock and took over at the easel. In the meantime, the first child had joined the group working at the store. She became a customer. The college student did not observe all the children nor the entire school day. Probably some children remained with one project for the full time. The point is that many of the children were choosing and changing throughout the period with a minimum of help from the teacher. More than change and choice were happening—and they were happening in a happy, practical, and realistic situation. This smoothly functioning class is a practical goal. The method is not a visionary goal. It is a workable method. It is an essential element of the art of kindergarten instruction.

Summary

Responsible choice is not difficult to develop in the five-year-old. The teacher who has helped her children develop a sense of freedom and an understanding of the limits and responsibilities involved in the daily program, can work major elements of choice into all phases of the day's activities. Exactly how much choice the child has will vary with the activity. He will probably have greatest freedom in the large blocks of time devoted to individual and small-group activities. The teacher takes an active part in all phases of the program and learns much about the needs and abilities of her children by what they choose to do. The choices of children become an immediate stimulus to their learning and an indication to the teacher of their probable readiness for new experiences.

CHAPTER THREE

Choice and Responsibility on the Primary Level

A second-grade girl had transferred from another school district. During her first day there came a period when the children all had seat work to do. The teacher explained to the newcomer what the other students already knew: She could choose from an assortment of games and activities when her work was finished. The child looked up, wide-eyed and questioning, "Do you really mean it?"

There are at least two implications in the question. The first is that there must be teachers who do not give the kind of choice offered to this little girl. Most of this chapter concerns this problem. The other implication may not have been intended. The child was not speaking suspiciously. As stated, however, there is the possible implication that the girl had learned not to trust teachers.

That choices offered must be honestly offered cannot be stressed too much. To motivate a child to accomplish what he basically wants is reasonable and need not be deceptive. To help a child see that there is relevance and interest in some things he must do is legitimate. But to pretend that choice exists when, in fact, none does, is not teaching choice but deceit. To pretend a choice and then manipulate the children into "making the choice" that the teacher has already determined is a very effective way to teach the brighter child to be suspicious.

Perhaps a teacher has no thought of deceiving a child, but she may not have any real concern for children's feelings and choices. A group of prospective teachers watched a teacher and her first-grade class write an "experience" chart about a recent trip. Over and over the children suggested various ideas in sentences that were striking and vivid. The teacher usually responded with, "That is fine, but wouldn't it sound better this way." After the class, the college students asked about the chart, and the teacher admitted, with apparent pride, that she had picked out each item for the chart and the 'best' way to describe it, while on the trip. The final result was exactly the one predetermined by the teacher. Giving the children a choice as to what ideas were important to them was an illusion. To this teacher this was simply good planning. The college students were troubled by the incident. (The fact that they were may be one of the hopeful indications for the future of education.) The children appeared to be frustrated and depressed. Whether or not they saw through the deception, they lost the excitement of a true learning experience.

Teachers can provide useful and honest choices. They can do this, however, only if they, themselves, understand both their responsibilities and their choices. Clear, hard-headed thinking and discussion is usually needed if the teacher is to understand the first. Teachers always have responsibilities and always teach within limits. These will vary somewhat dependent on the state, locality, local administration, and other factors. A teacher can never forget that the education of students is the teacher's major responsibility. All that occurs in a classroom revolves around this priority. When this goal is kept in mind, there can hardly be a set of circumstances that leaves the teacher with no choice. Nor will circumstances ever be so binding that the teacher can provide no honest choice to students.

Alternatives Open to the Teacher

Too frequently teachers' reactions to any suggestion as to how to bring choice into the classroom have been negative—"We can't do that!" It never seems necessary to ask, "Why not?" The teachers have their answers on the tip of their tongues: "The state regulations require us to teach such and such"; "The superintendent said . . . ."; "The teacher next door wouldn't like it." Let us examine some of these very real but usually oversimplified limits.

Opportunities for Choice Within the Framework of the School Relationships

The organization and work of the state departments of education differ from state to state. It is common practice for state committees to formulate general curricula and for the state departments to apply these decisions in the form of suggestions or guidelines. How limiting these guidelines may actually be in intent differs in every state. Take the choice of readers as an example. A local school system may be required to use one set of texts, or certain sets of texts, or may have the privilege of selecting from an extended list of possible choices. Or the limiting factor may be more subtle. The question may not be what the school system can use, but what will the state and/or local units of government pay for.

There are reasons for some form of regulation on the state level. In an older and simpler day it used to be said jokingly that if the state did not set up guidelines as to topics in the social studies program, a child might study nothing but Indians from kindergarten through eighth grade. Whatever the regulations are, subject to possible error as all regulations and choices are, the original purpose was legitimate. Teachers usually like to know what is expected of them. When one does find abuses to common sense in schools, they are as likely to be by teachers who are "out of bounds" as by those who are overly conscientious. For example, an elementary teacher turned a major portion of each day into recess periods. Such an abuse makes state requirements necessary. Another teacher, probably in all kindness, kept a small boy in every recess to help him with his arithmetic. She too was ignoring state requirements. One can function adequately within the bounds of state requirements. They are not usually rigidly binding. A retired supervisor in North Carolina claims that never once in over twenty-five years was she ever refused permission to try an innovation. The state today is pleading with school districts to experiment with new approaches.

But even if one assumes the requirements are rigid and the enforcement vigorous, this would not block a resourceful teacher from trying anything within reason. Suppose, for example, that the state regulations call for a study of community workers and that a text is to be used. There will be no regulation as to how the text is to be read, what kind of projects may be undertaken in the study, what additional materials may be employed. Nor will state regulations cover resource people to be used; the tracing of individuals, normally employed locally, who are now in the Armed Forces; the discoveries children may make about where the skills employed in the community originated; or where the goods and tools used came from geographically and historically. It does not take much imagination to realize that the problem is one of limiting choice to what the children can manage. Theoretically, there are not one or two, but over a thousand possible combinations within the choices named. Any teacher who will think through a situation looking for choices should be able to find many.

Most superintendents of public school systems have little time, unfortunately, to think about classroom procedures. In some states the office of superintendent is a political office. In others the superintendent is chosen by a school board, usually from among individuals who have qualified educationally. In either case, the superintendent has to live with an electorate or the elected representatives of the people. In addition, he has to live with a number of other problems, such as, state and federal reports, pressure groups, vandalism, and ad nauseam. In even a moderate-sized district, he probably has an assistant who is more directly concerned with classroom problems. Assistant superintendents in charge of instruction tend to be, if anything, too agreeable. They are aware of problems but sometimes are helpless to make changes.

One minor problem may be the fact that the superintendent sometimes makes statements to maintain a public image. Two different superintendents reportedly issued official notices that every child should "get through all the books."

But what about covering all the material with the slow learner. Here the teacher notes the directive and considers both its intent and the children with whom she is working. In almost every case the intent is that the child learn the concepts basic to the texts. In arithmetic, for example, a child has not in any meaningful way covered a text because he has done something on paper with the problems in the text. He has covered the text only when he has gained insight into the meaning and processes involved. If a certain child needs more experience manipulating rods or any of a wide variety of concrete objects, doing this may be "covering the text" more effectively than having the child (or the child's parents) plod through every item in the book. Illustrations could be multiplied from any subject. The conscientious and imaginative teacher can find meaningful ways to cover necessary material, whatever the level of ability of her children. Almost always this can be done in such a way that the official texts are involved in the process as useful teaching tools. Used in this way the slow learner gains in both confidence and competence.

Principals are more closely in touch with the situation in their schools than their superiors. Teachers in the primary grades are most fortunate when they have a principal who really knows what early childhood education is all about and is a person with whom one can communicate. It is helpful to be able to exchange ideas with an understanding superior. When the principal does not understand this area, he may set limits that are not helpful. He is probably interested chiefly in good classroom management. Good teachers, also, want good working conditions. Choice, handled competently, does not mean confusion.

In almost all school districts there are staff people attached to the central office who assist in some phase of the program of instruction. They may be called specialists, supervisors, consultants, coordinators, or be designated by some other term. They may work in a specific area of instruction or a certain level of education. Sometimes such individuals may cause problems for the teacher who wishes to provide choice for her class. The music specialist, for example, may know more about music than about the purposes of early childhood education. Some general supervisors may lay undue stress on a rigid adherence to a course of study. Most have no desire to restrict the innovative teacher. Normally, all of these people are resources for the teacher. They will gladly offer suggestions and help to secure materials. Even with supervisors who seem restrictive, the teacher can find areas of agreement and other areas still open to experimentation.

Teachers have to live with other teachers. Some teachers seem to be resistant to new ideas. This is an understandable and human reaction. Within limits there is value in caution with reference to untried approaches. It still remains that there is tremendous need for innovations in teaching. Not all of them will work. Even those which are proven successful are more likely to be accepted when presented with tact and without direct confrontation. One primary teacher was known to lose her job by pressuring for an individualized reading program. Her idea was good and it worked for her. She lost her job, however, because her approach was too dogmatic and unbending with the other teachers. With reasonable tact and common sense there is almost always some way the teacher can provide freedom of choice within her own classroom. In doing so she will be conscious of the feelings of others, will speak out when there is a chance that to do so may be helpful, but will not give needless offense.

In some school situations noise from one classroom may disturb another. A new teacher's class may make more noise than usual. In addition, the teacher may find herself the recipient of the results of annoyance for matters that are not of her making. The reaction may seem out of proportion to the disturbance. Schools are not usually places of deathlike stillness and should not be. Besides the normal classroom noise there may be other kinds that are beyond the control of the teachers. Apart from the shouts from the playground and the walking of groups of children down the hall, lawn mowers may roar just outside; pile drivers pound within sight and sound; airplanes zoom overhead; the intercom interrupts; and high school marching bands practice nearby. The bit of extra noise next door may be the proverbial "straw." The new teacher remains courteous and tries to do some problem solving on her own. Some activities that might disturb can be scheduled for a time when they will be least disturbing or perhaps can be moved to another location. There are choices available to teachers that involve no disturbance.

Teachers, especially beginning teachers, tend to fear parents. It will help the teacher to remember that the parent is probably afraid of her. When a teacher has a conference with a parent, her job is partially to help the parent relax and relate. The teacher and parent share a mutual concern for the child.[1] A kindly, honest, open exchange of ideas usually helps. Perhaps the parent has some suggestions for the teacher. He has known his child longer than the teacher and can supply the teacher with background material about the child that she will find valuable in dealing with the child in the classroom. A teacher should not criticize a child's work or behavior unless she has positive suggestions to offer. The opposite extreme must also be avoided; the teacher should not give false assurances. Very often the most beneficial result of a teacher-parent conference is the decision that both teacher and

[1] See J. Frances Huey, *Teaching Primary Children* (New York: Holt, Rinehart and Winston, 1965), Chapter 16.

parent will experiment with a modified approach and then confer as to results. Almost never is any parent critical of a teacher who has some rational reason for the method she is using and is willing to explain why she is using this approach.

Pressure groups, too, affect a teacher today and the choices she makes within the framework of the school. If pressures come, a distinction should be made between the teacher as a citizen and the teacher as a public employee. As a citizen, the teacher should be free to take whatever personal stands are required by conscience and common sense. In the classroom there is need for appropriate honesty. If one wing of the school building was burned down the night before, it does not make sense, even on the first-grade level, to pretend that everything is beautiful and fine. It makes more sense to talk about personal safety, the social climate in that first-grade classroom, the possibility that the children, by what they learn, may eventually be in a position to help solve some of the long-range problems. It is not appropriate for a teacher to espouse any partisan view or action in the classroom.

Some problems that result in misunderstandings with the general public require clarification. For example, to some people "social studies" means "communism." A brief explanation may be all that is required. If that doesn't work, explain to the children that they are studying history and economics and geography. Some pressure groups are demanding more academic emphasis. Even this is hardly a problem. The teacher is at least as much concerned with the depth of the learning experiences of her children as the group concerned. The question becomes one of making teaching effective. Whatever the teacher tries can be done with the understanding that if it does not contribute to more effective learning, it will be willingly abandoned.

Opportunity for Choice Within Social and Personal Limits

To some extent the limits discussed are more illusory than real. They may serve as convenient excuses for the teacher. It is easier to blame the system than to plan for worthwhile alternatives. Limits of a slightly different nature should always be in the forefront of a teacher's thoughts.

Teachers have a responsibility to society—represented in part by the school system, in part by pressure groups, but more accurately and subtly by the expectations of society. These expectations deserve consideration. Public schools belong to the public. If the teacher is unwilling to consider the relevancy of content and method to traditional values, then simple honesty would seem to indicate some alternative to service in the public school system. All kinds of questions can be raised about the stated premise and its possible application, but the fact remains that the teacher has a responsibility to her society. Although there is wide latitude for interpretation of this responsibility, there can be no reasonable doubt that those who pay the bill should have something to say about how the job is done.

Teachers have their own limitations.

1. They differ as to personal needs, intellectual capacity, creative ability, and sense of security.
2. And they differ in their backgrounds, experience, and economic circumstances.
3. Teacher education is sometimes more traditional than inventive.
4. Initial teaching experiences are sometimes disappointing.
5. Fellow teachers may exude defeatism.
6. Women who teach may have what amounts to a full-time job after school caring for their families.
7. Men may find that they have to "moonlight" to support a home.

These and other matters may "turn the teacher off" so that he begins to rely on routine and drill that seem to require less involvement. All teachers need to keep alive intellectually. The problems for each individual differ, but most limits are in the mind and attitude of the teacher—and can be overcome.

There are also limits that stem from the experiences of children in decision making. It is just as hard to exercise responsible choice if one has had no previous experience as it would be to read French if one had never seen French. If the children are used to rigid authority, and no opportunity to make their own choices, they can be instructed in the skill of decision making but this cannot be done instantaneously.[2] A gradual and prolonged training period may be necessary.

An Attitude of Search for Choice

There are always possible choices. It is easy for the teacher to feel fenced in. The fence is there, at least figuratively. It may even be a fence in depth. And possibly, there is an area just inside the fence that has an assortment of "booby traps." One cannot deny its existence. To return to the figure, however, part of the teacher's problem may be an obsession with the fence. Thus she may not see that the yard enclosed is expansive and beautiful and offers many possibilities. Figuratively speaking, she may not see that there are both openings in the fence and helicopters available to take her over and out. But it is her task to see just that. There are always possibilities.

The teacher takes into account the realities and explores the possibilities. She discovers her alternatives and implements those that serve the purpose. Partly, she does this by asking herself what it is that state committees, administrators, and parents really want for the children. The second question is whether or not the present method of teaching is doing the intended job. If not, an alternative always exists that can be tried out. If the teacher has this attitude toward work and life, then in many aspects of the program there will be choices for children.

[2] Paul R. Hunt and Elvin I. Rasof, "Discipline, Function or Task?" in Robert D. Strom, *The Inner City Classroom: Teacher Behaviors* (Columbus, Ohio: Merrill, 1966), p. 131.

Choices for Children

The teacher who realizes that her freedoms are not as rigidly bound as she may have thought and who is concerned with more than going through the motions of teaching, will provide choice for her children. As in the case of the younger children discussed in the last two chapters, such choices will sometimes be unexpressed. The teacher who discovers that her children both enjoy and learn from certain types of activities has given a real choice even though it may not be put in terms of "Which would you rather do?" On every level, furthermore, there are opportunities to let individuals and groups of children make their own choices.

The nature of choice depends in part on the kind of organizational pattern that there is on the primary level.

Nongraded, Team Teaching

Whatever the merits of the nongraded concept[3] and/or team teaching[4] as an organizational plan, the situation differs from the traditional graded, self-contained classroom concept. The authors support the two concepts but recognize that even the combination of team teaching and nongradedness does not in itself insure freedom of choice. In fact, it is possible that the application of these concepts can leave fewer options open to the personal decisions of children than the one-room classroom. A team of teachers, with the best motives in the world, can plan a program designed to meet the needs of the children in their varying levels of ability in a range of subject areas so thoroughly that while a child is moving from one interesting activity to another, the personal choices of the child as to what he will do with any part of the time are never considered. Options are created by broad level programs, but the options may belong to the teachers. This can be avoided, but to do so requires conscious intention and planning.

In one such program a problem was handled with tact and a degree of pupil choice. In a team-teaching, nongraded project, there were a variety of reading levels for the second-year group. Three little boys were failing to keep pace with the slowest group in the second-year program. They were invited to visit another group—a group in their first year in school. The boys agreed to the visit and participated in this group's activities. The invitation was repeated several times at intervals. In time the boys found that they were more successful there. Gradually they became acquainted with the other youngsters and felt more at home with the lower group. By a process that involved their own consent and decision they came to consider themselves

[3] See John I. Goodlad and Robert H. Anderson, *The Nongraded Elementary School* (New York: Harcourt Brace Jovanovich, 1963).

[4] See Judson T. Shaplin and Henry F. Olds, Jr., *Team Teaching* (New York: Harper & Row, 1964).

part of the younger group. (This account does not fully illustrate nongradedness. In a truly nongraded situation there would have been wide-ranging interchange in the program.)

For choice to function in the team-teaching approach, as in the self-contained classroom, the team must plan for choice. If one member of the team is more of a specialist in arithmetic than the other (or others), she could provide more opportunity for choice through her teaching method because of her wider knowledge of math than the one classroom teacher. The team also needs to plan periods that are open to a variety of choices. Included in such planning is time for subjects that are conducive to choice. Within both science and the social studies there is abundant opportunity for groups, self-selected on the basis of interest. These are areas in which heterogeneous grouping may be especially helpful.

In a nongraded situation there are times when it is feasible to ignore age as the criterion for forming groups. When older children are in the group, they can help younger children and at times not only do the job more effectively than the teacher, but in the process learn many things themselves. For the older children this can be a voluntary activity, giving an added dimension to choice.

First Grade

The listing by grade levels in this volume is questionable. However, most American children still enter a graded program, and thus the decision was to recognize this policy. The concepts to be expressed could apply equally to a discussion of children by age level. The reader may, if he wishes, substitute six-year-old instead of "first grade." However expressed, it is possible that the teacher of a single class unit working on her own may have more freedom than the team teacher, though she will usually not have as many resources as the team in providing for choices.

For some of these choices it is recommended that the reader review the chapter on the kindergarten. Many children in some states enter first grade with no previous schooling. This does not mean that they have no previous learning. It does mean that they need a transitional experience in which they can show what they can do and are given the opportunity to adjust effortlessly to the school program. Even in districts where there are kindergartens some type of transition should be provided for the children entering first grade. The school gives no choice but failure to those children who for whatever reason are not prepared for the program offered. The program must be adapted to the need. Part of this adaptation may include choices in the use of materials and equipment of the type used in kindergarten.

In the first grade, as in kindergarten, manipulative equipment is a standard requirement. Even those children who have made progress in the academic skills need contact with a variety of objects and materials to substantiate the abstract concepts that they are learning. Choice can be provided for all combinations of ability.

Choice also encompasses choice among more formal academic pursuits. First graders cannot choose to read in the full meaning of the term until they have learned to read. Still, almost all first graders bring with them some elements of reading skill. From the very first day that they enter first grade they will enjoy choosing books. Naturally, in the beginning they will select picture books. They will want books with stories they know. In most first grades there are "readiness" books that can be used in various ways. Sometimes these can be sent home with the child to be used in telling a story at home. Sometimes they can be cut up and used on a flannel board. Games can be made from them.

Not only in reading, but in every area of the curriculum even a first grader can be given choice. One principle might be to keep open the options that the kindergarten children enjoyed and add to these as the skills develop. As the year proceeds, first graders can do many more things and hence make many more choices than kindergarten children.

Second Grade

The second grade offers both more danger of limited choice and the possibility of exercising greater choice. The ever present danger is that choice may be neglected because it seems less necessary. Most second graders are reaching that stage of skill development in which there is pleasure in just exercising a skill. Most will read whatever is assigned with pleasure. They will usually do seat work with less discomfort or need for variation. Besides being more mature, they are more apt to be submissive. All of this makes it possible to "get by" with a regimented program. Such a program may seem "educational" on the surface, but at a minimum it contributes to a downgrading of education as an outreach to discovery into passive receptivity. Many child development experts feel that such regimentation of the already passive second grader, or seven-year-old, may contribute to more severe problems later.

The possibilities of choice grow out of the greater maturity and more responsible conduct of the second graders. These youngsters can accept responsibility for more freedom of choice and use this freedom to their own advantage educationally. They can now read. They can use the library more ably and select books according to needs. The type of projects that they are capable of undertaking is more involved and offers more choice for individual responsibility. The greater skill, perseverance, and resourcefulness make many kinds of choices possible and practical.

Third Grade

The usual third grader is an independent, outgoing person. If he has not experienced too much failure in school and life, he is ready to conquer the world. He may, in fact, need protection from himself, for he is likely to attempt too much. This does not mean strict regimentation, but cooperative planning. Nor does it mean shielding him from all failure. Learning to live with a measure of failure is part of living.

In the third grade, free, wide-ranging, honest choice can be open to the children. Even in a reading program choice exists. Third graders should have available reading materials suited to varied interests and ability levels. Individualized reading programs are very effective at this age level.

There are many third grades where freedom of choice is not permitted. Contacts with eight-year-olds have shown that they are capable of responsible choice. Happily, elements of choice have been noted in third-grade classrooms. However, neither memory nor survey of literature indicates that wide-ranging choice is characteristic on this level. Could it be that too often the danger noted with regard to second graders has become grim reality for most third graders?

Limiting Choice May Limit Responsibility

This chapter has tended to deal with the practical problems of choice as they seem to be viewed by some teachers. Teachers may themselves avoid attempting to improve their methods in fear of the responsibility of making personal decisions. This attitude is neither conducive to good mental health on the part of teachers or to stimulating classroom environment for children. Choice always involves some willingness to accept responsibility for whatever the results may be. Teachers need to exercise discretion in their classroom management. They need not assume that every experiment they attempt will prove successful. They should recognize that when children choose, they do not always choose wisely. Anyone bold enough to undertake the task of teaching can hardly hope to serve well if unwilling to experiment with caution, to try an occasional new idea, to make and acknowledge occasional mistakes.

The child who has no opportunity to make personal decisions as to what he wishes to learn and how is being "molded" into either a passive, indifferent student or a discouraged and defeated one. Some conform and are outwardly successful, but they do not learn by such processes in school to be eager seekers of knowledge. They cannot be expected to accept any major degree of responsibility toward learning and life insofar as all decisions are made for them. We have stressed that school and life are cooperative ventures. Freedom is always limited, but some degree of freedom must be given to children if they are to learn to accept responsibility for their lives.

Summary

All teachers work within a framework that includes responsibilities to nation, state, community, school administration, parents, and, even more importantly, students. Whatever the limits, there are always options. Often the chief limitation is in the understanding of the teacher. The dedicated teacher will recognize her responsibilities to all, particularly to herself and the children whom she serves. Part of this responsibility includes the willingness to make decisions herself and to accept responsibility for those decisions. Part of her responsibility is to teach her children responsibility by permitting them at least some degree of freedom in their educational experience. Responsible choice is important and practical for all children—nursery school, kindergarten, primary school or advanced levels of education.

problem solving and knowledge

The people there were more open minded. . . . They listened to the message with great eagerness, and every day they studied the Scriptures to see if what Paul said was really true.

Acts 17:11, *Good News for Modern Man*

1 2 3
4 5 6

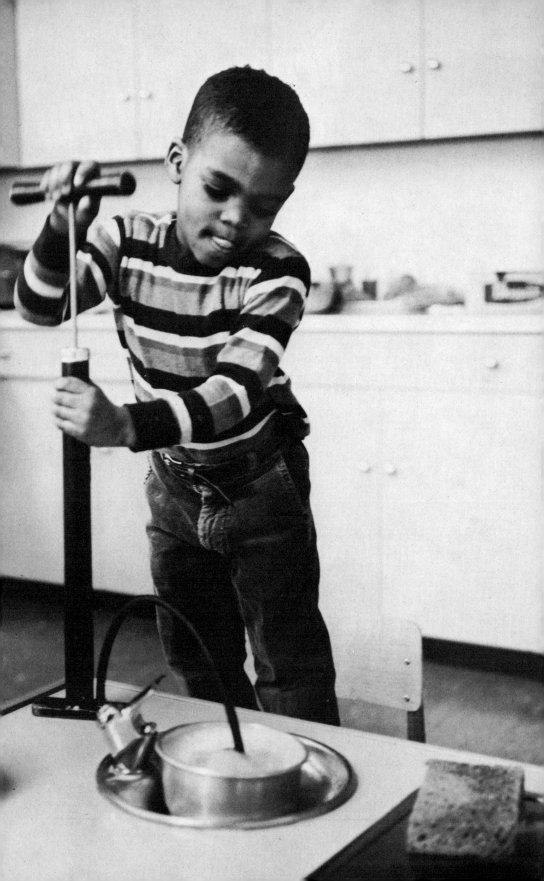

Problem Solving and Knowledge—Basic Principles

The concept of problem solving is central to all learning. Many other terms are used to identify the concept. Some writers speak of procedures for developing "inquiry skills"; others have spoken of the "experimental approach," or "the scientific method," or the "inductive method." Each phrase shares the common element of the active involvement of the learner. "Problem solving" seems a more inclusive and basic term. For some people this term, as any other term, has disagreeable or objectionable connotations. It can only be explained that the term is used in this text with very practical implications. No claim is made that all learning is problem solving—only that all meaningful learning involves some element of problem solving.

What Is Problem Solving?

Problem solving is a reaching out for knowledge. It involves a known problem and a search for solution.

Problem Solving Begins With Felt Needs

Any attempt to fill in a gap in knowledge or to find a way through a difficulty is problem solving. This is a broad definition. It can deal with something as simple as how to make a letter "o" or as difficult as how to establish lasting peace. It can range from which blocks to use for a construction project in the nursery school to the choice of a lifetime vocation, or mate, or religion. In many instances, the individual concerned requires additional information so that he can follow a course of action. There are other occasions when the basic requirement is the application of that which is already known to a new situation. Usually both the application of that which is already known and the search for additional information are required.

As used here, problem solving cannot exist unless there is a problem solver. The world is full of problems, but most people are not actively involved in the search for solutions. They cannot be so involved unless they feel that the problem is in some sense their problem and that they can contribute to its solution.

Problem solving encompasses the emotions and attitudes, which does not imply that the student who is inflamed with passion is thereby the best problem solver. Emotions can become so overwhelming that the emotion becomes the problem. Anxiety, fear, anger, and love can block problem solving. For example, a mother became very concerned because her third-grade son had practically ceased all school work. Observation and interrogation led to the conclusion that her eight-year-old son had fallen in love, not with a fellow third grader, but with the very attractive student teacher. The student teacher and the boy worked through this problem without loss of mutual regard. Other problems involving the emotions are much more difficult, and they may be present in the classroom on any level. Problems of this nature often require both some lowering of the emotional level and channeling the emotional drive toward problem solving.

The much more common difficulty in the classroom is the assumption that if interest is of importance in problem solving, it can be ordered into existence. Motivation is much more complex. We do not mean to imply that the skillful teacher never cultivates a latent interest in children. One primary teacher, for example, instead of announcing, "Boys and girls, we are going to study about Mexico for the next six weeks," started preparation months in advance. She had made a trip to Mexico and had brought back numerous articles used only in Mexico. At different times during the term she placed various ones in strategic spots in the room but said nothing about them until the children began asking questions: "What is this?" "How is it used?" "Where did you get it?" "Why is it called that?" Before long the children were pleading to study about Mexico. They became personally involved and were anxious to fill in the gaps in their knowledge.

The start in problem solving may begin with a child—his problem or his interest. The skillful teacher will take into account the relationship of any problem to the children. If the basic involvement is already present, there is no need to develop motivation.

In clarification it may be noted that "problems" in mathematics may or may not be problems to the student. This does not refer to the form of the "problem," as, old math, new math, math story problems, or numeral problems. No problem exists if the child is too confused to find any sense in the statement; neither does a problem exist if he already understands the statement fully. Suppose that in "old-fashioned" terms a child were asked to multiply 9 × 7. If he not only knows the answer but understands the underlying assumptions of the multiplication, for him there is no problem. Whatever terms are used, this is not problem solving. It is drill. On the other hand, the student who lacks either the information or the assumptions has a problem. Let us assume that the pupil has merely forgotten that 9 × 7 is 63, a variety of approaches could be used. He could ask someone who knows; look at a multiplication table; multiply 7 × 10 and subtract 7; add a column of nine 7s; arrange nine sets of 7 blocks and count them. Any of these approaches is in some sense "problem solving."

Problem Solving Reaches Out for Solutions

Problem solving goes beyond the sensing of a need. If problems are to be solved by a pupil, he must do something about them. There must be a reaching out for solutions. Meaningful answers to problems can seldom be simply furnished by teachers. At a minimum the pupil must have some degree of interest in finding a solution. He must put something of himself into the search for meaning. He thus becomes an active seeker, not merely a passive recipient.

Even this is, in part, the result of an attitude. Children do not attempt to solve problems unless they feel that the problem can be solved. The sense of confidence needs constant encouragement. Across the centuries there have been a number of individuals who made slow starts in life and were later outstandingly successful. The question may be raised as to how many potential geniuses are being lost to the future by branding all children failures who do not quite keep up to a predetermined pace. No child need be a failure. If he is bright enough to attend school, he can learn. If he learns what he is capable of learning, he is successful. If he feels successful, he is willing to attempt the problem just beyond his present grasp.

Both teachers and students can be deluded into thinking that problem solving is taking place when in reality only a guessing game is in progress. John Holt points out both the humor and tragedy of the current school situation in his book, *How Children Fail*. Particularly in the chapter headed "Strategy," he discusses his own observations of the guessing game as it is frequently carried on in the American classroom.[1] This appears to be a result of the school emphasis on right answers rather than on thought. There is even evidence of this on the college and graduate levels. If there is to be any significant reasoning about educational content, educators must shift the emphasis from speed and passing (attained by giving the prescribed "right"

[1] John Holt, *How Children Fail* (New York: Dell, 1964), Chapter 1.

answer) to depth and understanding. Perhaps if children can see immediate profit in true problem solving, they may eventually learn to work in the fashion advocated even when the reward is not as immediate.

Problem-Solving Skill Develops With Practice

The teacher will need some concept of the techniques of problem solving for her own purposes; however, the text will not detail these techniques. It is unlikely that the primary teacher will present these concepts formally. What she attempts, instead, is to encourage habitual ways of thinking and acting. She listens and helps the child clarify the problem. Her attentiveness and assistance may be enough for the child to discover that there is a way to finish the job or learn the answer. He is praised both for effort and solutions. If he cannot proceed on his own, he is helped to consider other possibilities. As ideas develop, the child is encouraged to test out his ideas, to double check them, and, if possible, to apply them to new problems. *In this way problem solving becomes a habitual way of looking at problems.*

Why Is It Necessary to Emphasize Problem Solving?

In part, the answers to the question as to why schools need more emphasis on a problem-solving approach have already been suggested. Four answers are discussed below.

1. *Schools have not been as effective as they should be in training students to think rationally.* Note the vocal minority of young people who have behaved as though democracy consisted of silencing all opposition. Or look at the many newspaper headlines that seem to indicate that most of the American public demands simple solutions to complicated and misunderstood problems. Our public schools are not the only agencies responsible for these attitudes, but they certainly had an opportunity to influence most people, young and old.

Indeed, somehow, schools have succeeded in teaching children not to think. One of the authors was a counselor for high school and college students for many years. He administered, as the occasion warranted, several hundred individual intelligence tests. The young people with whom he worked tended to be "bright." One group of questions in the test required a combination of reasoning and simple arithmetic. There were exceptions, but most students "blew" that particular section. Out of curiosity the examiner asked many of the students to explain how they had arrived at their answers. Almost invariably, each student had searched in his mind for some formula to apply, but he had been unable to find a specific one that fitted the particular problem. Instead of then "working" out the problem by reasoning, he either guessed at the answer or just omitted it. Apparently, each student performed just as he had been trained: "Don't reason a problem out! Look for a formula to try." There are no statistics to back the conclusion, but the author involved is quite certain that his deduction is valid.

John Holt tells of working with a fifth-grade girl to help her solve a problem.[2] He kept making the problem simpler and simpler, hoping to find the level on which she could function. As he watched the expression on the face of the girl, he realized that she was neither troubled about solving the problem nor was she attempting to think. She was waiting for a clue as to the right answer.

A mathematics major earned part of his way through college by tutoring in his field. One summer he worked with a boy named George who was to enter the seventh grade in the fall. George not only was unable to do sixth-grade arithmetic, but he was not even very good with third-grade material. What disturbed the tutor even more was that on any level, George had no idea whether or not his answer was right or how he could find out if it were correct.

One day the boy surprised the tutor by indicating that he had made an effort to memorize the multiplication table. This did not harmonize with the tutor's educational theories, but he gave due credit for this show of initiative. The tutor, then, attempted to make use of the memory work. Below is a brief quotation from his report:

After repeated mistakes, I asked George to show me how he could find the answer to one of the multiplications without the use of the tables. He looked at me as if I had asked him an impossible question and after five minutes said, "I don't know." I then asked him to think about it and try to show an example of one of the tables. This question made him nervous. . . . For some reason when I asked him to think, he went into a different world. He sat there, looking right at me without any appearance of thinking. He seemed to be in a trance. . . . I was dumbfounded. Did he have such little trust in his own judgment that any attempt to think turned his mind off?

The questions for all teachers would seem to be, "How do we keep from turning minds off?" And, "How do we turn them back on if they are already tuned out?" At least part of that answer seems to be "turn children loose" to work on problems that concern them.

2. *Education is only meaningful when it opens the door to learning as to how to cope with life.* The problem-solving approach is not the only element of meaningful learning, but it plays a major role. It trains the problem solver to look for a relationship between what he already knows and the problem. In the process of seeking solutions the student asks himself what it is that he already knows that can be applied to his problem.

With regard to young children the point was made that what was taught was not abstract principles but the development of a habitual way of attacking the unknown. In part, it is this attitude that transfers. There is little need to

[2] Holt, *op. cit.*, pp. 24–25.

emphasize that teachers cannot possibly furnish even their brightest students with all the information they will need for the future. Teachers can give them an approach to life that will enable them to reach out for solutions to the unknown problems that the future holds. Thus, it is not implied that nursery school children or third-grade students will at these levels deal effectively with major social problems. If they discover that present problems within their range of competency can be faced successfully, there is good reason to believe that they will be able to move on to face future problems.

3. *Problem solving can be a major motivating force.* In fact, in so far as individuals face felt problems and feel that they can do something about them, problem solving is probably the major motivating force in learning. This is true in all of life. The truth of this fact does not rule out the need of teachers, other adults, books, or any other means of learning. What it involves is the very important and serious attempt to make use of the present problems the student faces as a motive for integrating and applying present knowledge, and then moving on to learn more. Nor does this mean that the teacher always uses only the stated problems of students. Many problems may not be openly stated. The young child, for example, may not be able to clearly formulate in words what he needs to know. The sensitive teacher will not only make use of the evident problems, but also those she suspects to be present in the lives of children. It may be utopian to believe that all of school learning can be clearly related to problem solving. It is practical and down to earth to look for ways in which the problems on or just below the surface can become the basis for learning projects. If teachers and children can find ways to move out together from the problems children face, they save time and effort, and side step the danger of artificiality.

4. *Problem solving helps a teacher make material relevant to students.* Problem solving as a means of relevance is not so much a different topic as a different emphasis to what has already been stated. The child gains knowledge only as it serves his own purposes. He can only organize and reorganize the present learning, and those learnings he reaches out toward in terms of his own frame of reference. He can assimilate in his search for a solution only that which has a meaning, and thus relevance, for him. What is relevant differs for all people, be they adult or children. The factors making up what is relevant are too complex to be understood completely by anyone. The teacher does her best to understand the thinking of the child, but she may never be completely successful. Her task is to accept the problem that the child raises and support him as he seeks to work through it and seeks to relate it to his own frame of reference.

To take only one comparatively simple aspect of the problem. A very great age gap always exists between teacher and student. It comes as somewhat of a shock to a new teacher just out of college that in the terms of the first grader she is an ancient person. She is three times the age of her pupils. This age differential, for the nursery school child and the experienced teacher, can go beyond twenty to one. The greatest tragedy that can happen to a child is to place him under the direction of an adult who ignores his childhood and his frame of reference. It is the nature of the child that he neither thinks nor expresses his thoughts in adult terms. Likewise, it is almost equally tragic when an adult becomes so accustomed to children's ways of expression and what is relevant to them that the adult ceases to think and talk like an adult. Either extreme can be prevented. The most effective way is to permit children to learn as children, supported at all points in their endeavor by competent adults.

Summary

Problem solving involves both attitude and training. There must be a felt need for a solution. In addition, the attitude must be present that problems can be solved and are worth solving. With these basics children can develop an habitual approach to problems that considers relevant facts, discovers what is needed for a solution, searches for the elements that will make the solution possible, checks solutions found, and applies them to new situations. When the problem-solving approach is made an integral part of learning, present educational failure can be reduced. The educational process becomes more relevant to life, more easily applied in new situations, and a stronger motivating force in the acquisition of new knowledge.

CHAPTER FOUR

Problem Solving and Knowledge in the Nursery School

The little girl of this story is now a mature woman. She would not remember the night when shortly before her third birthday she looked up into a clear night sky, saw the moon, and reached for it. She tried to jump to it, and then loudly demanded that it be brought to her. Part of her attempt is no longer impossible. Man has reached the moon, but by a very long and complicated cooperative effort.

In some ways the young child is still reaching out for understanding of a vast and complicated universe. No adult can hand all this to him. Neither can he attain very much entirely on his own.

Problem Solving Before Three

To the best of anyone's knowledge, the newborn baby enters a world that is so vague and undifferentiated that it is not yet even confusing.[1] However,

[1] Paul Henry Mussen, John Janeway Conger, and Jerome Kagan, *Child Development and Personality* (New York: Harper & Row, 1969), pp. 155–156.

he is not quite as helpless as once thought. But helpless, dependent, and uninformed he is. He does not know his own mother; he is not sure that his arms and legs are a part of him; he is not aware of the existence of anything not in his immediate focus.

Help a Necessary Ingredient

It is self-evident that the baby faces many problems. It seems equally clear that he has very little with which to work. An adult might wonder, facetiously, why the baby does not give up in advance. Quite apart from the obvious need of at least one more mature person to take care of the baby's physical necessities, babies may and do "give up" unless there is something more. It takes affection and stimulation from others to keep a baby thriving. Thus the baby does not "give up" in advance partly because he does not understand how far he has to reach. But more important, he keeps on at the apparently impossible task of learning because someone accepts him in his helplessness and tries to help him come to terms with his environment. Not only does someone help him, but this someone has confidence that he *will* someway learn all that is expected of him. More than even this is involved, though.

Maturation and Experience

The human infant is born with a few abilities, but almost all that he learns is dependent on maturation and experience. Maturation, in the sense used here, means primarily the development of the central nervous system and all the other systems that make up the human body. Hereditary factors do affect development in countless and highly complicated ways. This is basic to all learning, including the ability to solve problems. Equally true, and more important from the standpoint of the teacher, is that all learning depends on experience. Experience is more important not because anyone can be sure that the experience has more influence on the development of the individual, but because it is the experience that can be altered.

Exposure

There seems little doubt that much in the experience of the child up to the age of three influences his later learning. Somehow almost all children learn a great deal before their third birthday. One is unable to speak too authoritatively about how the young child learns because the child cannot explain. Others can only watch what seems to be happening and make the best assumptions possible.

Through observation of very young children, educators and psychologists have found that familiarity with people and "other perceptual aspects of the environment" precede recognition.[2] Some things that appear "silly" may

---

[2] John Holt, *How Children Learn* (New York: Dell, 1969).

be rather good educational practice. The parents who talk to their children before the children are able to understand may be on the right track. And the more they talk to them as if they were grownups, the better. Reading to a baby may be good. Over and beyond the value of clear and continuing contact with a meaningful adult, there is value from the baby's becoming familiar with the sound of words. At some point very early in life the very young child begins to retain something from this type of contact. Whatever this "something" is, it seems to have value, as does the play interactions between baby and adult. Providing the young child with safe toys and various types of objects also has its place. This exposure to speech and other types of sounds, and to various kinds of objects is part of what the adult can do for the child. In providing such an environment, the mother or other adult caretaker is performing a function very similar to the later work of the nursery school teacher. She is providing the support and environment in which the child can solve some of the most difficult and important tasks he will face in all of life. One of these tasks is that of communicating with others. The adult cannot provide the full solution and should not attempt to force the child beyond his abilities, but the adult is essential to the solution of the problem.

Self-effort

Apart from what others are doing to help, the young child attempts a thousand things on his own, and some things he tries over and over and over again. Very early be begins to learn by imitating and by experimenting. It does not matter which comes first, provided it is recognized that both are there. The baby hears voices; he hears words; he hears sentences. By the time he is three he can usually do quite a bit on his own with all of these. In the process he may have invented and discarded elements of a private language. He has tried out all kinds of sounds, words, grammatical combinations. Watching all this, we might say that the "impossible" task of learning was not quite as difficult as it first appeared. It looks as though this helpless newborn creature has brought with him into the world a great potential, a drive toward competence and understanding, and the almost infinite patience needed to reach his goals.

An article in a popular magazine refers to an experiment by a mother who concealed a tape recorder in the bedroom of her two-year-old son to record what he said at night before he went to sleep.[3] Among other things, she found that the little boy played with words and word patterns: "What color blanket. . . . what color mop. . . . what color glass." "Block. . . . yellow block. . . . Look at all the yellow blocks." "I go. Bobo goes. We go." Apparently, the little boy was both drilling himself and experimenting not only with words, but with grammatical formations. Here the youngster without

[3] Carol Barach and Caroline Bird, "How Babies Learn to Talk," *Woman's Day*, XXXII (September 1969), 62–63, 101–102.

prompting or help was making an effort on his own to solve his problem of communication with the world around him.

Problem Solving by Three- and Four-year-olds

It is a reasonable assumption on the evidence available that children, with such help and support as is available to them, learn actively and persistently in the early years of their lives. Whatever nursery schools do they must not block off this eagerness for learning. Staffs of nursery schools must never lose sight of the fact that children change in various ways quite apart from any formal aspects of their educational experience and these changes will influence their learning pattern. In addition, there are no uniform growth patterns. One can assume a general pattern of growth only. Too many other factors, such as traumatic experiences, peculiar to the child enter the picture to allow the nursery school teacher to expect uniform development.

Child development specialists emphasize varying factors in the changes that occur with growth. Two of the theories seem particularly pertinent to the purposes of this chapter. One of these is Erik Erikson's concept of developmental tasks.[4] The first two of these tasks are the development of "trust" and "autonomy." There is no one magic day in which the first task ends and the second begins. They overlap and continue. Still, it is possible that the young child is concentrating on learning to trust not only people but a world that has organization and meaning. The lesson is never over, but the emphasis shifts to the learning task of autonomy. This increasing pressure to find himself as an independent person may give an added dimension to problem solving. The child may seem strongly compelled to find solutions without interference.

Frances Ilg and Louise Ames emphasize a different but equally helpful factor in growth.[5] They have noted that there appear to be behavioral cycles in the developing life of the child. The timing and effect differs with the individual, but each child usually goes through periods of equilibrium, periods when they are more aggressive and outgoing, and periods of disequilibrium and withdrawal. Three- and four-year-olds do tend to differ as to their place in the cycle. In reference to a nursery school situation, one difficulty with the three-year-old is frequently how to persuade the child to become part of a nursery school group. The problem with the four-year-old may be how to keep him from skipping out to explore the rest of the neighborhood.

Social Problem Solving

If the child who has been making rapid progress at home seems to backtrack somewhat on entering nursery school, this is not necessarily a cause for alarm.

[4] Henry W. Maier, *Three Theories of Child Development* (New York: Harper & Row, 1969), Chapter 2.
[5] Frances L. Ilg and Louise Bates Ames, *Child Behavior* (New York: Dell, 1955), Chapter 2.

There may be elements of social learning involved in such a shift that are so big and important, or even so frightening, that other forms of learning may be hindered. A very big problem for the three-year-old may be that of *learning to accept separation from home.*[6] With this social problem children may need help. For many three-year-olds it may be necessary to make the parting a gradual process. It probably is helpful if the nursery school for three-year-olds can begin with short sessions or fewer sessions per week. Children with a major problem of separation from the home must work it out. Other problems may have to wait until this is overcome. Resolving being away from home may be a problem at four or five, but it is much less likely to be so. Whatever the age, skillful teachers and parents will give support to the child as he works through his problem.

For the three-year-old there may also be the problem of *living with and working with other children.* Child development theory distinguishes between the "parallel" play of the usual three-year-old and the cooperative play or work of older children. Anyone who has watched a group of mixed-age children playing together will have noted exceptions. A three-year-old does sometimes play with an adult or an older child. What is under discussion is what is characteristic of his age group.

To some extent the social problem of the three-year-old may not be simply separation, but "all the other children." The teacher can help by not forcing participation or any kind of friendship on the child. This, of course, applies for all children. Usually, familiarity has to come before acceptance and understanding. For example: For several days an adult passed a small group of young children. Each day a slight greeting was given and returned. Then one morning he walked past when only two little girls were playing. They had a kitten to show. It was admired and petted. The little girls then continued the conversation by explaining their feelings about each other. It seems that they had decided they would be sisters. Seemingly, familiarity with the presence of the adult opened the way to communication.

The child who has played with many other children and has visited the nursery school may adjust quickly. Others may need longer. Social and emotional growth continue after the child has adjusted to life in the nursery school. There are many interpersonal problems to be faced and overcome. Someone once defined the problem of the nursery school teacher as teaching the boys who hit, not to, and the ones who did not hit, to fight back. In a sense, the definition is correct. More realistically, it means letting children work through their problems on their own within reasonable limits, while guarding against danger to the other children. The working through of relationships with other people begins long before nursery school and continues for the rest of life.

It is a reasonable assumption based upon both observation and reported experiments that nursery school experience contributes to both academic

[6] Majorie Graham Janis, *A Two-Year-Old Goes to Nursery School: A Case Study of Separation Reactions* (New York: National Association for the Education of Young Children, 1965).

and social adjustment. In the past nursery schools have tended to justify their existence on the latter premise.[7] This is not to be abandoned, but nursery schools can and do contribute to other aspects of problem solving.

Academic Problem Solving

The solution of social problems is not strictly divorced from other learning. Problem solving in cooperative living may well demand the very highest kind of intellectual activity. At least, we are being constantly reminded that we are finding it easier to reach out to the planets than to our neighbors. There is, of course, the added but less seldom stressed fact that the vast majority of mankind can leave the reaching of the planets to a handful of assorted experts, whereas all of us are involved in social relationships.

More important from the standpoint of immediate concern is the question of applying pressure for academic learning to small children as against the concept that childhood is a time for fun. It is seldom noted that the area of actual conflict is between *pressure* and *fun* and not between learning and enjoyment. A negative illustration may partially explain what is meant by academic learning. A highly regarded nursery school known to the authors manages to avoid almost any provision that would permit the child to solve problems in such a way as to develop increasing academic content. It does this by providing good and expensive play equipment—swings, merry-go-round, and so forth. The children enjoy the equipment but its contribution to academic learning is minimal. The school then teaches by reverting to highly directed seat work, including listening to the teacher and coloring ditto sheets. There is in this both fun for the children and an attempt to teach them, but the two are not combined.

The good nursery school, what ever its orientation, attempts to lay a background and provide situations in which children can seek the answers to their questions about life. This includes opportunities to ask questions of adults. It includes opportunities to discover that there is meaning in symbols that will become increasingly clearer as the child actively cooperates in the search for meaning. It includes opportunities to observe, to investigate, to try out things within the safe environment of the nursery school. In such a situation the child is learning new facts and also clarifying what he already knows. He is also developing keener awarenesses as to categories and differences. Part of this is academic learning by almost any definition. Part is background for later skill development. For both kinds of learning, the good nursery school makes use of the child's problems, particularly his eagerness to understand his world, in providing for intellectual development.

Part of the strength of good nursery schools is that they are protective places for children. Parents looking for a nursery school are usually most concerned with a safe and happy place for their children. Having satisfied

[7] Katherine H. Read, *The Nursery School: A Human Relationships Laboratory* (Philadelphia: Saunders, 1966).

these requirements, they might have a further question. Is it possible that the nursery school is so artificially safe and happy that nothing of importance to intellectual growth occurs? Play is fine and good; children need it. But does play automatically insure adequate intellectual stimulation?

The most promising development in nursery school programs is the increasing possibility of providing a happy learning environment without bringing undesirable pressure. Nursery schools have an advantage over most homes in this area. Many articles in the home are dangerous for young children. A three-year-old is not ready to experiment with boiling water, steak knives, or power tools. Parents may have to say "No" more often than should be necessary.[8] Nursery school teachers must say "No" too on occasion, but not as often. The nursery school is built for the child. The materials are such that the child can use them with comparative safety.

An even more important aspect of the environment in the good nursery school is that the equipment and the materials can be secured with the learning potential of both in mind.

Methods of Teaching Problem Solving in the Nursery School

Methods and materials are not identical, but they are always interrelated, particularly so in the nursery school. Even more than in the kindergarten, perhaps, the nursery school teacher teaches by providing the appropriate materials with which to gain experience.

Opportunity for Free Exploration

The good nursery school has many materials that, within broad limits, can be used as the child desires. There are blocks, dolls, sand, water, paint, and clay. There may be a house with suitable furniture plus household equipment such as pots and pans. There is safe equipment for climbing on, or jumping off, or crawling through. There will be some understood regulations—stated clearly and as often as necessary. All the items mentioned (and others too)—introduced when appropriate to the needs of the children—can be used by the children to discover, to explore, to solve problems as they arise. They can be used by a child playing essentially by himself or by two or several children as they begin to cooperate in dramatic play. In each activity problem solving is involved.

Self-corrective Materials

The world has elements of freedom, but it also has order and regularity. Nursery school helps to teach the latter in many ways. Some of this teaching

---

[8] Bruno Bettelheim, *Love Is Not Enough* (New York: Collier Books, 1965), p. 14.

may involve the use of what may be called self-corrective devices. These range from simple puzzles that go together in only one way, to boards into which pegs fit in an order prescribed by the shape of the holes, to towers, stairs, pyramids, matching boards, exercises in the use of buttons and zippers, and much more.

For some things in life there is only one right way. Many kinds of skills should be practiced. If the child chooses his problem and decides the length of practice, he is exercising a degree of freedom. The foregoing are some of the kinds of materials that the Montessori schools use. These schools are sometimes criticized on the basis that they appear to exclude free play and limit interchange between children. Whether either criticism is valid, there is no problem if such materials are only a part of the total program.

For their possible usefulness in problem solving one might consider one of Maria Montessori's observations. She watched one day while a very small girl of three placed graded cylinders in a block designed for the purpose. The girl showed such concentration that Montessori tried two kinds of distractions. First, she had the other children parade and sing as they marched around the room. The child kept right on working. Then she lifted the chair in which the girl was sitting onto a table. The child clung to her apparatus and then continued working. It is stated that Montessori counted the repetition of the same exercise forty-two times. The same account of this experience adds:

Then quite suddenly she stopped "as though coming out of a dream." She smiled as if she was very happy; her eyes shone and she looked around her. And, strangely enough, after all that long concentration she appeared to be rested rather than fatigued.[9]

Apparently Maria Montessori regarded this discovery of the young child's ability to concentrate and the need to repeat manipulations many times as something almost mystical.

John Holt[10] may be both more down to earth and more practical in suggesting that doing something once is not enough to prove to a young child that things work this way or that he actually understands how it works. He needs many times and many trials.

Need for Varied Repetition

It was noted earlier that any child may need to perform an experiment over and over. He may also wish to return more briefly to the same experiment and perform it again the next day to make sure that it still works the same way. Anyone who has worked with small children will attest that more often than not the story that the young child will select to have read to him is one that

[9] E. M. Standing, Maria Montessori: Her Life and Work (New York: New American Library, 1962), p. 40.
[10] Holt, op. cit.

he already knows "by heart." He may, in fact, object strenuously if a single word is changed. Probably there are so many things the young child does not know that he wants to be very sure that some things remain the same. He needs to check and recheck.

An added dimension to take into consideration is that the same experiment can be performed with more than one kind of material. Sand pours, and so does water. Water can change form without losing volume within containers. Clay can change forms without loss of amount as one manipulates it. There can be three people, three boxes, three chairs, or three cookies. Children sometimes need to do the same thing with the same materials; they also need to discover that they can do essentially the same thing with different materials.

A college student taught a young child to write his own first name. She used several methods to accomplish this. Her greatest thrill came when an excited command from the little boy brought her hurrying to the living room. The boy had discovered in a television advertisement the first letter of his name. This is a step in problem solving, but part of it was done with help and part on his own.

Problem Solving and Time

There are times in life when all of us must rush and hurry, just as there are emergencies when children must do what they are told at once. The planning and explanation of limits should take account of both actualities of life and school. To be ready for the possibility, one can make a game of such matters with young children. A necessary interruption once in a while is training for life too. But many schools, more often those above this level, put a self-defeating emphasis on speed. Children are asked to hurry through one piece of work to start something else when neither work has any particular significance to the child. Sometimes teachers are much more interested in quick answers than in thoughtful ones.

Good nursery schools have few time limits. Snack time may, for example, call for total participation. Everyone must go home—usually at about the same time. But not everyone has to stop building a house or working on a puzzle because the music has started. Children absorbed in activities may continue while a story is being read. Some children listen better this way. Pressures for speed, for finishing this to do that, should be reduced to a minimum. Pressures for staying with a given activity are also held to a minimum. If the child has no present interest in a certain activity, many other worthwhile things can be done. If a child is absorbed in something, almost certainly, more than fun is happening. The child is learning something about the make-up, the feel, the way materials respond. He is solving an immediate problem that is part of the greater problem of dealing with life. Too often, children are hurried along for the adult's reasons.

Positives and Negatives for Teachers

Nursery school children are striving for independence; they want to solve their own problems. Part of the skill of teaching for this age level consists of "setting the stage" and then remaining unobtrusive. Children often need moral support. This is not intrusion; it is normal interest. Part of a child's problem is finding someone interested enough to listen and to understand. The nursery school teacher has a wonderful opportunity to become an expert at this.

There is also the opportunity to engage in meaningful interchange with the children. A simple direction or explanation may suffice. It may be the suggestion of possible alternatives or the question as to what other possibilities exist.

There is little demonstrating. The teacher's purpose is not to show off her own skill at problem solving; it is to encourage the child to try his hand. This is more likely to be achieved by praising problem-solving achievements and efforts than by showing how to solve the problems. Still, there are times when direct help is beneficial. A limited number of "You might want to try it this way" remarks can be stimulating rather than stifling. Chiefly, it is the sensing of needs, the provision through experimental materials, and the encourage- ment of self-discovery that accomplishes the goal of helping the child to solve the problems confronting him.

Summary

Children much younger than three engage in important problem-solving activities. The nursery school when organized to implement problem solving can permit more such activity than the home. Part of this activity is in the nature of social learning. Such learning is important, in itself, and contributes to other learnings. A good nursery school, however, will encourage more academically oriented problem solving through both self-corrective and variable-use materials. In so doing it may set a pattern of thought that will influence later learning. The nursery school should be a place where the child usually has all the time he needs to satisfy his present curiosity as to how things work. The emphasis here, as in all of school, should be on depth of learning rather than speed.

CHAPTER FIVE

Problem Solving and Knowledge in the Kindergarten

The query "How high a bridge?" asked by a child in a Head Start class in a mountain community illustrates almost all that this chapter attempts to present. The physical setting was quite satisfactory—a good-sized cheerful room for the number of children involved. The equipment was satisfactory, too. With the teacher and children together in the room, the cheerful atmosphere changed to one of dark gloom. The teacher was a disaster as far as her understanding of teaching young children was concerned. Each child was seated in a desk, far enough away from each other so that he could not touch or speak to anyone—except the teacher. The activities consisted of seat work—weaving a mat, making a Japanese lantern, or putting a handmade flower in a paper cup—mostly done by the teacher and her aid. These "accomplishments" were put on exhibit and eventually taken home to the parents. The children were regimented, frustrated, and very unhappy. If they were learning anything, it probably was to hate school and to feel themselves failures.

One day the teacher was ill, and the teacher's aid, an untrained assistant but well-meaning and kind, took over the class. She could not do much more than relax and let the children enjoy their temporary freedom. This is not to imply that there was good teaching that day. Nevertheless, the situation was so much better than it had been that it looked good by comparison. Not only that, but good things were happening. The children were free to explore, to experiment, and to try things on their own. For that one day they both enjoyed school and learned from the experience.

On the day that the teacher was absent, four boys constructed a bridge. They had blocks and other necessary building equipment, but they still had problems which they talked over with each other. (This was a good language arts lesson.) The roadbed of the bridge had to be wide enough and flat enough for cars and trucks, but since a river ran under the bridge and boats used the river, the bridge had to be high enough for the boats to pass under it and still level enough for the cars and trucks. Note that the problem is one of engineering with mathematical overtones. The boys were, also, in the midst of what might well be considered a very worthwhile science experiment. It was more even than science. This was a problem involving transportation, and that is in the area of the social studies.

One is tempted to stop here. The incident nearly says it all. Not only was learning going on related to academic content and language skills, but also the boys had chosen a project of interest to them. In this they had made a step toward maturity. They had done even more. They were solving a fairly complicated problem by using their pooled information and intelligence. They worked together as a team to accomplish their purpose.

The remainder of the chapter will attempt to make more explicit some of the necessary ingredients of problem solving in the kindergarten. There is overlap not only among these ingredients, but also with what has already been discussed in the previous chapter. But here a different age group is under consideration and the approach is different.

The Role of the Child in Problem Solving and Knowledge

At any age level it is the child who is the learner. The kindergarten child is, normally, the world's most eager problem solver—a truism that may partially result from what schools tend to do to children in the more "rigid experience" that lies ahead. Regardless, most children come to kindergarten not only eager to learn, but capable of competent problem-solving behavior. Most five-year-old children are calm, happy, and curious.

Problems Solved Through Action

The kindergarten child is still a *man of action*. This does not mean that he is not also a thinker. His mind is as active as his body. He thinks better when he can manipulate objects and materials. Thus, whenever possible, it is valuable to permit the kindergarten child to make use of hands and body. In working with paints, blocks, puzzles, construction materials, or any other media, the child will be solving some kind of surface problem. Usually much more than this is happening. The child is working on problems that involve understanding of time, space, numbers, symbolic meanings, communication, and so forth. The media used serve the problem-solving needs of the child both on a surface and a much more involved level.

Group Problem Solving

For most kindergarten children problem solving becomes a group activity—a natural development, if encouraged. Children in small groups, usually, exchange ideas. They do not face the same problems as older adults and children. They don't have to relax barriers to express ideas. Their minds seem to rove freely and more than one idea may be presented and debated.[1] Both free-ranging and critical thinking goes on spontaneously. Not only can kindergarten children express ideas to each other freely, but sometimes they foresee that certain ideas will not work. More often they try out ideas. When they find that they will not work, they try to figure out what the problem is and how it can be solved. They tend to be group problem solvers.

Problems of Relationships

Because of the characteristic discussed, *kindergarten is probably the best spot in all of life in which to work toward the solution of interpersonal relationships.* Humans interact with other humans in some way from conception to death. Young children are very much interested in other children. It is in kindergarten, in general, that children have developed to the stage of being willing and able not only to work together but with each other in projects without the complicating factors that enter into personal relations thereafter. Not all kindergarten work is cooperative, but cooperation is present in some stage. In this early stage some of the difficulties of interpersonal relationships have not yet grown to great proportions. The question of two sexes is present and related to the learning situation, but usually no excessive attraction or aversion is present. Race is there, but this is no problem to the children. Problems of differences in personality, ability, and interests are present, but they are not as much of an obstacle to cooperation as they may be later. Kindergarten is much more than a social learning experience. It is, also, potentially, a much richer environment for learning to solve problems of interpersonal relationships than is generally recognized.

Knowledge Comes Through Problem Solving

That knowledge is acquired through problem solving is an obvious conclusion that has been presented before and will receive greater emphasis in the next chapter. Consequently, the discussion will be brief here. An emphasis on problem solving, on any level, does not mean a haphazard program, nor

[1] Ruth H. Nixon and Clifford L. Nixon *The Art of Kindergarten Instruction* (Pembroke, N.C.: Pembroke State College, 1969), Chapter 4.

does it mean a nonacademic curriculum. Problems faced, of any kind, call for a consolidation of what is already known, which usually leads to the incorporation of new information into a reorganized body of knowledge.

Problem solving on the kindergarten level is both a purpose and a means. The most important aspect (and also the most evident) of the problem-solving method is that it teaches individuals to solve problems.[2] The ability to solve problems is the most important skill the school can teach. In addition, successfully facing and surmounting a problem adds something to any individual's feeling of confidence and probably to his willingness to attempt a new problem.

We cannot predict what lies ahead for the world; one can only predict that the world will be different. One also can predict that the world will face problems that no one can even imagine now. It follows that a teacher cannot possibly teach children all the facts or all the solutions. Hopefully, the children can be helped to learn to solve present problems and to be somewhat prepared to face whatever problems the future may hold. And the kindergarten teacher is instrumental in setting the child on the right path of effective problem solving.

The Role of Environment in Problem Solving and Knowledge

The present section deals with two factors that should be so well understood as to need no emphasis. But in actual practice, both are often either ignored or misinterpreted.

The Background of Kindergarten Children

In the illustration at the beginning of this chapter four little boys worked together on a construction project. It was not the kind of a construction project that might have occurred to children from an urban plains city. They were mountain children. These boys knew mountains, rivers, bridges, boats, and trucks. These were elements of their daily lives, not the Japanese lanterns that their regular teacher had them make. They made use of what they knew to do something they could understand and enjoy. The "known" led to the discovery of problems and the search for solutions and resulted in the addition of concepts and the feeling of successful experience.

All children come to school with a background. It may be a background that is very different from that of the teacher. She should allow children to work on the kinds of problems that fit their cultural backgrounds. It is a more fruitful way of leading on and out into the larger world of knowledge.[3] None

[2] For a full discussion of this at the kindergarten level, see Lorraine Sherer, *How Good Is Our Kindergarten?* (Washington, D. C.: Association for Childhood Education International, 1959), p. 15.

[3] See Frank Riessman, *The Culturally Deprived Child* (New York: Harper & Row, 1962), Chapter 7.

of us comprehends, immediately, that completely foreign and imposed projects may lead to indifference and discouragement.

One's background includes more than the home and community. In the illustration none of the children had been to a nursery school or kindergarten. The teaching experiences attempted in those brief weeks should have been both more flexible and better planned. Materials should have been included that would have linked more clearly background and the coming school experience.

The Environment of the Kindergarten Classroom

The teacher is the most important single element of the classroom environment. What she does in the classroom cannot be separated from her attitude. Her attitude needs to be one that not only includes kindliness and concern, but, also, respect for the child and his abilities. Such an attitude is conducive to the active involvement of the child in the learning process. Perhaps the greatest emphasis in this text will be given to the concept that *children learn not by being lectured to, but by involvement in the adventure of learning.*

Space and arrangement greatly affect the environment. There are many earnest and concerned kindergarten teachers who labor under impossible conditions. It takes space for separate, freely chosen activities. Children can talk to each other while engaging in other activities without disturbing each other, but not unless space and arrangement permit. If the children are too crowded, the all-pervading problem of the teacher then becomes how to keep an imposed discipline. Under these circumstances problem-solving opportunities for children are severely limited.

Appropriate materials are essential to problem solving. Everything said about nursery school materials applies here. Kindergarten children can work with more complicated puzzles, more daring apparatus, and more involved constructional materials. Included in these may be many kinds of self-corrective materials. Problem solving is built into these materials. There is no harm in learning that many times there is only one way to solve a problem. Materials, however, should, also, continue to include those which can be used for a variety of purposes. These lend themselves to a freer kind of problem solving. Probably this free-ranging problem solving is even more important to learning.

The Role of the Teacher

As we have seen, the teacher plays a central role in the teaching of problem-solving techniques. She does this in a number of ways.

Setting the Stage for Problem Solving

There are innumerable ways that the teacher can adjust the circumstances and environment so that a problem is solved. One of the finest science lessons observed in a kindergarten involved an aquarium inhabited by tadpoles. Possibly some child had brought the tadpoles to school. If so, the teacher had welcomed them as a possible resource for a lesson in science and had obtained the aquarium for them either from the school or from a child in the classroom. Possibly the teacher had checked as to what the class knew about tadpoles and what they would become. She may have given a few words of explanation. Whatever else was done, the tadpoles were placed in the aquarium, fed by the children, and allowed to develop. The children became fascinated as the tadpoles began to change shape, and they watched with intense curiosity. For several days most of their free time was spent in the section of the room where the aquarium had been placed. They just stood and observed. Probably the chief problem solved for each child was simply, "What was happening to those tadpoles?" The teacher may have added to what was being observed, but teaching science through problem solving can be as simple as permitting the observation of what is happening.

What not to do was demonstrated rather graphically by another illustration. Fortunately, the demonstration was a college class for kindergarten teachers. A young college student had prepared a demonstration often used with older children. She was going to give a "lecture" on "oxygen" first. It is, perhaps, enough to record the question of a fellow class member: "And what would the children be doing while you gave your lecture?" The experiment that was to follow the lecture and be followed by another lecture involved the old but useful illustration of the burning candle in a glass jar with the light going out eventually because of the lack of oxygen.

In terms of the kindergarten, the difficulty in the student's idea of a lesson is, partly, that the teacher's concept of teaching is talking. To too many teachers *teaching is what the teacher says and does.* The children are supposed to sit, and think, and remember. This method provides no clue as to whether the project has any meaning to the children, nor does it tell the teacher whether they have the necessary background or interest. In the mind of the teacher it is curriculum, but probably only the teacher would learn anything from the experiment.

Helping Only When Necessary

There is the constant *danger* in teaching anyone, but especially small children, *that the teacher will move in too fast. Problem solving takes time.* Rushing in with an immediate solution may rob children of a chance to try to solve their problem.

The parallel danger is of giving *too much* help. An illustration that could be given in many variations concerns a set of parallel bars on a playground to which kindergarten children had access. The bars had not been intended for kindergarteners, but the children were interested and the bars were safe enough. Some were able to mount the ladder and swing across the bar with no help. Others climbed the bar but were afraid to go further, or if they tried, they were simply not strong enough to hold on all the way across. An interested adult saw their dilemma and offered to help. Not much help was needed and this not for long. A few ounces of lift was all that the weakest child needed to make it across. After a few days of practice every child felt competent—and actually was—to make the journey himself. The point is that a little assistance was all that was needed, but this little bit was helpful.

Being Part of the Action

Rather than moving in and taking over, or providing more help than is needed, the teacher becomes a part of the action. Perhaps the children are building a house they want to get inside of—most kindergarten children will try this some time or other if the proper materials are around. They will almost always run into difficulty. Materials strong enough to build a wall may hurt if they fall on them. A house big enough to crawl into may be hard to cover. Most of the time the wise kindergarten teacher will not supply the answer to the problem, but she will wonder with the children what might work. They, then, can experiment with possible solutions.

Sometimes the teacher helps to clarify a problem. She wonders aloud why something does not work or what more may be needed in the way of materials or information to get something done. She is not lecturing; she is not even telling. She is entering into the action to help clarify the picture or situation; she tries to visualize the problem as the children see it and to help them clarify their own thinking. Thus, she is teaching problem solving.

An observer of a kindergarten scene was particularly impressed by a "happening" in the classroom. A few children were playing in the playhouse. The teacher was watching but not interfering. One child took it upon herself to suggest forcefully that the furniture in the house should be rearranged. The children working with her went along with the idea, but cooperation was not complete. The child who made the suggestion attempted to hurry matters up by moving a small dresser by herself. The teacher watched and listened. The dresser tipped, and the drawers slid out. Now the teacher did step in, but gently. She knocked on the door and asked what had happened. What followed was not a scolding, but a lesson in science and social studies tied into, "Why did the dresser tip?" and "How could it have been moved more safely?"

Putting Problems Into Larger Perspective

In the week before Valentine's Day one kindergarten teacher discovered that her children were concerned about how they could send valentines to their parents. She broke down the problem into two parts: how to make valentines and how to send them home. As the children were in the process of solving the first problem, the teacher with the enthusiastic endorsement of the children arranged a class excursion. With the help of the parents and the cooperation of the local post office, teacher and children visited the post office. They stopped on the way to see a postal employee picking up mail from a deposit box. At the post office they mailed their own valentines. They saw the stamps cancelled and letters sorted for delivery. On the way back to the school they watched a mailman making deliveries. The teacher, in this instance, provided much help in solving the problem and enlarging its scope. The children were clearly and fully involved in the project. In addition to satisfactorily resolving their concern, the children became involved in a social studies project and their knowledge and horizons were broadened.

In enlarging perspectives the teacher tries to move in the direction the children have set.

Aiding Children to Move in the Direction They Have Indicated

A kindergarten class was working together on a major project. For an entire class to be involved at the same time on a project is very unusual, but the class had been building up to it for days. One child had a friend in the hospital. He was permitted into the hospital, though not into his friend's room. His experience became part of a general discussion in the kindergarten and, someway, started a series of activities almost wholly initiated by the children. Several children had toy medical kits or nurse's caps at home, which they brought to school. All had visited doctors. Some had spent time in hospitals. No doubt all had heard their parents discuss related problems. The teacher, too, made countless contributions to the discussion of hospitals and illness. For example: When the need for a stretcher arose, the teacher found a ladder to serve the purpose. One day the children organized themselves into a rather complete and complicated health team. They had doctors, nurses, aids, dieticians, ambulance and driver, patients, policemen at the stop and go sign, and so forth. Every child had a role. The teacher had no official part, but she found herself needed as an ambulance attendant. The patient proved too heavy for the regular crew. Very seldom do you see every child taking on a role in a big setting of a situation. These roles kept changing. What impressed the observer in the classroom that day was the depth of understanding exhibited by each child in the role he played. It showed that each already had a good grasp of the adult world. Here was cooperative learning through group problem solving in the form of dramatic play. This is, also, problem solving combined with academic learning at what must be close to the best in kindergarten experience.

Summary

Problem solving in the kindergarten builds on the children's background and developing abilities. Kindergarten children can think more effectively and communicate more easily than nursery school children. Through action and discussion they can solve problems. The kindergarten, thus, becomes a center both for the interchange of ideas and for solving problems in the area of interpersonal relationships. The teacher's role in all problem solving is central, but she must be careful to give more support than direction. In this support she helps her children solve not only the problems at hand, but also helps them move out into more complex activities and learnings.

CHAPTER SIX

Problem Solving and Knowledge in the Primary Grades

Three young boys were eager to show a completed project to school visitors. They were proud, and they had every right to be. In group consultations they had decided on a building project. After designing it together, they found their own materials and even earned money to pay for whatever had to be bought. From beginning to end, it was their project. As they showed the finished product to the visitors, their pride of achievement was evident in every action. The visitors too were proud, for these were three extremely disadvantaged children. Up to this time their school record had not been very successful; to the contrary, their record, on the whole, had been below "average." Considering their background, the boys might easily have become sullen, defeated, and bitter individuals even at this early stage of their lives. But such was not so. Heads high, eyes aglow, and confident, all three were ready for new worlds to conquer.

The episode just related aptly illustrates two vital elements of teaching—furnishing children the opportunity in the classroom to work out *their* concerns and problems and according them recognition for their accomplishments. Such a course of action is basic to good teaching, and particularly so in areas where, unfortunately, it is often most neglected—with the disadvantaged.

Basic Concepts the Same

Problem solving encompasses the whole range of questions that a child brings to the school or that the school brings to the child's awareness. The questions may be problems in the strictest sense; they involve things troubling a child. They may be problems from the standpoint of deciding on a procedure as to how to carry through a project. They may be problems only in that the child wants to know more about something he does not understand or has no prior knowledge of.

In the latter sense, problems are sometimes created by the teacher. The child has to be aware of things before they can be problems. It has been noted that problem solving leads to a search for new knowledge and that knowledge already possessed is used in the search for solutions. If there is an added element here, it is that some knowledge, sometimes a great deal of knowledge, is necessary before one is aware that a problem even exists.

Very few teachers are in a position to always work from the present concerns of students out to new areas of knowledge. Sometimes the motivation can come in other ways. But much blood, sweat, and anguish on the part of both students and teachers could be spared by putting the emphasis whenever possible on the relevant interests of students. Many a student's academic life could be saved in the process. A principal "caught" one of his pupils by a river bank during school hours. He restrained the impulse to order the boy back to school. Instead, he sat down by that boy on the river bank and both questioned and listened. As he listened, he discovered that the boy knew a great deal about the outdoors, though in school his demeanor was one of boredom and defeat. That conversation, followed by altered classroom procedures, changed a potential dropout into a successful student. He became a college graduate and professional success.

Problem solving on the primary level involves the growing ability to think. Memorization is not thinking; in itself it is not wrong. Drill can be fun, and some drill may be necessary whether or not it is fun. Most of the reactions in life are of necessity habitual. No one would get very far if he had to think deeply about every step taken. The danger is that routine and drill can become so much a part of life, and of school life in particular, that there is no time left to think when this is what is needed. If one ever learns to think, he learns by thinking. All thinking is related in some form to problem solving.

As with the nursery school and kindergarten child, the primary child is not ready to bear the weight of the world. He is being prepared to face more difficult problems by dealing with those he is currently able to understand. This may call for many difficult decisions on the part of the teacher. How much can young children understand and when, if ever, does she stifle an interest? A capable and ingenious teacher arranged a tour of a local water system. It included a short trip to the river that served as a source so that the children would know exactly where their drinking water came from. Next they toured the plant that filtered and purified the water. This reassured the children that the many pollutants and other foreign bodies did not flow from their faucets—that is, until a sharp-eyed boy discovered a small turtle in one of the already filtered pools. That created interest and excitement—and many questions and doubts. Among other things the children wondered if the turtle would appear in their drinking water. The teacher tried to reassure the children that there were more filterings before the water reached the faucet. Should she have done more? Perhaps not, but a teacher must be alert to when a child can assimilate more than she is giving.

Problem-solving Abilities Increase

The theme of this section seems to emphasize the obvious. However, too often in such situations we all tend to ignore the complications that can arise from an obvious situation.

Complications

Some entering primary children are in actual age only a few days older than some entering kindergarten children. They are younger than many kindergarten children will be at some point in the school year. On this basis, alone, it would be reasonable to expect them to need the same kind of problem-solving experience that kindergarten children need. Some six-year-olds may easily be three years younger in mental age than some kindergarten children. This is a conservative statement. One wonders how any teacher or administrator could fail to recognize that *not all first graders are ready for the traditional first grade.*

The above is obvious. There are more complex factors. For example: Jerome Bruner, the strong advocate of intellectual content in teaching, is an equally strong advocate of the inductive method of learning (i.e., problem solving).[1] He has experimented with children older than those under consideration, having them work with sticks, unmarked and graded on a different scale than any known to the students. One purpose was to learn what underlying principles of mathematics they could formulate. To a casual visitor to the classroom during the experiment, the activity might have looked like nonsensical play. In reality, it was a study of complicated problem solving. The point is that manipulative materials even at the primary level may serve more complex functions.

[1] Jerome S. Bruner, *Toward a Theory of Instruction* (New York: Norton, 1966), Chapter 3.

Children in the primary-age range need to be able to experiment with materials and objects.[2] They need to see, visit, and make firsthand contact. Some of such activity may lead to learning that did not occur in nursery or kindergarten. Some of it, however, may be advanced learning made meaningful by experimentation. As in kindergarten, if painting, or manipulation, or exploration is part of learning, they are valuable work experience, not play. If there is fun in the work, so much the better.

In a different area, but related, is the problem of social learning. As the nursery school child may need to accept the separation from home, the presence of strange adults, and more children than he is accustomed to, so *the first-grade child from a disadvantaged social environment may need even more time and tactful help to adjust to a new situation.* In some ways he may act like the three-year-old. However, the reasons for his behavior are different. As John Holt[3] suggests, he may have learned to keep quiet until he has studied the situation and decided on a course of action. He may have been taught to fear the school, or to hate people of other races, or to be belligerent. The problem is not simple social immaturity, though this too may be part of the difficulty. The problem is, in part, previous learning, and that may be much more difficult to overcome.

In the primary age range, even in first grade, children too often on the surface seem to have conquered the fundamentals of problem solving. When one takes the time to investigate how the child *really* arrives at his "answer," one discovers that all that has been learned is a formula. William A. Brownell, former Dean of the School of Education, University of California at Berkeley, used to tell of working individually with children concerning their difficulties in mathematics. One of the points he made had to do with teachers who attempted a few years back to break children of the habit of adding by simply counting up a scale, i.e., 4 plus 3 is 7 because 4 plus one is 5, plus 1 is 6, plus 1 is 7. It was usually the child who managed to hide the fact that he was carrying out the same process in disguise who was rewarded. Most good teachers would encourage children to use fingers, or blocks, or marbles, or anything else as long as a prop was needed until the child really understood the relationships involved. Disguised similarities can take many and more sophisticated forms.

Maturation and Problem Solving

The teacher who has worked with first-grade children and then with older children will notice many differences in their rate of learning and their method of problem solving. Usually, the older the child the more involved he can become in working through a problem. Not only will he want to go into it more deeply, but he will be able to stay with a project longer. In addition, he will be able to work independently to learn more of what

[2] Jean Piaget, Foreword to Millie Almy, *Young Children's Thinking* (New York: Teachers College, Columbia University, 1966).

[3] John Holt, *The Underachieving School* (New York: Pitman, 1969), p. 105.

he needs to know. In short, the older child has additional abilities that he can apply to a subject.

In part, problem solving is different as children grow older because they have increased skills and knowledge.[4] Nursery children do ask questions, but they have difficulty in understanding and in expressing their ideas. Kindergarten children and most first graders are capable of learning more by questioning, and can report many things with a high degree of accuracy. They have a better chance to learn and apply their learning to the solution of problems. Third graders may not only be able to ask more probing and relevant questions, but they can, if necessary, write the information. They are more able to read reference materials and make notes on what is needed.

Problem solving is different as children grow older because *they are increasingly able to work together.*[5] They cooperate with the teacher in the search for solutions. More and more frequently they use the inductive method to solve problems. For example, in the study of phonics the teacher can cover a chalkboard alone or with the cooperation of the children with words containing the letter "c." The children will then attempt to figure out when and why the letter "c" sometimes represents the speech sound of the letter "k" and other times it represents the speech sound of the letter "s." From this discussion they can generalize to formulate working principles. Thus, when appropriate, most primary children can cooperate as a class in problem-solving activities.

Problem solving is, also, different as children grow older because they are *increasingly able to engage in many kinds of group activities.* They can, for example, engage in simple forms of "brain storming" in which all children express ideas which are received without criticism, then the ideas are reconsidered to find the ones which can be tried out. Third graders ordinarily enjoy committee work. Within the group they show leadership, ingenuity, and persistence in group projects. A worthwhile project effectively conducted develops responsibility and discipline. One fourth-grade teacher was regularly assigned children below grade level, including many categorized as "trouble makers." Many of these children were underprivileged. To encourage the interest of her class the teacher made use of appropriate projects. It took a few weeks, but invariably a transformation occurred in the classroom. Those frustrated, trouble making children became welded into a purposeful, cooperating group. The teacher's immediate attention for purposes of discipline was no longer required. The children were deeply and personally involved. Leadership developed. Skills and talents appeared that other teachers had not been able to bring to the surface. Class members made more than expected academic progress almost without realizing that they were learning anything.

[4] See Jean Piaget, *The Language and Thought of the Child* (New York: Meridian, 1955), p. 139.

[5] Grace Langdon and Irving W. Stout, *Teaching in the Primary Grades* (New York: Macmillan, 1964), p. 51.

Changes in the Thinking Process

To add a slightly different dimension, problem solving on the primary level is different because the process of thinking changes. Three-year-old Ellen casually met one of her father's visitors to her house. When she first encountered the visitor, there was only an exchange of names. On the third encounter over a period of time Ellen took over. She showed her possessions, talked about her dolls in personal terms, hosted an imitation tea party for her guest. Throughout, she was a bubbly "hostess." Five years passed until the two met again in Ellen's home. Nothing as dramatic as the first encounter took place. Ellen, now eight years old, could visit coolly and calmly. She was interested in events at a distance in time and space. During her conversation with the visitor she discussed other children with both kindliness and critical insight. She explained what they were doing and failing to do at school. She could even tell one with apparently sound logic what the teachers were doing wrong in their handling of other children. The girl was the same; still bright, attractive, and charming. Her mental processes, though, were clearly different in kind.

Jean Piaget, the Swiss observer and theoretical thinker, concluded that there were three distinct stages in the thinking of children.[6] He believed that the child went through a "preoperational stage," roughly the time from the child's first use of language to the development of such skills as reading and writing. It was Piaget's observation that the child's concern in this period was the manipulation of things, or objects, through action. Some symbols are used. Language is included, but most abstract concepts are beyond the child's comprehension. Piaget thought that the most important abstract concept that the child could handle, and the one that marked the child's movement into the second stage of mental thought, was the concept of reversibility.[7] For example, he noted that children tended to think that a tall, narrow glass contained less water than a short, wide one. The variations of this are many.

Apart from questions about Piaget's method and his failure to use control groups in his original study, three questions have been raised about his conclusions. Is this change in thinking the result of maturation or of experience? The answer is an old one as applied to all learning—it appears to be both. At least, there have been experiments that indicate that the concept of reversibility, or more simply, that matter can change shape without being different in amount, can be taught.[8]

[6] Jean Piaget, *Six Psychological Studies* (New York: Random House, 1967), Chapter 1.

[7] Jean Piaget, *The Construction of Reality in the Child* (New York: Basic Books, 1954). See also Henry W. Maier, *Three Theories of Child Development* (New York: Harper & Row, 1969), Chapter 3.

[8] Annemarie Roeper and Irving E. Sigel, "Finding the Clue to Children's Thought Process," in W. W. Hartup and N. L. Smothergill (eds.), *The Young Child: Reviews of Research* (Washington, D. C.: National Association for the Education of Young Children, 1967), pp 84–94.

With young children, the question of verbal expression versus under-standing is pertinent. Holt points out that the child may not understand the wording of the adult or may not be able to explain his own thinking. Apart from these possibilities of misunderstanding, the child may be trying desper-ately to make sense out of adult nonsense. Thus, Holt wonders: "If someone suddenly asked me [as many people do ask children] if there were more males or people in my family, I would probably answer (1) 'Say that again, please.' (2) 'Are you kidding?' (3) 'What do you mean?' I certainly wouldn't expect that the questioner wanted me to take such a silly question literally and seriously."[9]

Holt raises the question related to the accuracy of Piaget's experiments. Children were given toys and asked to put those together that belonged together. They made very interesting classifications that were apparent nonsense to the experimenters. But when told to put the toys back in the box, they separated them by kinds with no difficulty at all. Holt surmises that the children interpreted the first direction as one to use their imagi-nation. The second direction was more in line with the children's concept of orderly arrangement.

Whatever possible objections there are, Piaget called attention to an important concept. It is important for the teacher to remember that a child thinks in different terms at different ages. The application to this chapter is that normally, *with increase in age and learning, a child develops more advanced modes of thinking.*[10]

Most pertinent to the teacher of the primary-age child is the second of Piaget's stages of mental development in distinction from the first and third. The terminology is less important than the concepts. As Piaget spoke of his first stage as "preoperational," so he speaks of the second and third as the stage of "concrete operations" and the stage of "formal operations," respectively. Part of the distinction is that in the second stage the child still thinks in concrete terms. He needs to manipulate objects, but he does this to accomplish a purpose and to clarify his thinking. Later (Piaget felt that this did not begin before the age of ten[11]) in the stage of formal operations the child is able to think in a more completely abstract and symbolic procedure.

Piaget did not hold that a child passed from one stage to another on a given moment. He recognized that even in terms of transitional periods, these periods differed greatly from one child to another. However much this chapter has oversimplified Piaget and however much Piaget may have oversimplified what he observed, as applied to problem solving, it would appear that children are capable of quite different mental processes at different periods in their lives. Thus, the primary child is gradually developing

[9] Holt, *op. cit.*, p. 66.

[10] For further discussion, see, David H. Russell, *Children's Thinking* (Boston: Ginn, 1956), Chapter 9.

[11] Jerome S. Bruner, *The Process of Education* (New York: Vintage, 1960), p. 37.

ability to express his thought in speech, in writing, and in numbers. Unless he is an exceptional child, he is still very dependent on the use of actual experience and the manipulation of objects to solve his problems.

What some developmental educational psychologists refer to as "verbal mediation" becomes an important aspect of the child's learning in the primary years. By this is meant the child's developing ability to think with words and symbols. This is a valuable skill to be cultivated and encouraged. The danger is that the primary teacher may assume too much. The child's rote memorization may be accepted as thought. Memory is involved in all of thought, but there is something more involved. Hence, while duly gratified by any child's ability to use symbols in thinking, the teacher will not rush this process. With both words and numbers the child should be able to check the abstract symbolic operation against concrete experience. If the primary child is permitted to do this kind of checking, he will increasingly use what he knows to build toward the kind of "formal reasoning" that Piaget expects to develop after the primary age level has been passed.

The Teacher's Role in Problem Solving

Much of what has been stated applies to a discussion of the teacher's part in the problem-solving activities of children in the primary-age group. Possibly, even more of the suggestions made as to the teacher's part in the problem-solving activities of kindergarten children are pertinent. In this section points already made will be restated, but with a different approach. A group of concepts that may help clarify the problem are discussed. The concepts are separated in an attempt at clarity. In the teacher's classroom experience they often overlap.

Prediction and Planning

Even a beginning teacher should be able to predict some things about the children she will teach. Knowing the age level provides one basis for prediction. Knowing something about the socioeconomic background of the children gives some clues. Here school records are frequently useful. Rarely will a teacher walk into a regular classroom without knowing in advance something about the children in her class. Anything known can be used in predicting the needs and interests of children, and in planning.

The teacher can set a climate for problem solving very early in a school year. Not only must the teacher make it known verbally, but, even more important, her actions must convey that she is more interested in what the children learn than in what she has to say. No teacher is infallible. When she does make mistakes, the climate in the classroom should be such that the children are encouraged to discover them. It should be known to the class that when problems arise requiring information none of them possess, the teacher and class will search for solutions.

Verbalizing these concepts to the children may be of more value as a reminder to the teacher than as clues to the children. Through classroom experience the children will discover the reality of the attitude implied. The teacher needs to study her own concepts of teaching. A student teacher was "giving" a science lesson. Her lesson planning was faulty in that it planned only for demonstration and discussion. Among other things the student teacher had not considered that something might go wrong with her experiment. She planned to show how a needle would float on water. The difficulty that developed could have been turned into a problem-solving situation. The needle did not float. It sank! The student teacher was at a loss. The children, on the other hand, became interested. They could hardly stay in their seats. Had the student teacher been interested in the children's learning, she could have explained what should have happened and then suggested ways to check for possible variables: temperature of the water, size of the needle, size of container, water from various sources, and so forth. Then, if not in the classroom, the children could have experimented at home to find the one thing that made the difference. Instead of this, the student teacher could only half sob, "It worked at home," and turn to other matters.

Identifying Problems and Adjusting Programs

As the teacher establishes rapport with the children, she will find that they will talk freely about personal problems. These personal problems may be more shocking to the teacher than to the child. They may need the teacher's understanding. Many things happen to children. Some children are deserted, or neglected, or mistreated. When there are agencies that can help, the teacher will make use of such agencies. In the classroom, just the acceptance of problems and being able to relate them to a trusted person sometimes makes them tolerable enough so that the child can more ably enter into class work.

Some problems can be easily handled by the teacher if she is alert to them. A third-grade boy brought a coconut to class one day. It was admired and discussed, then placed on a shelf where it could be seen by all. For hours the little boy was "just not there." The teacher noticed it, but she ignored the situation. The student teacher took a more direct approach. She took the boy aside and asked what the problem was. It turned out that he was under orders to bring the coconut home that night. The boy could not reconcile the seemingly contradictory directions from the mother and the teacher. Reassured that the coconut could be taken home when he left school, he entered wholeheartedly into the school work. The sequel might be guessed—it was the student teacher who had to make a dash to catch Dave and give him the coconut as he boarded the bus for home.

It is more difficult for children to talk about *educational problems* than social ones. Perhaps the children sense that both they and the teacher are threatened in this area. Children need to feel free enough to report that they do not understand what is being taught. It is natural that they have difficulty explaining what they cannot understand. Here the teacher's task in identifying what is wrong becomes more complex. She has to be alert to clues. Perhaps available specialists may be of assistance. Some learning problems relate to hearing difficulties or sight difficulties. Speech problems may require help beyond the competence of the classroom teacher. Even in most of these situations, the classroom teacher will have a role to play. A child with speech difficulties, at the very minimum, can be helped with the cooperation of the class to feel comfortable and accepted.

Commonplace difficulties may involve complexities. Why do some children have trouble with spelling, for example? Is it some lack of perceptual ability that must be improved? Could they learn if they could be taught to visualize a word? Most children can, but not all. Would understanding phonic principles help? It would some children. Would analyzing specific difficulties work? This approach is helpful for some older children. Just noting and studying, not whole words, but the elements, usually the single letter misused, may be helpful. For a very limited number of children tracing and retracing words provides the kinesthetic feeling that seems necessary. A gentleman who always had been a very poor speller in school did not realize until years later that writing a list of words twenty times each had meant nothing to him, not even boredom. There was always something more interesting to think about. For him, spelling had to be a problem-solving experience, and no teacher even hinted that such could be the case. Teachers need to identify the problems of children. This identification goes far beyond the concept of whether the child can get the "right" answer. It involves his process in reaching an answer and whether or not that process is meaningful to him.

For problem solving to occur, the problems must be clearly identified and delineated. Prediction and planning are adjusted as needs are revealed and analyzed. For every group planning entails some programs intended for all children, others for certain groups of children, and work for individuals. Teachers need both daily and longer-range planning, but both should be subject to revision. One teacher planned a lesson in science for the whole class. She planned well in advance and introduced the lesson at an appropriate time. Her basic question was, "What could be learned about friction?" She had gathered materials to be pulled by means of rubber bands over various kinds of surfaces. These surfaces included smooth desks, cloth, sandpaper, and so forth. The children worked in small groups with the materials on the various surfaces. The teacher allowed the discoveries and discussion to develop spontaneously. At the end of the day as she thought back to the experience she made a discovery herself. Every concept that she had in mind as a possible discovery and some that had not occurred to her had been pointed out by the children.

Including and Involving Children

If a class is to provide a learning situation for children, the children have to feel that it is their class. No special philosophy of education is implied. Nor is the implication that the children alone set the curriculum or method. "Their class" means that somehow the children feel both included and involved.

Very often it takes just a little "give" on the part of the teacher to create such an atmosphere. As a treat for her class, a primary teacher brought an electric popper to school and popped corn for the children. Even though she intended it only to be a treat, the children turned it into a lesson. They identified problems. How hot did the popper have to be before the corn started to pop? Why did the corn pop? Why did some kernels not pop? This group of six-year-olds had "the time of their lives" studying a science lesson.

The importance of including the children in the program of problem solving cannot be overemphasized. Children themselves will bring problems that will open up a world of learning. Sometimes the problems are just below the surface ready to be tapped. One student teacher attempted a unit on the planets with a very bright third grade. Perhaps, if she had been more able, she would have either predicted the results more wisely and have avoided the topic, or have planned to turn the unit over more completely to the children. For the children, the topic was just right. The student predicted this much correctly. Her problem was the old prevalent one of feeling that teaching was "telling" and that she must do the telling. Unfortunately, there were thirty students and only one student teacher. As a group they knew more about the topic than the student teacher. It was a wonderful learning situation if only the student teacher had been able to get out of their way and encourage them on. As it was, she kept on trying to lecture to a bored and increasingly distressed class.

Summary

Children from six through eight need some of the same kinds of problem-solving experiences as do younger children. Not only will many need transitional activities, but most are still in need of opportunity to check mental processes through the manipulation of objects. Even more important is the need that children feel involved in the learning process. Such involvement grows most readily in a climate that accepts and considers the children's needs and problems and encourages their active participation in the search for educational answers.

structure
and creativity

No doubt, then, that a free curiosity has more force in our
learning these things than a frightful enforcement.
St. Augustine, Confessions

1 2 3
4 5 6

Principles of
Structure and Creativity

Possibly the idea of indicating the interrelationship between creativity and structure came from Jerome S. Bruner. In his deservedly famous *The Process of Education*,[1] Bruner is concerned with structure in the important, but restricted sense of the structure of subject matter. In his use of the term he is speaking of the basic principles of a subject. He does not use, at least, in this immediate context, the term "creativity." He does speak of the need of "imaginative" search for effective methods, of intuitive grasp of principles, the "training of hunches," the "shrewd guess," the "fertile hypothesis," the "courageous leap to a tentative conclusion."

It is generally recognized that in the literal sense of creating something where nothing existed before, only the Divine Being can "create." The human can only rearrange the existing into new forms. In the broadest sense, he creates for himself a new body of knowledge as he reorganizes the known through altered concepts. The individual creates whenever he uses his mind and body to produce something that he has not himself possessed before. There is a sense of constructive vigor, of imagination, of adventure in the word "creativity." It is logical to recognize that creativity can be used for negative purposes. In this text the concern is only with positive creativity.

[1] Jerome S. Bruner, *The Process of Education* (New York: Vintage, 1960).

Consequently, creativity normally produces something of worth to humanity. One accepts as creative effort, however, anything that is new and prized by the few or even by the one who made the effort.

Structure and Creativity in Harmony

"Structure" will be used in Bruner's sense to refer to the basic principles of subject matter, but it will also recognize the relevance of the structure of society, of the educational system, and the child. Existing structure will be considered here in its relationship to creativity.

Creative Possibilities Within the Social Structure

The events of the past several years have forced in upon the consciousness the flaws that have always existed in our social structure—in our "American Way of Life" or in our "Free Democratic Society." Neither the structure nor the flaws are static. They will both be somewhat different even a month after the reader has read this printed page. In spite of the flaws that may exist, there is a purpose in our society to support the development of creative potential. We have in the past missed this goal, but we have had a society in which if the creative genius was not universally admired, neither was he universally condemned. In theory, and to some extent in fact, we have supported those who dared to be different, to imagine new possibilities, to try new forms.

The society in which the individual lives always influences his creative efforts. Even the most highly gifted artist bears the stamp of his time and place. If this were not true, the critic could not place a picture in an approximate period of time and as belonging to a certain school of art. It is also true, however, that the social structure of which the artist is a part was in itself a source of his skill and his creativity. The novelist draws upon the social structures of his time (or of some time). The musician is influenced by the social structures in which he creates. The scientist only discovers when the "time is ripe," and that, too, is related to the social structures of his day.

The Purpose of Educational Structures

The purpose of the school system is to provide an environment in which children develop in security and freedom. In theory there are compulsory attendance laws to protect children from exploitation. The implication is that freedom comes through learning; slavery is the lot of the ignorant. Insofar as the system works toward this purpose, the school is a place in which the child's right to search, to solve, and to create is cherished and protected.

In all free societies some structures must be involved. The rights of one individual cannot infringe on the rights of all. There is little freedom in the midst of anarchy. The structure of the school can protect the child's freedom to explore the fields of knowledge, to try out his skills, to create his own literature, or art, or other legitimate product. It is essential that this right not be infringed upon by the needs of parents, the greed of exploiters, or the violence of crime.

The Value of Structure in Subject Matter

Structure is essential in the study of any skill or academic area. Information must have a framework for support or it becomes meaningless trivia. The relationship to creativity is, at least, threefold. However arrived at, there is discovery, a feeling of at least re-creation, when one sees basic structure in a subject. Bruner would carry this a step further. He suggests that any student learns most effectively when he discovers this structure for himself. He points out, for example, that the child discovers much of the fundamental nature of his language long before he hears of rules of grammar. He would like to see more elements of this experience of discovery in the school experience.

There is a third implication in Bruner's theory. He refers to Benjamin Franklin's proposal for the Philadelphia Academy:

. . . It would be well if they could be taught every Thing that is useful, and every Thing that is ornamental: But Art is long and their Time is short. It is therefore propos'd that they learn those Things that are likely to be most useful and most ornamental . . . .[2]

Bruner's proposal differs, however. He would stress the structure of subjects. Presumably, this would protect the pupil from the stifling weight of information now forced upon him. At the same time it would provide the time and freedom to explore creatively in the directions that the student might choose. Structure, thus, becomes not only an important discovery reached through a process related to creative research, but it also frees the student from drudgery to more individualized creative effort.

In moving on from Bruner's concept of structure, it should be noted that the authors employ the term "structure" as applied to the student or child, the educational system, and to society in a slightly different but related and legitimate way. The definition that covers all the uses of this term is the fourth one given in The Random House Dictionary of the English Language.

Anything composed of parts arranged together in some way, an organization.[3]

[2] Robert Ulich, Three Thousand Years of Educational Wisdom: Selections from Great Documents (Cambridge: Harvard University Press, 1948), p. 444.
[3] The Random House Dictionary of the English Language, unabridged edition (New York: Random House, 1966), p. 1410.

Some of the definition of structure that Bruner seems to have in mind—the basic framework of a subject—also carries over into our other applications of the term. Most organizations prove on close examination to be so complex that only the most basic elements usually are observed. This will be especially true in speaking of the structure of the child.

The Relevance of the Structure of the Child

Structure, not only the structure of subject matter, but the structure of educational and social organization must relate to the structure of the child. The child has a basic human structure. This biological structure is in a particular stage of development, or rather each of many separate systems within the child is at a certain level of development. Even this will have been influenced by the experiences of life. But a different dimension of this organization is the personality structures that have developed as the result of heredity, environment, experiences, decisions, and so forth. All this and much more is part of the child the teacher seeks to help in his educational endeavor.

At various places in this text the point is made that a child cannot be taught until he is prepared by development and experience for this learning. Bruner emphasizes another concept. He is concerned that the subject be broken down into fundamentals that the child can grasp. He is, also, convinced that the concept of "readiness" has been misapplied. Some educators emphasize the relationship of readiness to development almost to the exclusion of experience. Present thought acknowledges that no child would be ready for any academic learning if he were not prepared for it by previous experience. Most would go further and emphasize that the child is always ready for some form of learning. The question is what can he learn now. If today he cannot be taught to read, he can be taught some perception or sequence that is a step on the road to reading.

Almost every child can be taught. He can be taught in terms of the structure of a subject if we understand that structure and the structure of the child. If the two are in harmony, the child is not held in check. New areas of creative learning are opened to him.

Structure and Creativity in Discord

Thus far only the positive relationship between structure and creativity has been examined. Unfortunately, life rarely evolves so that only positive results occur when structure and creativity mesh.

Pressures

The plight of the creative person can be tragic. There is pressure from society to conform. With the fifth-grade student, it may be pressure to conform to an age and sex group. The high school student is influenced by an adolescent culture and by a special clique. Some students of ethnic groups may be held in a kind of mental serfdom by pressure groups. There are reasons and sometimes values in pressures. The adolescent may need the support of the clique on his way to independence. But often pressures, especially if not understood and faced, produce conformity rather than creativity.

There are also pressures exerted by parents and school people. Both are interested in the kind of conformity that leads to academic achievement. Both can be insensitive to creative endeavor that does not fit into the usual pattern. Even on a more ordinary plane the same principle can apply. Holt rightly notes that a child who brings home an original drawing may be received with little warmth by the parent.[4] If he brings home a work book, he is immediately praised. This type of pressure comes from both home and teacher. Anything that looks like school work is fine. Drawings carry some connotation of the useless and the contraband.

Rigidity

Jacob Getzels and Philip Jackson point out that creative, nonconforming individuals learn as well as brighter, conforming students, but the teachers too often do not appreciate them as much.[5] Some teachers may not appreciate creative students because they test out the limits of any structure. Such individuals always know another way to do something, perhaps six other ways.

From the standpoint of educational structure, the problem is that people unconsciously accept structure as all-important. They forget why a rule was established—what becomes important now is the rule, or the institution, or the public image. Institutions, committees, lodges, can become much more interested in perpetuating themselves, or their way of doing things, than in responding to people's needs. School people can get bound up with trivia—schedules for lunch and buses, the enforcing of regulations, the established penalties for various infringements—and in the process forget the child. John Gardner notes that someone has said, "the last act of a dying society is to get a new and enlarged edition of the rule book."[6] How true!

The Absoluteness of Authority

One of the difficulties rulers have faced through the centuries is that once a man has reached the top, who is going to tell him that he is wrong.

---

[4] John Holt, *How Children Learn* (New York: Pitman, 1969), p. 135.

[5] Jacob W. Getzels and Philip W. Jackson, *Creativity and Intelligence* (New York: Wiley, 1962), p. 31.

[6] John W. Gardner, "The Ever-Renewing Society," *Saturday Review*, 46 (January 5, 1963), 92–95.

Progressive businesses go to great length to keep lines of communication open, and then frequently fail. Some years back a major automobile company lost millions of dollars in recalling and repairing a defect an employee reported when the first cars went through. And in the U.S.S. Pueblo incident the United States government had to sign a document (and thus say it was true) while it simultaneously proclaimed its falsity through the news media. They did this to secure the release of seamen sent on their way in spite of warnings lost in the maze of organizational structure. The illustrations could be multiplied. There are times in life when authority must be obeyed and when life itself may depend on instantaneous reaction to ingrained responses. Most of the time most teachers will be right. The principal's decision is probably justified. The more true this is, the less reason to fear the divergent thinking of the creative student. He may need help in learning how to survive in a world that can be rejecting and cruel. He may need support in thinking through a problem to his own solutions. There is little need to demand that any child accept something as true because a teacher or book says it is true. Conviction seldom comes by submission to authority, at least, not for the creative individual.

Summary

The structure of the subject adapted to the structure of the child provides a basis and framework in which the child can be creative. The structures of society, including that of the educational system, are intended to be, and should be, both the basis of creativity and the source of protection to the individual in his creative effort. The danger is that such structures may be misused. They serve not to support, but to thwart creativity when pressures, rigidity, and authority become more important than the individual.

CHAPTER SEVEN

Structure and Creativity in the Nursery School

The relationship between structure and creativity in the nursery school is important, though this importance may easily be missed. Primarily, the nursery school teacher structures her program in such a way that there are many opportunities for spontaneous expression by the children. The structures of society will have influence but, fortunately, most of society is not yet concerned with establishing rigid structure at this level. This leaves the nursery school teacher relatively free to work within the framework of the nature, capabilities, and structure of the children in her group. Even though it is repetitious, it seems worthwhile to note that vast differences exist between the reactions of an individual child who is just attaining the age of three and the same child about to become five. Such differences also exist in the reactions of individual children the same age. The nursery school teacher seeks to provide opportunities for the kinds of experiences that encourage the development of creative expression suitable to her particular children.

The Creative Nursery School Teacher

Throughout, it has been emphasized that the teacher is a vital element in the child's learning experience. This has been stressed because the teacher's role does not coincide with the popular concept of a teacher's work. To almost everyone, a teacher is someone who tells, demonstrates, or directs. On all levels, there is validity for this description. Most teachers do just that, and most adults were taught by such teachers. There are circumstances on any level when there is a need for directed learning. In the broader context, the concept implies that individuals learn chiefly by being "told"—but they seldom do. The concept is especially misleading in all areas of early childhood education. *The younger the child, the less effective is "telling" and the greater the need for self-directed learning.*

The discussion applies with special force to the encouragement of creative activities. The teacher, on any level, who values imaginative thinking and expression must be especially careful not to criticize, or direct, or instruct in ways that inhibit. The teacher of small children plays a vital role in their creative experiences, but her part is not like that of the stereotype teacher.

The Creativity of the Teacher

Other things being equal, the more creative the nursery school teacher is the better. An attitude of free adventure breeds such an attitude in children. The ability to see potential in a situation makes it possible for the teacher to plan for creative experiences. Some creative exercises by children demand a willingness on the part of the teacher to enter in the activities in ways that would be impossible for the less flexible adult.

The nursery school teacher does not have to excel in her creativity. The form of creativity she needs is more an appreciation of artistic endeavor, and an awareness of the possibilities in children, the situation, and the media. That is, the teacher does not need to be a gifted dancer to be able to encourage children to express the feelings music suggests to them. She is more in need of the freedom to plunge her hand into a container of paint than the ability to draw artistically. It is more important that she be a free, self-confident human being, able to permit messiness at appropriate times and places while preventing it at other times than that she understand the psychological implications of such artistic endeavors. It is helpful if she can play the piano and to catch with that instrument the melody the children are composing, but her playing need not be flawlessly perfect.

Frank Barron views creativity in one of its aspects as vitality turned to constructive service.[1] Possibly, this is the essence of the creativity needed by the nursery school teacher. *Implied is a love of life that is structured toward the adventure of encouraging children in their quest for selfhood.* Involved here is a warning of a possible misuse of the creative urge.

The Creative Teacher Does Not "Mold" Children

Adults influence children. If they had no influence, there would be no need for schools. But the idea of the child as clay to be molded is carrying

[1] Frank Barron, *Creative Person and Creative Process* (New York: Holt, Rinehart and Winston, 1969), pp. 7 and 8.

the idea of influencing children much too far. The creative teacher is not using as her model the figure of "the clay on the potter's wheel." She is not working with inanimate matter; she is encouraging growing persons to express their ideas and emotions in constructive ways. Perhaps even this is not the ultimate purpose of creative activities on the nursery level. Alicerose Barman expresses the concept intended when she says:

Every child, even the most unattractive at first and second encounter, has an individuality which grows best when something in it is approved by an adult. Self-image remains with one, when finger plays and painting techniques, favorite stories and juice-passing rules are long forgotten. Positive self-image is a necessity to a free citizen in a democratic society; nursery school is that society in microcosm.[2]

Every good nursery school teacher is concerned with seeing not only potential, but confidence develop. In this limited sense, she is "molding children," but *she never forgets that the personality she wants to emerge is the individual's own, not her creation.*

The Creative Teacher Keeps Structure at a Minimum

Several forms of structure are present even in the creative activities of the nursery school. Much of the structure is inherent in the developing mind and body of the child. Probably no child could draw anything if the child had not first had experience with some related media. A child could not make up rhymes and tunes unless he had already learned to talk and had some acquaintance with melodies.

Other structure is involved in the situation. Work with "messy" materials can be confined to areas where interference is least and cleaning up easiest. Acting out feelings in response to music can be kept within whatever general limits are required for the happiness of all involved. Free play with sand and water requires a few regulations. It may even be necessary to demonstrate some things that can be done with clay, or paint, or wet sand, or blocks.

What is not involved is a lesson in art, or architecture, or music. John Holt describes an experiment with a child not quite three.[3] He thought, rightly, that the child might enjoy the bright, colored Cuisenaire rods. When he dumped the rods on the floor, the child gathered them up and clutched them possessively. Holt says that he looked like a miser with a horde of gold. Then, Holt reports, he made a mistake. Aided and abetted by the child's father, he tried to show what could be done with the blocks by building a simple structure. He persuaded the youngster to relinquish the rods for the demonstration. To his surprise, the child walked over and scattered the rods in all directions. The experiment was repeated several

[2] Alicerose S. Barman, "Four-Year-Old Development," in Joanne Wyle (ed.), *A Creative Guide for Preschool Teachers* (Racine, Wis.: Western Publishing Services, 1966) p. 16.

[3] John Holt, *How Children Learn* (New York: Pitman, 1969), pp. 86–87.

times with the same results. Possibly, the child was objecting to another's use of his materials. More likely, he resented the adult showing how much better he could do the job.

Structure in the art involved will develop. Freedom in its use must come first. The teacher encourages this. That encouragement may be no more than to encourage a child to see how clay feels or to scribble in any way he wants on a piece of paper. It may be demonstrating that it is all right to get one's hand dirty and to smear paint on paper. It is *not* insistence that a brush be held a certain way, or a picture be drawn realistically, or that a clay animal conform to a picture in a book.

The Creativity of the Nursery School Child

Depending on your point of view, the nursery school child is either non-creative or highly creative. From the standpoint that one speaks of creativity when he thinks of the great artist or writer, there is not much creativity in evidence. What does a sand castle, or a doll house, or swirls of paint have to do with works of art? What does a child's doggerel have to do with literature? What is the simple tune evolved by the four-year-old in the field of music? The answer may be that none of these things are even a beginning toward greater things in art. The present production is far from being a work of art, and most young artists fail to move on from these simple beginnings to major creative achievement.

But from the standpoint of the nursery school child and his present capacities, important creative activities may be in progress.

It Is New

To the three- and four-year-old child many things are creative in the sense that they are new experiences to him. The feel of sand is creative if a new sensation is involved. A mark on a piece of paper is creative if he has never used a crayon before. The perception of color, of texture, of shape may, also, include elements of creativity.

As the child moves out into what may appear to be very rudimentary drawings, simple dance steps or movements, or whatever the activity may be, it is creative to him because he is doing something he has never done before. He is moving out on the basis of past experience into a new adventure. It is not necessary that the child know what he is painting for it to be creative. He may be learning the feel of paint and the pleasure it gives to spread it over a sheet of paper. He may be experimenting to see what sizes and shapes he can make. Or he may be, as true artists do, drawing something known to him as it appears to him. Whatever the media and the expression, if the child is moving out into new territory, it is a creative experience, which in itself is important. It matters not that the child become an artist, but *it is important that he carry on into life this zest for discovery and joy in experiencing the new.*

It Is Uninhibited

The creative activities of children are usually uninhibited. It is even more accurate to say that children are not inhibited in the ways that most adults are. Until someone makes fun of their effort or shows indifference, they are normally willing to try their hands, or bodies, or voices at endeavors within their comprehension. They are usually willing to paint as they discover the uses of paint, enjoy the process involved, and are proud of their productions. They will, once they understand what is permitted, devise their own ways of expressing a rhythm, for example. They will make up verses of a song and sing it without self-consciousness.

The freedom from inhibition must be, however, supported by an accepting atmosphere within and without the nursery school. Haim G. Ginott tells of a boy taken to visit a kindergarten class who looked at the pictures on the wall and demanded loudly, "Who made these ugly pictures?"[4] Ginott adds that the mother was embarrassed and started to scold the boy. The teacher, sensing the meaning behind the question, explained that here it was not necessary to paint pretty pictures. One could paint what he felt. Apparently, even by the age of five, Bruce had discovered that creative activities were subject to criticism. He needed assurance that they would not be in that room.

Creative expression needs protection as well as encouragement and stimulation. . . . The child, like the painter, reveals all of himself in every movement of the body, in every stroke of the brush, or in every movement of the pen. Often, of course, these expressions do not emerge in the form an adult may desire. But if creativity is suppressed because parents and teachers do not understand the meaning behind the expression, or if one child's efforts are compared with those of other children, the spark of genius may be forever lost.[5]

Nor does the concept of lesser inhibition mean that all children are the same in their reactions. Anne Shaaker Schulman observed children in a small nursery–kindergarten, a parent-sponsored project. In a book describing her experiences on facing pages are two pictures, each with a brief comment portraying scenes that occurred at the school. The first picture shows three children at an outdoor table beginning to experiment with finger paint. One child has plunged right in and is painting vigorously, but the other two are not painting at all. They are absorbed with the feel of "this slippery stuff." The second picture shows the two children who had earlier been

[4] Haim G. Ginott, *Between Parent and Child* (New York: Avon, 1965), p. 22.
[5] As quoted in Lillian M. Logan, *Teaching the Young Child* (Boston: Houghton Mifflin, 1960), p. 310.

absorbed with the sensory feel of the paint busy at a cooperative painting project. The boy who had entered in with such initial enthusiasm is no longer on the scene. The textual comment reads in part:

In the end, it is the most cautious and skeptical who stay longest and gain most from the experience. Such movement, in only minutes, from anxiety to hesitation to complete involvement, is what makes teaching at this level rewarding.[6]

A story is recalled that is only remotely connected to the concept of creativity, but it does point up the danger of an adult missing the beauty in a child's acts because of his own structures. The little girl involved (Jane) was an impoverished nursery school child privileged to attend a demonstration school conducted to train Head Start teachers. The nursery school teacher was a young, imaginative, and empathetic person. She noted that the child, having been given a piece of gum, treasured it and chewed it for the balance of the morning. When lunchtime came, the child had a problem. She did not want to part with her gum, but it would interfere with eating. Her solution had elements of creativity in it, and it took close observation to detect what she had done with it. She stuck the gum to her own forehead.

It is the sequel that usually shocks teachers. They are not wholly wrong, but they see only one side of what happened. It was during lunch that the other nursery school children, equally impoverished, noticed the gum and began to reach for it. Jane, thereupon, took the gum from her forehead and divided it among the children at her table. Granted, there is something lacking in hygienic precautions here; there is also a lack in the view that most adults take. They see the spread of contagion. *They fail to see a spontaneous act of generosity.* Amazingly, the young home economics major in charge of that group of children saw beyond the implications for health and beyond the humorous aspects of the act to the beauty of the spirit displayed.

It Is Developmental

Children's creative expression is developmental in at least two ways. (1) There seems to be a general developmental pattern. (2) Much of the learning of young children involves creative art. In their book, *The Psychology of Children's Art,* Rhoda Kellogg and Scott O'Dell, after comparing drawings made by children throughout the world, assert that "all children pass through the same stages of development." They add that, "These stages may vary from child to child, or overlap, like the waves in the sea."[7] They carry the

[6] Anne Shaaker Schulman, *Absorbed in Living: Children Learn* (Washington, D. C.: National Association for the Education of Young Children, 1967), pp. 20 and 21.
[7] Rhoda Kellogg with Scott O'Dell, *The Psychology of Children's Art* (New York: Random House, 1967), p. 13.

thought on by suggesting that the child begins with a scribble that even in this early stage contains the idea of a "figure-ground relationship" and has the beginning of pattern. By the age of three, the child "has entered the stage of outline shapes." He then begins to draw circles and ovals. They have found that the child seems to move quickly to the ability to put shapes in "structured forms" in which the child may, for example, put an X inside a rectangle. As Kellogg and O'Dell see it, sometime between the ages of four and five, the child moves into "the pictorial stage." These early drawings may be only suggestive of form. The forms gradually become more realistic.

The other sense in which the creative art of children is developmental is that it is an important part of the learning experience of children. All that follows in this section of the chapter bears on this: that art, creative music, movement, verbal forms, contribute to personal and intellectual growth. They are not interludes in a day's activities. They are essential parts of the young child's learning experiences.

It Is Revealing

Whenever the child expresses himself in any free creative activity, he is revealing all of himself. Probably, no one activity or any combination does quite this, but the creative activities of children offer clues to the perceptive teacher. The possibility always exists of misinterpreting an artist. No one picture, or any other creative product, should be considered conclusive of anything in and by itself. The tune the child sings may have been made up by someone else, for example. Still, the freer the child is in expressing his feelings with paint, or word, or movement, the more clues he gives as to how he feels about himself and his world. This is a special extension of the concept of freedom of choice discussed earlier. The child shows what he likes and what he can now do by what he chooses to do. He does this when, for example, he draws a picture, but he does something more. He reveals quite unintentionally something about how he views things, which may be more important in the nursery school than ever before, or ever again. The child is reaching a stage in development in which he can begin to picture in his own way what is important to him. He cannot usually explain his thoughts or feelings in words, either with or without the picture. The teacher knowing the child and his background can read the message conveyed by the child's creative expression.

It Is Therapeutic

The creative acts of children and adults are a helpful means of releasing tension. Children do more when they create. They work on their problems, at least some of the time, in their art, music, and dramatic endeavors.

Sometimes children draw animals or mythical creatures that represent fears. They may then draw fences or other forms of barricades to represent protection from the danger. Some pictures show the reverse of this. Children may be afraid of what they may do and "fence themselves in." It may be possible to say to certain children, "Maybe you are afraid you may hurt your baby brother." Chiefly, the classroom teacher helps by permitting the children to work through their problems in their own creative media. Thus the teacher affords her pupils the opportunity to express themselves. Sometimes she can give support and understanding. If wise enough, she can avoid pressure and still emphasize the positive aspects of the children's feelings. "You know you will not hurt the baby, though sometimes, you would like to."

Many teachers oversimplify the ideas just expressed. They seem to think that free creative expression is sufficient therapy for major emotional disturbance. Nothing could be further from our thought. *Anything done with a deeply disturbed child must be done under the supervision of competent specialists.* Creative activities may not even be possible for such a child. Even if they are, the specialist's diagnosis and counsel is essential. Neither the creative act itself, nor the attitude of the teacher is therapy in the professional sense of the term.

It Is Preparatory

Creative activities are also *ways of developing skills and insights*. The child who imitates a kangaroo is developing physical agility in the process. The child moving in harmony with the mood of the music is developing, or at least laying a background for, musical appreciation and understanding. Making up simple rhymes is a step toward poetic expression. Any form of art contributes toward the development of perception. As the child begins to draw the simplest forms, he is teaching himself to see form and to control movement. Some place in the process, presumably when realism begins to enter gradually into his frame of reference, the child is ready to perceive the form of letters, or words, or numbers.

Creative expression fits into the total developing pattern of behavior. Creative skills provide background, and even drill, in the perceptions and controls essential to the more academic skills that lie ahead.

Creative Activities in the Nursery School

There are no hard and fast lines between the creative and the more prosaic activities of life. Nor is there a clear distinction between freedom of choice and problem solving, or between problem solving and creativity. For young children there is a creative element to most activities.

Movement and Exploration

Children of nursery school age seem to be constantly on the move. In the playground they may crawl through barrels, jump into boxes, and climb up on platforms. They seem to love the feel of sand and water, mud and clay, or any other thing of substance. The most popular play center in one nursery school for a time was a pan of water with some detergent added and an old-fashioned egg beater. With such materials, children gain knowledge of the feel of things. They explore places and sensations. Even mud puddles may serve exploratory, sensitizing, tension-relieving purposes.

Patterns and Perception

There is an element of creativity in the *young child's sensing of structure*. The taste of peppermint; the smell of spices; the pressure of wind; the sound of the drum; the feel of snow; the shape of a truck; the appearance of an adult; these and countless other perceptual experiences are exploratory and basic to creativity. Looking at the experience from the above standpoint, one can see creative problem solving in a child's question about a rather tall visitor, "Is she still growing?"

The element of discovery of structure is present in problem-solving activities of the Montessori pattern. Putting anything together for a first time may be a creative experience. Some of this may tinge successive efforts. Furthermore, the product of such endeavors may have beauty for children.

Music and Dance

There are other activities in the nursery school that fit the names, if not the concepts of adult artistic endeavor. Music and dance would be so classified. We have mentioned that it is helpful if the nursery school teacher plays the piano and knows enough music to pick out on the piano the tunes and rhythms that children make up. Children greatly enjoy making up their own songs and adapting the words to rhythm and melody. To have the teacher play the tunes on the piano and sing along with them is a very satisfying, creative, learning experience; whatever the limitations of the song and the musicians, the experience fits into the category of the creative arts.

But lacking this kind of musical ability, the teacher can still give her class an opportunity to express themselves through music. There are many good children's records to which children can tap out or clap rhythm. It may take demonstration and encouragement, but children can quickly learn to respond in their own way to the mood and rhythm of the music. This may come by gradual steps. Just learning a song from the teacher or a record may come first. This might be by imitating the teacher. They may experiment, tentatively, with musical instruments available. The children can also explore wider limits of creativity through freer and more individualized bodily movements to music.

How far the good, but general, nursery school should provide experience in either music or dance is open to question. Much more can and has been done by specialists. Young children can become proficient in certain phases of either or both music and dance, but this would not seem to be the concern of the general nursery school. Thus, in speaking of "dance" in the nursery school the authors have in mind activities which might not be so classified in other situations. Everything the child does that leads to greater physical coordination has some relationship to the topic. There is an added dimension when the physical activity is associated with rhythm such as marching to music, or individualized movement in response to the mood of certain music. Musical games, also, belong in this category. There may be a place for very simple folk dances. The danger in the latter is that the emphasis can shift from creativity by the children to premature drill. The nursery school is a place for spontaneity.

Rhymes and Stories

Rhymes and stories made up by the children themselves are expressions of creativity. Rhymes and stories from books constitute an important part of the children's experience and form a background for what the children do, but a feeling for words and what one may do with them grows out of the children's own verbal experiences. If in this early school experience the children begin making up their own rhymes and find enjoyment in the sounds of words, a step in the direction of creativity has been taken.

The stories that the four-year-old tells may be highly creative and filled with imagination or fantasy, but so is all fiction. A child's story should not be labeled a lie. Young children need time to distinguish between reality and fantasy. The nursery school teacher may be able to help with this, not by correction or attempts to distinguish between the two. Rather she can praise the story as a story. In the nursery school it may be told to the teacher alone, or in time, to a group of children. In either case, it is creative fiction.

Role Playing and Dramatic Play

There is creative role playing on the nursery school level. Probably most of such role playing can be more accurately described as dramatic play. The nursery school child will do little of the interpretive "acting out" of stories. Most of this belongs in the kindergarten and primary levels. Still, he does play roles as he knows them. The young nursery school child may be limited to a role in which he plays independently. When he loads a truck with blocks, it is conceivable that this is all that is happening, but it is also possible that the child is "a trucker." One nursery school boy put on a long dress, sat in a small rocker, and rocked slowly back and forth. He "was" his grandmother. As the children reach a stage of cooperative play, groups of children frequently engage in dramatic play. Roles taken may be so engrossing that for the moment the child must be approached as he is in his role. A group of children playing house may refuse admittance to another child, and then readily admit the same child when the nursery school teacher introduces the child in a role appropriate to the situation. There is more than creativity here. The child is indicating his view of adult life. But creativity is evident and it is related to the possible later creative interpretation of the feeling and actions of others.

Pictures and Scenes

Pictures can be presented through many media and in many different forms. By the time a child has entered a nursery school, he has probably had much experience in arranging and rearranging a barnyard, or a doll house, or equivalent settings. In arranging his props the child is not thinkng in terms of what looks most artistic. Still, in arranging and rearranging a setting, design and form are present. This type of activity continues on into and beyond the nursery school age.

Before most children enter nursery school, they have also experimented with some form of drawing. Younger children "scribble" on a piece of paper. The boundaries of possible artistic effort are enlarged both through the developing abilities of the child and the resources of the nursery school. Nursery school children may continue to use crayons and paper and the sand box for pictures, but their horizon for such artistic expressions is enlarged by the availability of finger paints and brushes. The broadening of their scope may only go as far as watching the splatter of paint on paper. It may end with coloring a sheet of paper with one color and coloring over that with another color. This will merge into more evident designs and artistic productions that will be labeled paintings by teacher and child.

Sculpture and Architecture

Most nursery school children are inclined to remain with the comparatively simple with regard to structure. They tend to enjoy building with large blocks, or pieces of boards, or cardboard cartons. They may design elements of landscape in the sand box. They love the feel of clay, and if no one is critical of their products, they will begin to mold it into crude shapes. Some nursery school children will move well beyond these rudimentary designs.

The overlap between primary-age children and the kindergarten-age group noted elsewhere also works in reverse. If in a certain school program children must be nearly five before they enter kindergarten, then some nursery school children will be much closer to six than they are to four at the end of their nursery school experience. Consequently, some of the children in nursery school may be bright kindergarten-age children for part of their nursery school experience. They may be ready for much more advanced forms of music, drama, art, and architecture than has been discussed here. For such children, the discussion of Creativity in the Kindergarten is more appropriate.

Summary

The nursery school teacher should be a creative individual, but her creativity is used to support and encourage children in the development of their own confidence, competence, and creative freedom. The creative expressions of small children may take forms that would not be recognized by the untrained adult as worthy of notice. With proper encouragement such creative acts can be means of building self-esteem and skills while relieving present tensions and helping some children work through personal conflicts. Creativity enters into almost all the activities of the "free" nursery school. Creative activities include elements of all the creative arts.

CHAPTER EIGHT

Structure and Creativity in the Kindergarten

On the day before Easter vacation a kindergarten teacher suggested that the children draw Easter cards with the symbolic bunny for their parents. One child seemed to the teacher to be having difficulty with his drawing. She quickly sketched a rabbit and gave her drawing to the boy to color. He accepted, but an onlooker overheard him protest, "But that's not my rabbit!"

Reviewing the incident, one suspects that the teacher made several mistakes. In terms of this section of the book she may have permitted a *social structure to assume too large a place.* If Easter bunnies have any place in the life of a child, that place should be a matter of fun and games. Why should every child be asked to draw a rabbit? *The teacher also imposed her own structures*—the child's rabbit must look like her idea of a rabbit. And it seems probable that in the whole process *the teacher was yielding to the pressures she felt in her situation.* The children should take something home to the parents. That something should look good, even if it were the work of the teacher and not the child. The teacher had overlooked the need of the child for choice, for success, for creativity. The incident is important only from the standpoint of its implications. The teacher seems to have overly structured a situation. A job had to be done in a certain time and certain way. There is structure in the kindergarten—several kinds—but the structures of the child are the most important.

The Structure of the Child and Structure in the Kindergarten

As noted in earlier chapters, kindergarten children influence the program of the kindergarten by showing the sensitive teacher what they can do and what they are eager to learn and accomplish.

The very nature of the normal kindergarten child lends itself to a special kind of structure, which most certainly is not that of the professional artist. The kindergartner is still a child. Exactly what kind of a child he is will depend on many things. His chronological age may differ from other children a great deal in proportion to his total life span. His rate of development in all its variations will be different from that of other children. The kind of home and community he comes from will effect his behavior. If he has been shouted at and knocked around at home, it will take him awhile to adjust to a different kind of treatment. His language will reflect both his home and his explorations as a four-year-old. In such a context, not all kindergartens and not all kindergarten children fit into a neat category.

The Kindergartner Is Orderly

It still remains true that for most children the kindergarten age is a "comfortable" age.[1] Five-year-olds tend to like order. They seem to have as much fun putting things back together as in taking them apart. They know where things belong and put them in place with less effort than the teacher. Their likes and dislikes are not set as to certain kinds of work. The child who takes on the job of cleaning up the sink is just as proud and happy as the child who helps put the store in order. This may not come automatically. It takes cooperative planning between teacher and children. To a relaxed teacher and the usual kindergarten group it comes normally, naturally, and easily.

The Kindergartner Is Responsible

The kindergartner seems a very "grown-up" person, at least viewed in relationship to the nursery school child. His increased maturity partially accounts for his actions. But, there seems to be something more than this. The typical five-year-old has reached a somewhat peaceful plateau between the turmoil of earlier years and the pressures and irritations that too often follow. He has learned most of the basic characteristics of his society, has a usable language, can communicate most of his ideas, and accepts more responsibility for activities than he formerly did. As yet he has not learned to fake and dodge as well as older children. The kindergartner can be and usually is a very responsible person.

[1] Frances L. Ilg and Louise Bates Ames, *Child Behavior* (New York: Dell, 1955), p. 44.

The Kindergartner Is Cooperative

The kindergarten child usually wants to please adults, including his teacher. He will go along with the teacher's ideas, especially if she has shown that she is interested in his. At five he can cooperate more easily and freely with other children. With other children he is more often supportive than competitive. He can take and give ideas. He can understand more fully than the nursery school child the necessity of recognizing the rights of others. When another child or adult is hurt he is more likely to respond with sympathy. Although he may need help from time to time in give and take and empathy, if there has been a minimum opportunity to learn, the help can be easily given with emphasis on the positive.

The Kindergartner Is Purposeful

In a very important sense, all children display purpose. There are underlying needs and purposes involved in the outreach of children of all ages. The understanding adult can recognize these needs and respond appropriately, regardless of the age of the child. Such understanding is necessary in the kindergarten. It seems that there is something even more outstanding, or perhaps just more apparent, in the work of the kindergarten child. It may be granted that to the uninitiated many things take place in the kindergarten that appear to be play and trivial. But, as we must repeatedly stress, to the teacher and children they are not play, but work. Children who choose their work usually give themselves to it with both a will and a purpose. They are accomplishing something of importance to them. They may not wish to be interrupted and should not be hurried or stopped too abruptly. They are involved in important work—to them.

Thus, it should be evident that there is structure in the kindergarten. In part, it grows out of the situation. In part, it is based on the conventions of society. In part, it has to do with the background, temperament, training, and skill of the teacher. But to an even greater extent it is there in the nature of the five-year-old. If we assume a true kindergarten situation, structure is a minor problem. However, it will require commitment and planning to see that structure does *not* suppress creativity.

Structure That Supports Creativity

Arthur W. Foshay has suggested that creativity may be considered as composed of a number of phases—though not necessarily distinct stages.[2] The first phase involves an openness to new experience. Included in this open-

[2] Arthur W. Foshay, "The Creative Process Described" in Alice Miel (ed.), *Creativity in Teaching* (Belmont, Calif.: Wadsworth Publishing, 1961), pp. 22–40.

ness are such concepts as divergent thinking, tolerance of ambiguity, ability to see possibilities in raw material. Some of the concepts may be too involved for the kindergarten experience, and much of the discussion may be more relevant to older children, but there is some application to kindergarten. Foshay speaks of the necessity of first bringing focus to bear on relevant information or materials and then proceeding to the hard work necessary to produce the poem, or music, or story, or picture. Whatever product evolves from the endeavor should be accepted, modified, or rejected by its creator.

Acceptance, modification, or rejection—all enter into the creative act and can be spoiled at any phase of the operation. The chief service of the teacher in aiding the child to express himself creatively is not to tell, or criticize, or even demonstrate; it is to provide the setting that makes creativity possible. Even by the age of five, it is very easy for the child to begin to learn not to take risks, not to expose himself, not to try to do something different. At a minimum the kindergarten teacher can provide a setting in which intellectual and artistic risk taking are not "dangerous" nor frowned upon.

The kindergarten teacher creates the opportunity for creative expression by exhibiting an attitude of basic acceptance of the child's own form of expression be it a "nonsense" story, a dance interpretation, or a work of art. An essential ingredient for artistic endeavors is *time*. The five-year-old must not be rushed. In addition, he needs the space in which to work and the necessary materials for most forms of art expression. To repeat, *the teacher is teaching creativity by providing the opportunity and the atmosphere.*[3]

Because various forms of creativity were discussed with reference to the nursery school and will be considered again in the context of the primary school, the balance of this chapter will be limited to the area of art as an illustration of creative activity. Application can be made to any of the other forms and disciplines involving artistic endeavor.

What the Kindergarten Teacher Does *Not* Do

Many years ago one of the authors went home from kindergarten in tears. She became a failure at the age of five. There may have been other factors involved, but one factor was recalled vividly by a glimpse into a kindergarten much more recently. In that scene of over fifty years ago, the children were being directed to make Japanese lanterns. The task had no meaning for the author. She did not know what "Japanese" meant and had no interest in or aptitude for the task. In addition, the job was hard—

---

[3] Association for Childhood Education International, *Creating with Material for Work and Play,* Bulletin No. 5 (Washington, D. C.: ACEI, 1957), Inserts 1, 2, and 4.

too hard for most five-year-olds. It is mentioned because a similar project was observed in a little mountain school visited in the summer of 1967. The teacher of the mountain school was committing the same error as the teacher of the past—involving her children in activities that had no relevance for them. In a class for kindergarten teachers the major problem the teachers seemed to be concerned with was not how to stimulate the children to creative expression, but what the children could take home on the first day to impress their parents. Some wanted ideas for projects the children could make and take home *every* day. Parents deserve the finest treatment possible. They certainly deserve honest respect. Foisting off on them as the work of their children what is obviously primarily the work of the kindergarten teacher is not an evidence of respect. It does not indicate that the teacher has much self-respect or respect for her position—nor for the abilities of her pupils.

Parents almost always cooperate with a teacher who respects them, loves their child, and is willing to explain what she is doing and why. This does not mean that there may never be a few ditto sheets around that the children can color if they choose. For some children, just coloring a piece of paper is a first step. Coloring in a design may or may not be a good second step. Generally, if a child wants to color a prepared design, let him. A teacher may want such materials or similar ones in the classroom for children to use when they have a few minutes to wait for something better to do.

Overall, ditto work or any other similar directed activity is poor. It is poor because (1) there is little experimentation possible; (2) the children probably have better coloring materials at home; (3) it is busy work; (4) the children are seldom involved; (5) it is all the teacher's idea—if that. One could go on, but if this were all that happened, it would chiefly just be poor because nothing really happens. There has been a bit of busy work for a few minutes.

What the Kindergarten Teacher Does

Part of what the teacher does derives from her own attitude. If she is interested in freedom of choice and is interested in the child's developing ability to solve his own problems and to accept responsibility for his own behavior, she then can understand the child's involvement with process rather than product.

For her art program the teacher will need both long- and short-range planning. The teacher with foresight will order more materials than she expects to use. It is impossible to judge requirements exactly—better a small surplus to use the following term than a lack of supplies. In addition to the type of materials that the children are acquainted with for a particular project, the teacher occasionally will help the children begin experiments with a different form of expression and different materials. Rarely on the first day of school will a large array and variety of materials be "out" and available to the class. Children need time to get accustomed to a room and what it offers. They also need time to grow accustomed to freedom within limits before they are handed materials that mark and spatter.

In introducing new art projects the teacher will work with individuals and small groups. The other children in the meantime can work with other media with which they are already familiar and interested. Architecture is an art too. If most of the boys are happy in a building project, let them stay with it. If several children, for example, are engaged in dramatic play in the house or store, they should be free to stay with this while the teacher works with other children. In most instances it is more effective in kindergarten to demonstrate to a small group than to a large group. The other children will learn from the first group, and this has its values.

In planning her art projects the teacher should have a varied program, introducing a number of art media a little at a time so that over the months the children will have a choice as to both media and what they do with them. In this type of a program a teaching assistant is a great help. While the teacher is demonstrating the new art form, the assistant can oversee the rest of the class. If no assistant is available, a parent or other person could be called upon. A parent dropping in for a half hour, if the arrangement and situation are understood in advance, can have fun and be most helpful. But a good kindergarten can function with no one there but the children and the teacher. If all the children have a job to do that they feel involved in, they can work ahead on their own for short periods of time. The teacher is then free to work with a small group on a specific art unit.

The teacher will initiate the art program by introducing basic supplies first such as crayons and paper. With these two tools children can experiment with color. How they handle them and what they do with them will enable the teacher to assess their maturation level. From their actions the teacher will learn other things as well. If a child has never had crayons, he may just scribble. Another youngster may color the entire paper with one color. Others may use many colors. Some may even make designs—but that is not necessarily what is important. While working with the crayons and paper, the children are experimenting and getting the feel of creating. They are learning.

A Head Start teacher found herself with *no* supplies for art work. Another teacher gave her some tempera paint. In their impoverished home environment the children had had little experience with art supplies and were not ready to draw or paint a design, but they did love that paint. They painted all the paper that the teacher could provide, even though it was only newspapers in the beginning. The teacher hung the papers up in the room, and the children beamed with pride. Their work was on display. Next the teacher collected scraps of wood—and the children painted these. Was it art? Who can say. Was it creative? At least it was their work and they were fascinated with it. A little later on they were more ready to handle some of the supplies that began to come in.

Clay is not hard to introduce. Put some out on a table. As children become interested, they will try it out. Various types of clay must be kneaded into a pliable form—the children are usually delighted to assume the job. A teacher may suggest what else can be done with the clay, but the children may already have ideas of their own. These ideas gradually change as they discover their limitations and the possibilities in the media. Some children are content to simply enjoy the feel of clay. In a brief time some may go to something else. They may come back another day.

Fingers may or may not come before brushes in painting. Finger painting engenders a sense of freedom and brings enjoyment for children. A teacher, too, can get enjoyment in getting her own hands "dirty." Finger painting can be done on an easel, on the floor, or on a table. Some children may be afraid to finger paint—after all, they might spot their clothes. They should not be forced to participate but encouraged. Let them watch the others. In time (it may take days or even weeks) various children will dip fingers in the paint and be on their way—not only in this form of art, but perhaps to a less constrained life.

How many different types of art should a teacher try? It depends on the circumstances. The children will lead the way. Some children enjoy just dropping paint on wet paper or dry paper. Others like to blow paint through straws on various kinds of paper. And still others like to fold paper over on drops of different colored paint. There are many variations of any idea to be tried. Almost any of these within the comprehension of the kindergarten child could be right at a particular time.

Creativity and Structure in Life and in Skills

When considering the art of the nursery school child, the observation was made that the child through his art may be expressing his fears, feelings, and needs. Often this phase of artistic endeavor is overemphasized. No such overemphasis is intended in stating that art in the kindergarten is therapeutic and revealing.

Art and Self-disclosure

The artist at any age expresses something of himself.[4] There is value in this, sometimes there is release. All have problems on the subconscious and conscious levels. Probably at both levels artists of various ages sometimes find a measure of release. The kindergarten teacher will watch her children's art as she watches all behavior for possible clues to trouble or growth. She will refrain from making conclusions on the basis of one picture or one act. A picture, like an act, may give a clue. One kindergarten teacher collected

[4] Miriam Lindstrom, *Children's Art* (Berkeley: University of California, 1959), p. 11.

pictures from her children. One showed the family. The mother was very large; the father was small; the other siblings were smaller. The kindergarten artist pictured herself as "tiny." Her self-portrayal may or may not have indicated a subconscious evaluation of the family and of herself in relationship to the family. One would not decide on the basis of the drawing, but one might wonder. Another girl filled her picture with a likeness of herself with the rest of the family stuck in here and there, all much smaller. Possibly, the child was drawing a picture of herself and added the rest as an afterthought, or she may have been revealing something of her self-concept.

The same kindergarten teacher in plain view of two girls busily painting turned on a tape recorder. One of the girls was highly verbal. Though she knew the recorder was there and understood its use, she was soon talking away without the slightest evidence of self-consciousness. She sang and talked as she painted. When the teacher played back the tape, in places one could clearly tie in the voice and the picture. At other points on the tape the picture evidently represented the same feeling if not the same content. The child was gaining skill in painting, and she was verbalizing. Between the two she told much about herself. Art, then, may not only provide release for the child, but help show the teacher what else she can do to help and teach.

To some extent, then, the young child is revealing himself and his views of himself and his world through what he depicts. As noted for the nursery school child, this is not all the therapy a disturbed child needs, but it is therapeutic and self-enlightening for the relatively normal kindergartner.[5] There is even more involved in this seeming play with crayons and paint.

Preparing for Academic Achievement

More is happening than is obvious when a child engages in any form of creative endeavor. When a child uses his fingers, or a brush, or a crayon, he is developing motor skills essential to handwriting. Writing and reading both involve perception of form. As the kindergarten artist works, it is sometimes possible to see almost a repetition of the historical development of writing. The scribbles of the two-year-old become the forms and figures of the preschool child. A picture may be just a picture, or it may tell a story. And in the kindergartner's story all kinds of things can begin to get mixed up in the story, such as letters and numbers copied from the surroundings. A further development adds the name of the artist or a title for the picture. It is a logical progression to move from one's own drawings to pictures in a book that tell a story and then to words that go with the pictures. The *creative expression*— art and all the other forms of the creative arts—*is a bridge to the development of skills and knowledge.*

[5] Helen Fisher Darrow and R. Van Allen, "Independent Activities for Creative Learning," in Alice Miel (ed.), *Practical Suggestions for Teaching* (New York: Teachers College, Columbia University, 1961), p. 5.

Summary

There is structure in the kindergarten, but it seldom needs to be imposed with a heavy hand. The structure of the kindergarten child is ordinarily such as to make it possible to structure a program that protects and encourages creativity. In this chapter the art of the kindergarten child was used as an illustration of the value of creative expression. Such expression is both of present value to the child and a means of developing the perceptions and dexterity required for the learning of the skill subjects.

CHAPTER NINE

Structure and Creativity in the Primary Grades

"Boy! When you get that teacher, you paste and paste and paste all year!" This remark was overheard through an open school window. The boy exclaiming was referring to a dedicated teacher who had explained a few weeks earlier that she had found a way to teach her first graders that kept them too busy to make trouble. She dittoed four simple drawings on a sheet of paper and below these four or more simple sentences of the Dick and Jane type. The pupils had to cut and paste the right sentence below the right picture.

The idea had merit. It was not the only technique that the teacher employed. Nevertheless, at least two things were wrong. The boy who made the opening statement implied both in the one sentence: "Boy! When you get that teacher, you Paste, and PASTE, *AND PASTE* all YEAR!" The teacher overdid a good thing. In addition, the boy probably had realized that he was chiefly doing "busy" work. It took time to get the supplies, cut out the sentences, paste them just right, throw away the scraps, put away paste and scissors, clean off the desk, and wash his hands. Probably some valuable learning was going on but at least one bright child was going to remember not this learning, or even fun, but PASTE.

The illustration hardly begins to express the dangers that lie in wait for the child in many an elementary classroom. The problem has already been discussed in the chapters on choice and problem solving. The pressures to achieve the curriculum imposed and the rigidity of personnel may lead to defeat, frustration, and failure for the primary child.

In terms of this final chapter on structure and creativity, the emphasis is stated in a form in which the danger and damage are clearest—and the most often ignored.

Creativity Endangered by Structure

Creativity works in and through and is supported by the right kind of structure. Structure in organization and individuals makes possible the accomplishment of goals. Too easily, though, structure can cease to be a means and become the primary goal. The effective teacher never allows the structure of the class to suppress the creativity of the class as a collective whole or the child as an individual.

Overstructuring the Primary Experience

Frequently overstructuring takes the form of a goal (not usually admitted) of producing docility and conformity. The child is expected to be sweet and obedient.

One of the authors observed a supposedly well-managed first-grade classroom. The teacher was outwardly pleasant, her voice carefully modulated; she was usually smiling. Beneath this seemingly pleasant exterior, she was an absolute dictator. Structure was carried to an extreme. In a handwriting lesson the children were to sit erect in their seats, wait for orders to arrange their paper, wait for orders to pick up or put down a pencil, wait for orders to start writing. "Do everything at exactly the same time and as far as possible in exactly the same way," were the instructions the class received. If a pupil picked up a pencil before he was so directed, the teacher kept right on smiling while she slapped the offender's hand. Apparently, in this room it was, also, a misdemeanor to even finish an assignment before the time was up. One small boy closed a workbook and picked up a book to read. This time the smile faded a bit and the voice lost some of its careful modulation. "Put that away and finish your work!" the teacher ordered. "But I have finished my work," said the boy. "No, you haven't," declared the teacher without checking. "Put the book away." So the book was put away and the boy stared at his workbook in what appeared to be total frustration. This teacher was highly regarded by superiors and public. Why not? Her room was neat, orderly and quiet!

Most teachers are not like our "exemplary" teacher. At least, they do not carry their benevolent dictatorships to quite the extent this teacher did. One must be constantly on guard not to submit to the *subtle danger of completely teacher-dominated activities.* Such domination is possible, and comes easily, because young children will usually submit. Besides, the teacher is under pressure to control.

There are less obvious ways to crowd out creative effort in a classroom. The most usual forms come from equating "talking" with "teaching" and crowding every moment of the day with assigned activities. To this can be added the increasing emphasis on product (on the right answer as understood by the teacher) rather than on understanding and process. The result is an "over"-structuring that leaves no room for creative effort.

Unfortunately, one does not have to look far to find multiple illustrations. One need not even look beyond the supposedly creative art experience. One teacher solved the whole problem of the six-year-olds' drawing of the human figure by telling her class, "You just make a hay stack like this. Then you draw a circle up here for a head. Then you draw lines here and there for arms and legs. See how easy it is." This is an imposed structure that produces a certain kind of result. For humorous purposes in a limited context, there might be some value. In this case the children were still drawing people like haystacks a full year later. Marie M. Hughes graphically illustrates this type of stifling of creativity in two instances.[1] A third-grade class was constructing paper fruit and vegetables for a large cornucopia to symbolize the Thanksgiving season. One boy was carefully drawing cherries. The teacher intervened: "Here, fold your paper like this and you can cut many at one time." It made no difference that the boy had in mind the cherries that he had picked on his grandfather's farm or that he wanted to make them different.

The other illustration comes from a slightly older group of children, but the principle is the same. A boy had drawn the inside of the university field house. The field house was empty except for a lone figure on the court holding a ball. The art supervisor took one look and said, "You haven't filled the spaces. Here, let me show you." Then the supervisor sketched in figures in the court and bleachers. As he turned, he heard the sound of tearing paper and he ordered the boy out of the room. As the boy left, he was heard to mutter, "I was all alone. I was practicing, and it was a little scary."

The points in the three illustrations differ. In the first two the question is production for ease and speed with resulting lack of any creativity. The last is simply the imposition of the structure in the mind of the art teacher on a boy's attempt to depict something of meaning to him. Sometimes even the structure of reality can be brutally and unnecessarily imposed. A third-grade teacher asked a class what color an elephant was. "Pink," replied one boy. "You know you have never seen a pink elephant," declared the teacher and proceeded to get the right answer from someone else. The boy in frustration turned to various members of the class. "I know," he pleaded, "I've seen pink elephants." No doubt some correction was called for, but it could have been done in such a way as to preserve the boy's dignity and recognize the fact that probably the very books the school was using had pink elephants.

[1] Marie M. Hughes, "Integrity in Classroom Relationships," in Alice Miel (ed.), *Creativity in Teaching* (Belmont, Calif.: Wadsworth Publishing, 1961), pp. 77–105.

There are pink elephants in pictures, cartoons, movies, and the toy counter. For that matter, live elephants have been colored pink for display purposes.

The Influence of a Developing Realism

The teacher needs to be particularly concerned as to the danger of stifling creativity in the primary grades because of the child's increasing awareness of the gap between his production and reality. Further on in this chapter the positive aspects of the child's developing abilities will be discussed. In the present context there are at least two factors to note. E. Paul Torrance quotes from the limited available research indicating that there are rises and falls in the creative inclination of children.[2] Part of this may have to do with transitional periods through which the child passes in his own development or because of the organizational structure of the school.

It is hoped that in the future the first grade will not involve as abrupt a change in the life of the child as is now common. In most areas of the United States the first grade is another new beginning. Kindergarten and first grade are too often very different. Moreover, first grade is actually the first school experience for about one third of American children. Periods of major adjustment are not usually times of high creative effort. Teachers of such children should make a major effort to permit and encourage what creativity remains possible.

There is also a growing realism on the part of children that often outruns skill. At least some six-year-olds can see what is wrong with their pictures, but they may not be able to improve them to the extent that they wish. Such self-criticism increases with age. The eight-year-old may be especially critical of himself and in great need of support and assurance. If he can be encouraged to find enjoyment in his improving abilities, he is less likely to abandon creative effort.

The older child faces the additional risk of the possibly stifling influence of the gang or clique; the primary child faces a related danger. Not only is he critical of his own work, but other children and teachers are often critical. This criticism must be kept in check. Honest effort can be accepted for what it is. A little girl in first grade was puzzled because her pictures were never chosen by the teacher as one of the "best." The child could not understand why this was so. Perhaps she had reason to be puzzled. Why should not any six-year-old's honest effort be recognized?

The primary-age child needs opportunity for creative experience. Such activities continue to be an outreach to understanding of self and reorganization of the knowledge flooding in. It is vital that he be protected from the pressures for conformity from structures within and without. Still more is necessary. *The school system and the teacher should so organize the program that creativity is valued.*

[2] E. Paul Torrance, *Guiding Creative Talent* (Englewood Cliffs, N. J.: Prentice-Hall, 1962), pp. 91–92.

Creativity Supported by Structure

Several premises are intermixed in the thesis that structure supports and encourages creativity. One is the concept of encouraging all children to be creative. Another is the need to protect and support the highly creative child. Probably, as in other areas of life, there is no clear-cut dividing line between the two groups. When Jacob Getzels and Philip Jackson conducted their experiments[3] to distinguish the characteristics and achievements of creative versus intelligent children, they did not sample the entire population of children. For their study they selected the most creative and the most intelligent. Presumably, by any test or selection the total population would have formed some kind of continuum. And, as with most other areas of life, creativity is not necessarily "all of one cloth." Children who are creative with words may not be especially creative with music or art.

As Alice Miel asserts, *neither teachers nor pupils must spend all of their time "being creative."*[4] Teachers must live with themselves and their own limitations. They may need to venture carefully into the possibly troubled waters of creative activity. Peggy Brogan suggests that the creative teacher "expects the unexpected."[5] Every teacher should, but the extent to which teachers can live with such a concept will vary, though the attitude can be developed in almost everyone. The very few who must have all plans worked out in detail and carried through exactly as planned *should not* be working with young children. But even the most creative teachers and pupils will do some things where the creative element is not the major factor involved.

Evelyn Wenzel points out various kinds of creative teachers.[6] Some "burst" with energy. Their classes are always providing programs, and their rooms are showplaces of various activities. At the other extreme there is the teacher who is not showy at all, but somehow supports the creative efforts of children while remaining almost a shadowy figure herself.

Need of Opportunity for All

As creativity has been defined for this section, it involves the rearranging of thought or materials to produce something new to the individual. So defined, all children must be creative if they are to learn. It thus becomes important that all children have the opportunity to continually revamp their experience. An essential ingredient is an attitude on the part of educators that cherishes the attempt of the child to think through what his experience really means. The teacher who begins to value this kind of creativity will be

---

[3] Jacob W. Getzels and Philip W. Jackson, *Creativity and Intelligence: Explorations with Gifted Students* (New York: Wiley, 1962), Chapter 2.

[4] Miel, *op. cit.,* p. 8.

[5] Peggy Brogan, "The Case for Creativity," in Miel, *op. cit.,* p. 13.

[6] Evelyn Wenzel, "Finding Meaning in Teaching," in Miel, *op. cit.,* pp. 41–47.

more interested in the work of the child who has given thought to a situation, even when his answer "appears" to be wrong, than to the glib right answer. She will value every evidence that the child is moving out on his own.

This attitude needs to be undergirded *by encouraging creative thought and expression in the usual subject areas*. The child's sincere question is important and should be considered. The teacher does not necessarily have the answer on the tip of her tongue, and when she does, she may not give it. Answers may come from the children. And in these answers they, too, need to be taught to value the questioning, seeking, and discovery approach. The child's story, illustration, and problem are all-important. The understanding of basic principles is worth many hours of unenlightened drill.

Special times must be set aside for creative activities. In these periods, criticism is even more rigidly excluded. One third-grade teacher prided herself on her ability to teach Creative Writing. The children were urged to write freely. But—the teacher then read their compositions aloud in class, criticizing every mistake in grammar and spelling. One could see the young authors cringing in shame at the front of the class. Creative writing is a time when one writes as he feels or thinks. The "author" should be able to ask for help with spelling or grammar. He should be permitted to read his own composition to his peers. If there is a grade, and probably there should not be, it should be for the attempt and the creativity—not the mechanics. Stephen Joseph found that even culturally deprived children down to the age of seven could write meaningfully when freed from the risk of ridicule.[7] Incidentally, children do gain skill more rapidly when this is permitted. There are times in any school for specific language instruction. It is both dishonest and brutal to tell a child to write his thoughts freely and then to proceed to tear him apart.

How different the picture is when children are permitted to read their own creations. In one team-teaching situation children read with the assistance of an amplifying system to a hundred or more children. They read proudly and interpreted their own meanings. The audience responded with appreciation and enjoyment. One of the teachers in the team, a very creative person, had remarkable success working with this large group in the area of creative writing. She used various techniques to bring out the group's creativity. For example, in the large room where the group met, there was a chalk board in the front of the room. As the teacher dramatized an imaginative incident, she drew various lines on the board until the outline of a giant ant emerged. Alongside this, in one corner of the board, she placed some tiny people. What, she asked the children, would each of them do if he were an ant 10 feet tall? As they began to respond, she told them to write it down. They did this with glee and gusto. In this incident the only problem proved to be that word spread through the school system of the "terrible

[7] Stephen M. Joseph, *The Me Nobody Knows* (New York: Avon, 1969), Introduction.

violence" imagined. No one seemed to have dared suggest that the violence must have been there all the time and that this expression was possibly therapeutic.

The principle applied to creative writing is equally pertinent with reference to all creative endeavors. The element of risk must be reduced to what the child can accept. This can be partly done by reducing criticism. It is also possible to emphasize the fact that all differ in special abilities. It can be done by permitting freedom in the use of media. There can be free periods in which children work on a variety of projects. Chandler Montgomery rightly contends that it is not robbing a child of his choice or infringing on creative thought to invite the child's interest and participation in certain types of artistic endeavor.[8] His contention is particularly true if there is an actual choice and the child can do something else if he prefers.

In such an environment, *children with no extraordinary talent may do some extraordinary things.* If the teacher sets the example by making up simple rhymes related to the children's experiences, they may soon start making up their own. If the teacher puts the rhymes to music, her children may do the same. If she shows interest in their stories, they most likely will make up more.

Protection, Support, and Guidance for the Highly Creative

It was noted earlier that creativity probably exists on a continuum. Out on the far end of the continuum the very creative individual faces special problems. Paul Torrance states the problem as follows:

Who can blame teachers for being irritated when a pupil presents an original answer which differs from what is expected? It does not fit in with the rest of the grading scheme. They don't know how the unusual answer should be treated. They have to stop and think themselves. Peers have the same difficulty and label the creative child's unusual questions and answers as "crazy" or "silly."[9]

Torrance suggests that the very creative student requires several kinds of help. He needs help to recognize that it is all right to think differently even though one is not always understood. Sometimes help is provided by the presence of some "sponsor" or "patron" who has sufficient prestige to support an individual in his differences. The principal, or the guidance counselor, or the teacher might play such a role. What is essential is someone to listen, to understand, to recognize the talent. Often the parents and some teachers require assistance in recognizing the worth of the divergent thinker. On any level highly creative people are a rarity. Such a child may need help in learning appropriate ways to interact with other children. He may need help in learning creative ways of interacting with teachers without being difficult. Whatever special gift the child has, it should be treasured and rewarded.

[8] Chandler Montgomery, *Art for Teachers of Children* (Columbus, Ohio: Merrill, 1968), pp. 163–171.
[9] Torrance, *op. cit.*, p. 8.

Structure Enhancing Creativity

The possibility of a stifling conformity exists in overstructuring by the teacher—a fact we cannot stress too much. The danger of doing so is increased by the developing realism and self-criticism of the child. Along with these negative factors, there are positive aspects of the situation. These include the many school systems and teachers who enthusiastically support creative endeavors.

Equally important and more pertinent to the present discussion is the developing ability, added experience, and vastly increased store of knowledge of the growing child. The third grader in comparison to the same child in nursery school is a much more competent individual. Both his changing structure and his grasp of the structure of his world make possible a vastly enhanced creative effort. As Helen Heffernan suggests,[10] creativity requires some kind of raw materials, some fund of information, some ability to use tools. All through the primary experience there remains the danger of discouraging the child by the rigid insistence on the production of adult imposed forms. But *creativity does require a structure within a child* and a grasp of the structure of the operation that the child wishes to perform. This comes gradually. Full fruition of any form of creativity is years away. Still, there are eight-year-olds who can draw or paint with more freedom and realism than many adults. There are children who can dance, or play the piano, or perform with artistry beyond the average adult. The application is broader than is implied here. Creativity touches on every area of life. Practically all children—creative or not—develop a variety of abilities that makes further creative experience possible.

The Creativity of the Six-year-old

The six-year-old child needs help and support in continued free creative endeavor while he acquires the skills that make a different type of creative endeavor possible. If protected in his originality, he will still be relatively free in his art work, although there is danger and possibility in his own self-criticism. Criticism should not be considered evaluation, for too often criticism is destructive. Evaluation connotes a constructive and positive approach. One form of evaluation is to consider the appropriateness of creative effort to a certain situation.

The six-year-old has more experience upon which to draw and has greater perceptual and manual abilities than the kindergartner. His art tends to have more realism, if less freedom. He continues to create rhymes with increased verbal accuracy and unique sense of humor. He enjoys dramatic play but with increased insight. His body responds more skillfully in rhythmic

[10] Helen Heffernan, *Guiding the Young Child: From Kindergarten To Grade Three* (Lexington, Mass.: Heath, 1959), pp. 252–315.

expression. He usually needs help in written expression. If the teacher sympathetically responds to his oral expression by writing down his thought, the six-year-old can be successful as a composer in the same sense as an author dictating to a secretary. Not only that, but he can almost always read back what has been written with significant oral interpretation.

The Creativity of the Seven-year-old

The seven-year-old child usually has reached a new plateau of calm purposefulness. The inherent danger for the seven-year-old is that he may be so thrilled with the simple fact of acquiring skills that he may regress in creative expression unless specifically encouraged. With encouragement he can bring both increased skill and creativity to all forms of artistic expression. The seven-year-old is increasingly competent in the use of writing for his own purposes. If given the opportunity, he usually begins to "blossom out" in his own brief compositions and poems. He is no longer as dependent on the teacher to write down his ideas. Like all other individuals, but more restrictively, he knows many more words than he can yet spell.

The seven-year-old also can more successfully take part in group projects. Such group work opens up possibilities for a variety of art projects, for example, either by the entire group or by those members most interested in art. Other children can make their contribution through construction or written work.

The Creativity of the Eight-year-old

Many contend that "the sky is the limit" with the eight-year-old. Herein lies a danger. He may attempt too much and grow frustrated through failure to reach his goals. Thus, the teacher of eight-year-olds is faced with how to keep projects within reasonable bounds without dampening the enthusiasm of the children. On the other hand, a teacher with a group of eager, creative children who have ample opportunity to express themselves may have to extend herself in keeping pace with their enthusiastic approach to learning problems. An eight-year-old is capable of participation in many forms of individual and group projects. He is frequently ready to move from the area of dramatic play to more realistic role playing. With practice in a relaxed atmosphere, he can learn to use hand puppets to good advantage. He can also help with the construction and operation of a puppet show. He can take part in more intricate group planning and do a more effective job on the individual parts of the group project. If given encouragement and stimulus, he can express his imagination through creative writing.

The assumption throughout is that practice of two kinds has occurred. One is *practice* in continuing *to be open to new experiences* and in daring *to express one's inner feelings and thoughts*. The other is *practicing the skills involved*. The child who plays the piano well at eight began learning to play long before. His practicing need not have been wholly drill. The piano teacher may have had the child working on a simple melody from the first lesson. Interest and drill are involved, but there is something more. If not by eight, at least soon thereafter, the child learns to experiment with his own interpretation and arrangements. He learns to play the things he hears. Perhaps he learns to hear within himself the melody that has not yet been written. Creativity and structure move on together if the eight-year-old-pianist is someday to become a composer or even a good pianist.

Creativity and School Achievement

Creative activities are more likely to improve school achievement than hinder. More real work is accomplished when creativity is respected and nourished than when rigid routines are followed. Children learn only when they are involved and they are only involved when their imaginations are fired. A first-grade class was made up of children from two very different types of kindergartens. One kindergarten was very formal with a great deal of seat work, chiefly of the ditto variety. The other kindergarten had an "experiential" type program. There the children had worked in the store or house, did art work as they wished with any media that they selected, and had been encouraged to express themselves. There was no "ditto" work of any kind. It was the children from this kindergarten with varied experiences who learned to read with more ease than those from the other group. These children were alive and eager; they had more complete understandings of their world. More formal evidence of the relation of creativity to achievement comes from the study by Getzels and Jackson[11] and is confirmed by Torrance.[12] They found that in spite of more negative attitudes by teachers in regard to creative students and in spite of lower intelligence scores in general, creative individuals demonstrated that they could do equally well with tests of achievement. The evidence is that *to encourage creativity is to improve the learning process.*

Summary

There is danger that the creative impulses of children may be thwarted by the misuse of structure. Pressures the teacher feels may smother creative expression. Other attitudes and pressures may make mockery of supposedly creative experiences. Even the child's own developing realism may prove a hindrance. If given support and encouragement, the child's increased competence makes creative effort more varied and productive in the primary grades.

---

[11] Getzels and Jackson, *op. cit.,* p. 30.
[12] Torrance, *op. cit.,* p. 59.

skills and insight

It is well done to make a child read and write, and learn and repeat—but it is still better to make a child think.
Pestalozzi, On Infants' Education

1 2 3
4 5 6

Principles Relative to Skills and Insight

Part IV is primarily concerned with the recognized academic aspects of the learning experience of the young child. The whole area of the how and why and when of academic learning greatly concerns educators today. In an earlier and simpler, but not necessarily better, day there was no evident problem as to whether or not schools taught skills or insights. Traditionally, the first three grades in school taught the three R's, the basic skill subjects. In the mind of the general public teaching the three R's was the school's reason for being.

Among educators, there has been almost as strong a tradition in the opposite direction with regard to what has been known as the "preschool" years. Traditionally, the nursery was a nursery or day care center. It was not primarily concerned with teaching. People had never given much thought to the fact that three- and four-year-olds were learning anything of importance. At the most they were kept safe and happy and helped to adjust to each other and the supervising adults. Some of the same concept carried over into kindergarten experience. That many states do not have public-supported kindergartens as yet is one of the many indications of the attitude that kindergarten is play rather than school. Probably these children in nurseries and kindergartens did learn, incidentally, skills and concepts that were related to later academic success. Traditionally, educators did not think in these terms.

Learning Basic Skills Early in Life

There has been a dichotomy in the thinking of the general public and to a lesser extent in the thinking of educators. Both have tended to think that in nursery and kindergarten children were learning, but nothing specially related to academic skills. Their thinking concerning the grades has been the opposite: they expected children to be taught the traditional academic skills; nothing more was expected. The dichotomy referred to between the so-called "preschool" and "school" experience is false. Learnings directly related to the traditional programs of the early grades begin much earlier in life than the age of six[1]—for that matter, earlier than three. We shall not discuss at this point when formal reading and the related skills should be introduced into the curriculum except to stress that such skills as reading are based upon the development of many preparatory skills. Whenever formal reading is introduced, there should have been many kinds of preparation involving both the development of skills and insights prior to its introduction. Today it is generally agreed that most children by the age of three have mastered much of the basic structure of their language. Thus, the child does not begin to learn the skill subjects in the first grade. He started on the path to learning the academic skills long before nursery school.

Different Rates of Learning

The dichotomy between preschool and school experience is false because *children differ*. Their readiness for any experience depends on both native endowments and previous experiences in life. At one time child development specialists overemphasized the interrelationship of learning with maturation in the development of readiness. Knowing more about readiness does not simplify the problem. If anything, it can aggravate the "problem," for "readiness" is extremely complicated. Even when it is recognized that children differ in chronological age, in motor and neural development, in social and emotional maturity, and in exposures to opportunities to learn, it is an oversimplification. Closer investigation of any one of these factors leads to the discovery that it is in itself a vastly complicated subject. It does not make sense to suppose that *no* child in the kindergarten should be taught to read or that *every* child must be taught to read in the first grade.

Skills Not Isolated Learning Experiences

The dichotomy that has tended to exist between school and preschool is also false because the basic academic skills are not isolated learning

---

[1] James Cass, "The Crucial Years Before Six," *Saturday Review,* LI, 24 (June 15, 1968), 59.

experiences. It is many years since the publication of the book, *Why Johnny Can't Read.*[2] Why, one might well wonder, has no one ever written a book entitled, *Why Johnny Doesn't Understand What He Reads. Word calling doth not a reader make*—a reader is one who reads. This implies reading with understanding, appreciation, feeling, curiosity, and eagerness.

What has been said about reading can be applied to other academic skills. One sixth-grade girl could work perfectly any page of arithmetic problems, provided she was told in advance what the process was. She had to be told when she came to the next page whether to add, subtract, multiply, or divide. She had been "taught" arithmetic. She was, mechanically, almost flawless. But she had no insight as to why any procedure was called for. She had learned a skill well but seemingly had learned nothing of insight or meaning. She is an extreme example only because she was so good in the skill, and so completely devoid of insight. Most children never get this much skill unless they have acquired insight.

Skill and Insight

When permitted, skills and insight develop simultaneously. Frequently a skill can be taught without the user of the skill understanding very much of the purpose of the skill. We speak of people as cogs in a machine. More and more we find ourselves in contact with computers in our daily living. Programmed by the skilled and knowledgeable technician, a computer can furnish an amazing amount of information in very little time. It can only do what it is programmed to do, however; it cannot plan its own work. And if something is wrong with the way it is programmed or with the information "fed in," it can make fantastic mistakes. (The reader probably has his own fund of stories: the man who received a check for over a million dollars in place of $1.15, or the girl who found she was signed up for only one college course, football.) It is difficult to develop people with "programmed mentality," but that does not stop many people, educators included, from doing so. Any time the teacher or parent demands, "Stop asking questions and do what I'm telling you to do," he is working toward the production of skill without insight.

The Infant

The infant begins his separate existence as a functioning organism. He has done an immense amount of growing and maturing, and probably some learning, even before birth. He still has much growing and maturing to accomplish. In this process almost every new fragment of skill shows some element of insight. Some activities seem reflexive or almost wholly develop-

[2] Rudolf Flesch, *Why Johnny Can't Read* (New York: Popular Library, 1955).

mental. Movement, for example, seems built into the human infant and is present before birth. It contributes to growth and learning. The learning seems to involve discovering a purpose for movement and then coordinating that movement to accomplish that purpose. The baby that finally succeeds at the age of six months in picking up a block does not appear to an adult to have accomplished much, but months of both development and learning have gone into that achievement. The baby may have no realization of the wonder of his achievement. If one has watched the eyes of the child as he has noticed the block, and then watched the uncoordinated attempts to reach it, and when reaching it, to pick it up, one can see that something akin to insight has been there and that skill is slowly developing.

Further Development

The combination of search for insight and skill proceeds throughout life. They are in full and visible progress before the beginning of nursery school. It is the job of the nursery school to cooperate with the child in his search for meanings and abilities. Nurseries serve other worthwhile purposes, but a nursery school is not a school unless it teaches. *It does this by cooperating with the child in his outreach for both skill and insight.* The three-year-old has much to learn. Most of his insights are sketchy and distorted, and his skills may appear minimal. Both, though, are amazing when compared to those of the six-month-old baby. The three-year-old can do many things that bear directly on academic skills. Thus, the teacher does not wait until the child is six or even five to teach the skills.[3]

The task of developing skill and insight is a continuous one. The value of nursery and kindergarten from this standpoint is that the environment can be arranged to encourage the more rapid development of both. How this is done is basic to the discussion of the next chapters. The teacher who understands the nursery- and kindergarten-age child accomplishes these purposes almost without seeming to teach. How far and in what directions such "teaching" leads depends on many factors, but in a good school very important learnings are going on.

It follows, therefore, that the primary school is not starting out on a new endeavor. *When the child enters the first grade or its equivalent, he should move on from whatever levels of achievement and knowledge he already has reached.* In the good primary school, then, the school adjusts to the child. If he already knows how to read, he is not started in a preprimer. If he is not ready for even a preprimer, he is given appropriate learning experiences as preparation for more formal instruction.

In either case, the skills will not be divorced from insight. Insight is even more important in learning to read than skill. Someplace in the learning of the young child he makes the discovery that symbols represent speech

[3] Esther P. Edwards, "Kindergarten Is Too Late," *Saturday Review,* LI, 24 (June 15, 1968), 68–70, 76–79.

sounds and that the sounds combine to form words (hopefully, words he already knows). This discovery of meaning and purpose provides the excitement in early reading. A charming story is told by Maria Montessori.[4] She had already taught some of the slum children in her early project to write through the sensory experience of tracing letters cut out of sandpaper which would lead them on to meaningful writing. Then she began to write simple sentences on the chalkboard. She wrote, "If you can read this, come to me," and similar sentences. She did this for several days. One day she looked down and there beside her was a "tiny mite of a girl" saying, "Here I am!"

Acquiring Skills

Given a purpose and a sense of success, most individuals will work diligently to acquire skills. In some ways babies are very persistent in developing rudimentary skills. Little children drill themselves in countless ways in acquiring language. High school band members not only practice music, but spend hours in intricate drill in order to perform their routines. College boys put up with a great deal of regimentation and hours of drill and struggle to perfect their skills as football players. In each case there are purposes served by the skill.

The Purpose of the Skills

The skills serve purposes. Sometimes a skill may temporarily become its own chief purpose. For the toddler the joy of walking may be for a time more important than where he is going; a child may run for the sheer pleasure of running. But underneath even this exuberance there is a purpose. The purpose may be momentarily forgotten, but it is there just the same. The academic skills are similar. There is a kind of triumph simply in being able to write an "a" or recognize one's name. The fact of skill may take precedence for a short interval, though even then there is some form of insight. He begins to understand that "a" represents something; it is the individual's name he recognizes.

The skills are intended to serve purposes beyond themselves. Usually part of that purpose is understood before the skill is fully achieved. The boy learning to play baseball is awkward. He does not use bat or glove with skill, but in all probability he already has decided that he wants to knock the ball over the head of the outfielder or put the batter out by catching the ball. Reading is important because it opens up new vistas of knowledge. It is an important skill, but it need not be simply a skill. So with all the academic skills—they are basically means to an end. They help us to understand, to communicate, to solve our own problems.

[4] E. M. Standing, *Maria Montessori: Her Life and Work* (New York: New American Library, 1962), p. 50.

The Thrill of Skill

It has already been implied that there is excitement in the mastery of skills. The individual who has learned to read will often enjoy demonstrating the new-found skill. The child who has learned to write will be happy to have an adult observe the product. Every child can have these successful experiences. The accomplishments should be treated with respect as significant achievements. This is true whether such success takes place in nursery school or much later. Progress in a skill is exciting and rewarding—and should be recognized.

The Variety of Skills

This excitement in learning a skill can be enjoyed by every child. Even the extremely retarded child is gradually gaining some skill. He will gain more if he is praised for what he learns, not condemned because he has less skill than others. The very young child is gaining skills that can be recognized as skills. The older child is gaining ground in countless ways and in varied rates.

The skills classified as academic skills are made up of many subskills. Reading involves perception and differentiation. It includes the understanding of auditory distinctions and the meanings of the distinctions. In our language it includes the discovery that words and sentences move from left to right and that reading proceeds from top to bottom. Carl Bereiter has attempted to teach slum children that every word has a beginning and an ending.[5] A vast complexity of insights and skills enters into such a skill as reading.[6] Among these preparatory skills there is necessary learning appropriate to the child's level of development. What is fundamental is that the child be given a successful learning experience so that he will be eager to extend his learning experiences.

The Danger of Teaching Skill in Isolation

Probably no one has even succeeded in teaching a skill without at least a little intermixture of insight. There is danger that, particularly on the primary level, the teacher may overemphasize the skill at the expense of insight. The result can be mechanical drill. Some drill is necessary in life. Children and adults drill themselves repeatedly to perfect skills for their own purposes. However, there is harm in imposed drill, particularly when the child's mind is not involved in the procedure. Such drill seldom accomplishes its purpose. Too much of it can make life very frustrating for anyone. The child should

[5] Carl Bereiter and Siegfried Englemann, *Teaching Disadvantaged Children in the Preschool* (Englewood Cliffs, N. J.: Prentice-Hall, 1966), pp. 38–39.

[6] Marian Monroe and Bernice Rogers, *Foundations for Reading: Informal Pre-reading Procedures* (Glenview, Ill.: Scott, Foresman, 1964).

be involved in a meaningful experience, related when possible to his own purposes. *Teachers tend to assume that the children understand what they are practicing and why.* If the children have not so learned, very little of value has been achieved. The numeral "7" may mean nothing to a child. Counting seven blocks or seven pennies is a form of drill also, but it may give the child insight into the meaning of the numeral. Skills are important but so is insight into meaning and purpose.

Summary

Both skills and insights are sought in all the learning of life. Both begin much earlier than nursery school and continue far beyond the primary years. One does not wait until after kindergarten to begin helping the child toward academic skills or to drop all other learnings when the child enters the first grade. Skills are sought when they have meaning. They are chiefly means to other purposes. *Skills must be rooted in understandings.*

CHAPTER TEN

Skills and Insight in the Nursery School

A three-year-old boy was struggling valiantly with a coat before going outdoors on a cold day. His arms were not going in the right places. When he finally got his arms in the sleeves, the coat was on backward. It could not be buttoned. He had wanted to do the job himself and after a fashion, succeeded. As we remember it, he was forced to accept a little help before being permitted outside. Whether the help should have been given is debatable.

Three-year-olds need help with many things. How much and in what way is central to the discussion that follows. If there is a lesson in the story itself, it is that the normal three- and four-year-old is eager to do what he can *on his own*. The teacher's task is to encourage his growing skill and self-reliance.

Skills and Insights Brought to the Nursery School

All should understand the importance of the infant and toddler period in the life and learning of children. As previously noted, learning is a continuum that begins at or before birth and goes on in some form until death. Thus, at every level in education, those working with children should know as much as possible about what has gone before and what will follow.

There is a further point that teachers on every level should remember. *Learning is broader than a school's curriculum.* Children learn much, for better and for worse, that no school purposely teaches. They learn some things in any school that are not intended. Even in nursery school they may sometimes learn that school is frustrating and, possibly, frightening. They also learn from other people besides teachers. It is generally accepted that parents have more influence on the attitudes of children than do teachers.[1] The effect includes the attitude toward learning. Parents may be very effective teachers of some of the academic skills. Children also learn from other adults, including the baby sitter, custodian, cook, relatives, and garbage collector. They learn from older children and their peers. Educators have been aware that children learn outside the school, but until recently too many have neglected to take such learning into consideration when they deal with children in the classroom.

Thus, children entering a nursery school have already learned a great deal. If one were to graph learning from conception through maturity using a ratio scale that considered learning in comparison to what was known at each preceding level, it is a reasonable assumption that the sharpest rise in the curve would precede the third birthday. When it is remembered how little the child can do at birth, his progress by the age of three is remarkable. Unless extremely retarded mentally or physically handicapped, he can not only walk but run too. Walking is a complicated skill; running is even more so.

The three-year-old will not appear quite as skilled in the use of his hands as with his legs. He may have difficulty with tasks that are not hard for older children. His perceptual skills and related ability to manipulate are poorly coordinated. Given a crayon, he scribbles and little organization may be evident. It is important to remember his limitations. He is making steady progress in manipulative skills. This progress can be encouraged. It will be if the adult appreciates the value of his sensory motor experience. For the child such experiences are valuable even when they seem to the adult to be unnecessarily repetitious.

Prenursery School Learning and the Language Arts

The rapid progress most young children make in the understanding and use of their native language has been indicated. As with all other learnings, it varies with the child. The variation may be influenced by many factors including native endowment, but also including all the experiences and relationships of life. There are a few children who do not seem to have made this rapid progress. Some children of nursery school age either cannot

---

[1] Margaret Barron Luszki and Richard Schmuck, "Pupil Perceptions of Parental Attitudes Toward School," in Jerome M. Seidman (ed.), *The Child: A Book of Readings* (New York: Holt, Rinehart and Winston, 1969), pp. 500–512.

or will not speak. If they can but will not talk, the problem may be social and the immediate need may be an adjustment to the situation. Such a situation is more likely to be true in programs for the culturally disadvantaged, but it may be true of other children as well. If so, giving the child time to become accustomed to a new environment, to feel safe away from home, and safe with other children may bring speedy recovery. The child who cannot speak presents a different type of problem. Diagnostic study and assistance beyond the capacities of the nursery school are probably required.

Most three-year-olds do talk, however, and they usually have an extensive speaking vocabulary. In addition, they understand many words that they cannot yet say.[2] They can speak in simple sentences. By fairly complicated thought processes they have learned many of the essential elements of English grammar. Whatever else is involved, three-year-olds have made great strides in the mastery of the language art skills. They still have a long way to go, but the amazing thing is the start that they have already made.

It is not as evident, but the three-year-old has already made a start in other language art and quantitative skills as well. (The discussion will not be concerned with the occasional three-year-old who can already read a book. Probably very few nursery school teachers will ever meet one. The problem to be faced by the teacher is not this, but in what way to help the child move on from whatever his level of achievement may be.)

Perceptual skill is closely related to language art. Possibly one can trace the beginning of listening back to the months before birth, but visual perception does not begin until birth. From observations of babies it appears that perception is confused and limited in the early weeks. But from the moment the baby first opens his eyes, he gathers visual experience that is preparing the way for many things including the ability to read. None of this is to imply that the development of the child's central nervous system, growth and changes in the body, and all the other phases of maturation are not essential. Learning the skills is a gradual process interrelated with other processes and greatly dependent on experience.

Most of these preliminary experiences and the development of essential subskills will come gradually and easily, without pressure or even a great deal of thought in most homes. Children gradually learn to identify and to distinguish. It is a well-known phenomenon that it is easier for a stranger to care for a very young baby than for an older one. The most logical explanation is that at about six months, or shortly thereafter, the baby identifies his mother as the most important person in his life. Being left by the mother in the care of a stranger can, then, become for a time a very traumatic experience. The baby has learned to discriminate. He can recognize his mother's face and voice.

All kinds of experiences and learnings take place during infancy. Most have some bearing on the learning of skills. An eighteen-month-old child

[2] Paul Henry Mussen, John Janeway Conger, and Jerome Kagan, *Child Development and Personality* (New York: Harper & Row, 1969), Chapter 4.

can readily be seen both understanding a mother and also figuring out whether or not the mother really means what she says. For example, two women with children were standing in front of an apartment talking. One woman was keeping an eye on a toddler. As he wandered up the street, she said, "Tommy, don't go any further." Tommy hesitated and appeared to size up his mother. To the observer, and evidently to Tommy, the mother seemed still relaxed and not angry or frightened by his action. Tommy continued up the street. When the distance began to grow too great, the mother's tone changed. Tommy stopped. He did not return, but he did stand and wait to be gathered up. Tommy was reading his mother with a fair degree of accuracy.

Thus, the so-called academic skills are made up of many parts, and, as we have noted, the child of three has learned many of these parts. He has learned much of the language he will later learn to read and write. He can use anything from a few to many hundreds of words. The child who has an extensive vocabulary has more of the "parts" of a reading skill than the child who has a very limited one. Some of this advantage is that he has learned how to put more speech sounds together to create meanings. In this he has increased the possibilities for thinking.

Even before the child has made discernible progress in understanding and forming words, he has been making babbling sounds that include all, or almost all, the basic speech sounds of every language. Even earlier than this, he has been following objects with his eyes and learning to perceive form. Something of the same kind of mental process that permits the eight-month-old baby to distinguish between his mother and some other person goes into his later ability to distinguish the form of words and letters. The ability to perceive, to distinguish, to develop memory for these perceptions has gone on from birth. It cannot be overemphasized that these perceptions and many other learnings are related to the development of academic skills and that the teacher must take these into account.

Familiarity Precedes Recognition

One other major emphasis must be examined before discussing the program of the nursery school. It relates directly to what precedes the work of the school and to what the school does. For most learning, familiarity precedes recognition. It has been implied above that a baby spends months becoming accustomed to his mother. The same principle seems to apply to other learnings.

The young child gradually becomes familiar with many things. Some of this familiarity becomes clear recognition. A child of three in a city may know that green means "Go" and red means "Stop." If not, he has been observing the changing of traffic lights for much of his life and the added learning as to meaning will probably come easily. Other matters may be only vaguely familiar; the clock, the calendar on the wall, the big words on the boxes and cans on the kitchen shelf. The child may not have learned to read a single word, but he has been growing accustomed to the fact that things are designated in certain ways. There are many stages between the first fleeting perception and full understanding of meaning. All of them form part of a developing organization. The child learns, at least in part, through a process that gradually leads from familiarity to understanding. A great deal of familiarity is already present in the background of the child's mind. Very seldom does a teacher succeed in bringing clear understanding of any concept that comes as a completely new idea to the student. Usually the teacher helps the individual see a little clearer what was already at least vaguely present. Many of the three-year-old's concepts are vague ideas. Nevertheless, they form a basis for further learning.

The Nursery School Teaches Skills and Insights

To say "the nursery school teaches skills and insights" may seem unnecessary. But this phase of the work of the nursery school has not been emphasized in the past. Other purposes have so dominated some writers in the field of early childhood education that they have sometimes sounded almost anti-intellectual in tone. This is not surprising, for the emphasis in nursery school has been exactly the opposite of the elementary school. Traditionally, their prime objective has been to provide a safe and happy environment for children. They also provide for important social learning experiences. Traditional nursery school educators are concerned that teaching skills in nursery school and kindergarten might result in turning them into poor imitations of first grade.

Since learning is a continuum, it is the function of the nursery school to teach insights and skills—but not by using the structure and methodology of a first-grade classroom, nor by exerting uncalled-for pressure on the child to learn the skill. Nursery school is neither the place for high pressure nor for inappropriate method. Good nursery schools in their seemingly unstructured programs provide many opportunities for intellectual growth. Some of the suggestions offered as possible approaches to teaching the three- and four-year-olds can be utilized without pressure or regimentation.

Nursery Schools Must Be Intellectually Stimulating

Good nursery schools further the intellectual development of children. This statement does not imply a departure from the programs already carried on in good nursery schools. Three considerations seem appropriate.

1. One of these is found in *the way children learned before entering nursery school.* John Holt has observed a variety of situations that seem to imply that children learn by many repetitions of manipulative and verbal practice; that they learn by imitation; that they learn from models.[3] Concern-

---

[3] John Holt, *How Children Learn* (New York: Pitman, 1969).

ing the latter, the model should not be too perfect. A great deal of tact is needed. Children usually correct most of their errors over a period of time without pressure from anyone.

Holt points out in his book that an adult must be careful in offering help to a youngster because the child might then feel the project was no longer his work. A teacher in a child development center noticed a four-year-old boy who was having a wonderful time working with clay. It was his first experience with clay and he was having difficulty making exactly what he wanted. Fearing that he might be overly frustrated, the teacher, an understanding and skilled person, offered what she felt was minimal help. As she tells the story, she showed the boy how to make legs for the dog he was attempting to shape. Apparently, the child felt that the teacher had taken over his project, and he lost all interest in it. Many days passed before he returned to the clay.

Time magazine reported on an experiment by Jerome Bruner with young children.[4] According to the article, Bruner believes that in spite of the young child's limited abilities, incredible skills and "the full splendor of intelligence" are already embedded in his nervous system. This and the suggestions given above form the first consideration for the nursery school teacher. Most children are ready and eager to learn, given the opportunity. Whatever the nursery school does, *the first rule should be that nothing should interfere with the basic drive of the child to learn.*

2. The second major fact to be considered is the present program. Included in this is the question as to whether or not children's enthusiasm for learning may be blunted, which may be brought about by overdirection or underexposure. Probably no nursery school offers all the possibilities of learning that could be provided. James Hymes has stated, "We expose, but we do not impose." He emphasizes the basic concept in his *Teaching the Child Under Six*.[5] There is always the possibility that a child who was in constant interchange with his mother in the home learning words, repeating sentences, listening, asking questions, following directions, may find himself in the nursery school with little exposure other than fun, games, and other children.[6] This is not to downgrade these activities, but they may not in themselves provide as much learning as the home did.

Catherine Landreth suggests the kinds of exposure a good nursery school could provide. Unfortunately, she is reporting not what she saw in the school that she visited but what she wishes she had seen.

Recently I visited a nursery school in which a four-year-old boy was having a birthday party. The "party" consisted of cupcakes and lemonade, and an each-to-his-own rendering of "Happy Birthday to You." Not a word about the fourness of

[4] *Time,* March 28, 1969, p. 56.
[5] James L. Hymes, Jr., *Teaching the Child Under Six* (Columbus, Ohio: Merrill, 1968).
[6] Roger Brown, "Three Processes in the Child's Acquisition of Syntax," *Harvard Educational Review,* 34 (1964), 133–151.

four. Why, I thought, couldn't they give the boy four hearty cheers or four loud claps. And why not have him blow out four candles and wear a four on his chest to show that what had been three was now four. Those cupcakes too, could have had all pattern variants of four decorations—raisins or whatever. Moreover, since four marked four years, why not four pictures on the bulletin board of the boy at one, two, three, and four to show that the units counted were large units in development and time?[7]

What valid criticisms! The excellent suggestions could have been made a part of the celebration with no pressure on the children in any form.

3. The third consideration for the nursery school teacher is what programs are being offered in nursery schools throughout the country. Are there concepts and techniques that can be utilized without violating basic principles? The answer is a qualified "Yes." There is, in fact, more in common among the very good nursery schools than there is between any of them and the unimaginative child care approach. It is to be remembered that the traditional nursery school was primarily a place to leave the young child in the safe keeping of kindly adults. There was little concern with learning, other than the social learning involved in adjusting to a new situation. While the approach to the problem by present day theorists and practitioners differs greatly, the trend among those who are offering new approaches includes recognition of the educational importance of the nursery school. It also includes an attempt to build from the child's present knowledge to more advanced learning and to make this learning experience both happy and exciting.

Approaches to Nursery School Learning

The emphasis in nursery school should depend on the needs and purposes of the particular school. *The content and method should be relevant to the kind of school and children involved.* Some schools meet only a few hours and only on certain days in a week; thus the child attends only for a limited time. The limited time would seem to make imperative a learning experience more intensive than the normal experience of the child who attends a nursery school daily. Some child development centers may even have a child for as many as nine hours a day. Their goals may include nutrition, health care, recreation, enrichment plus various learning experiences. Some children in nursery schools come from homes that have a wide variety of learning devices. These children need exposure to a different type of program than children from impoverished homes. One way to illustrate the different approaches to nursery school learning is to discuss some of the programs in operation.

[7] Catherine Landreth, *Early Childhood: Behavior and Learning* (New York: Knopf, 1967), p. 238.

The Traditional Approach

Traditionally, nursery schools have been concerned with the care and well-being of the young child. They have tended to employ materials and methods that were both enjoyable and conducive to discovery and growth. They have emphasized that the nursery school was not the place to force feed children academic skills. The importance of contact with interested and kindly adults has been stressed; so, too, has the importance of learning through social contact with other children.

The concern for the well-being and social growth of children has probably never or seldom been the sole purpose of the nursery school. All traditional schools have introduced elements of learning in various ways. There is learning in working with so-called "creative play" equipment. Rhymes, songs, limited exposure to numerical and verbal games have usually been part of the program. Nothing in the traditional approach automatically rules out innovations. It would seem to provide a basic frame of reference from which to consider other approaches. The parent would do well when seeking a nursery school to look first for the kind of concerns shown by the traditional nursery school people. There may be changes needed but not "revolution" insofar as the normal, competent, confident, and inquiring child is concerned.

The Montessori Approach

Earlier chapters have mentioned the great appeal of the ideas of Maria Montessori. Some of her ideas are in full harmony with much of the thinking involved in the present version of the traditional "American" nursery school. Montessori stressed leaving the child free to choose appropriate materials when they were available and to work diligently in the mastery of such materials. She suggested that young children love order; they want things to be where they belong. She believed that there are sensitive periods in the life of a child when he is especially open to certain types of learning. She loved and respected children and childhood.

The traditional nursery school has in recent years appropriated or improvised materials similar to those Montessori devised. One characteristic of Montessori materials[8] is that they are intended to be used in a certain way and in that one way only. Pegs fit only the right hole; pyramids go together in only one way. In many Montessori schools if a child is taught to set a table, it must always be done the same way. Dishes are to be washed in only one way. It may be that young children do need materials that can be repeated with the same results. Possibly many children need to learn well how to perform a certain operation. Buttoning and unbuttoning two strips of cloth has its useful implications for this age child. Usually in life there is only one way to do this correctly.

[8] See National Association for the Education of Young Children, *Montessori in Perspective* (Washington, D. C.: NAEYC, 1966).

It might be advantageous if all nursery school people were familiar with the procedures, materials, and, above all, the underlying psychology and philosophy of the Montessori program. It would be equally helpful if kindergarten and primary teachers knew more about this approach. Many teachers are using adapted "Montessori" materials, but what they may lack is an understanding of the purpose, value, and developmental design of the materials.

Many years before the days of B. F. Skinner, Montessori developed a programmed approach to learning. She did it in such a way as to make use of the natural interest of the young child in working with his hands and in developing his inborn potential. It is not an imposed program. The child chooses the materials he wishes to work with. It is a carefully prepared program to develop the sense perceptions of the child. In each phase it begins with the simple and moves toward the complex. Skills are broken down into their simplest components. As an illustration, the child learns to tie shoe laces with one white and one black lace. In this way directions can be given and understood more easily. When learning colors, he learns to distinguish the three basic colors, then all the colors, and from this moves gradually to the ability to recognize a whole array of colors and shades. The child learns to distinguish shape by sight and feel. Then he eventually learns the sight and feel of letters produced with sandpaper or the equivalent. He also learns to trace and fill in designs long before he attempts to produce letters. In due time he is able to draw on a wealth of previous experience in learning to write.

The Montessori schools, like some others, sometimes advertise their accomplishments more glowingly than may be justified. Montessori schools do teach children to read, but not necessarily at three, or four, or even five. What they seem to be aiming for is to provide the necessary prelearning skills that will enable a child to read as soon as he is ready for the experience. Needing students to maintain the school, they may sometimes stress the end results rather than the cautious approach.

There would appear to be restricted opportunity for social growth in the Montessori schools. Little provision is made for cooperative or dramatic play. The possible loss of the experience of free discovery and exploration is another factor to be considered. Montessori schools have not encouraged creative activities, though some of the schools are now attempting to include some of these activities in their programs. Most objectionable of all is the implication that the Montessori method is the only right way.

None of the objections voiced should keep the alert teacher in early childhood education from gaining new insights from the study of Montessori theory and practice. At a minimum, it would seem that with the many Montessori type materials that are available in nursery schools, kindergartens, and many primary classrooms, the teacher should know how these materials can be fitted into a program of readiness and/or enrichment.

The Bereiter Model

Perhaps the most controversial program to be proposed for the nursery school in recent years is that developed experimentally by Carl Bereiter and Siegfried Engelmann. The two men at the time of their study were associated with the Institute for Research on Exceptional Children at the University of Illinois. There are many categories of exceptional children, and all need different elements in their education. The program set up by Bereiter and Engelmann, which for convenience sake will be called the Bereiter Model, was developed for a specific class and need—disadvantaged children.

Bereiter noted, as have many others, that the programs of school orientation, such as the six-week summer Head Start program, did not adequately prepare the child for the rigors of a structured first grade. Such programs might help a child enter school with a better attitude, but the attitude was not likely to persist if the child met with rebuff and failure in school. The problem is very real, especially for the slum or rural impoverished child whose language background may be deficient or different.

Bereiter and Engelmann developed a structured learning experience specifically designed to enable the language deficient ghetto child to "catch up" in the skills expected by most first-grade teachers.[9] Fifteen children who from all indications were headed for certain school failure were selected to be in the program. All were at least four years and nine months old—that is, they were of kindergarten rather than nursery school age. The program lasted for nine months.

For these children representing the culturally and educationally disadvantaged, Bereiter developed a structured, highly directed, programmed approach. There were three teachers, each specializing in one area— language, reading, or arithmetic. Each teacher sought to create a directed, but exciting, interchange between teacher and child. All lessons were short: fifteen minutes each day at the beginning, and eventually, twenty minutes. Thus, the intense instruction in total amounted to not more than an hour a day. There was a break between the instructional periods in which the child could relax and play, though the attempt was made to have the instruction period the most stimulating part of the program. In total time the school day lasted only two hours.

The Bereiter Model has a programmed approach and specific goals. Discipline is achieved in three ways—interest, specific reward, and mild punishment. The interest in the original study, in theory at least, was maintained because each teacher had only five children to interact with. The teachers involved did not hesitate to make use of the child's background. One of the

[9] The rationale and method of the program are discussed in Carl Bereiter and Siegfried Engelmann, *Teaching Disadvantaged Children in the Preschool* (Englewood Cliffs, N. J.: Prentice-Hall, 1966).

language lessons, for example, dealt with weapons. Attention was rewarded by cookies—immediately, for attempted participation at the beginning of the school term; then postponed to the lunch break as the child became accustomed to the program. The child who did not pay attention was excluded temporarily from the group.

One further point may be noted. In the Bereiter Model the goals seem reasonable. In reading, for example, the goals included helping the child understand that words have a distinct "entity." Bereiter had noted that children with an impoverished background spoke in what he called "giant word" units. Words in phrases and sentences were blended into one indistinct whole. In view of this, the Bereiter approach included teaching that each word has a beginning, ending, and middle. Another minimum goal of the nine months of instruction was a *sight-reading* vocabulary of at least four words.

The exact wording of the fifteenth and last of the stated minimum goals of the program reads:

15. A sight-reading vocabulary of at least four words in addition to proper names, with evidence that the printed word has the same meaning for them as the corresponding spoken word. "What word is this?" "Cat." "Is this a thing that goes 'Woof-woof'?" "No, it goes 'Meow.' "[10]

Many questions can be raised about the Bereiter Model. For example, which was effective—the method itself or the fact that there was one competent instructor for each five children? Most teachers would be delighted to have an opportunity to work without distraction with five children at a time.

The more basic objection is the emphasis on "directed" teaching of young children as opposed to the emphasis endorsed in this text and by the majority of those concerned about the education of young children. Even though some differences in approach may be required in helping the disadvantaged child it may still be asked if equal results cannot be secured by less questionable methods. There is reason to believe that they can.

A third possible objection is the question of the almost certain misuse of the model. The Bereiter approach is remedial. As described in the original experiment, it is a carefully balanced prescription for a specific need. What happens if a teacher with less competence and training attempts to impose the structure unaided on a group not of 5 children but of 25 or 30? Carefully applied, Bereiter's remedy may be better than the disease. Misapplied, the reverse may be true.

There is the further question with regard to the concept of any child being required to "catch up" with anyone. The objection is not specifically to Bereiter. He points out that his program is designed to meet the already existing demands of society. The problem is larger than the controversy about

[10] *Ibid.,* p. 49.

the Bereiter Model and is discussed more adequately in other sections of the text. There can be less objection to the concept of society's attempt to "make up" to the child for deficiencies it has imposed on him—a point all teachers of the disadvantaged should ponder.

A Modified Developmental Approach

Rose M. Bromwich's approach to dealing with the problem of language learning by the disadvantaged child[11] expresses well what the authors advocate. Basically her suggestion is that even for the disadvantaged child there can be a gradual shift in understanding and use of language when several things happen. First, the child must discover that his own utterances are accepted and considered important. When his communication is accepted without criticism, the disadvantaged child becomes more verbal in his own medium of exchange. He also becomes more involved in the learning process. If involvement and acceptance can be maintained through kindergarten and the primary grades, the child gradually shifts for appropriate purposes to standard English in order to be able to communicate more effectively. This process leads to learning of skills and insight without the risks involved in the more prescriptive Bereiter approach.

The Bromwich model *brings the method of working with the culturally "different" back to the kind of learning many are advocating for those who are not culturally "different."* All children need to feel acceptance, to feel that what they say is important to adults, to know that they are successful in learning. If children are treated this way, from whatever ethnic and/or socioeconomic group they come, the teacher will be able to enlist their efforts in the learning of skills and insights.

Summary

The nursery school accepts the child at three or four. Ordinarily, the child has already acquired many skills and gained many insights. He is in some phase of the process of building toward the more academic skills. For most of these learnings there is both a general familiarity with figure and content, and the development of many sub-skills. One of the major purposes of the nursery school is to contribute to the continued development of academic skills and insights. Traditional American nursery schools have always made some contribution to these purposes. They are now in the process of reexamining their methods in the light of increased understanding of the learn-

[11] Rose M. Bromwich, *Developing the Language of Young Disadvantaged Children* (Washington, D. C.: Department of Elementary-Kindergarten-Nursery Education, National Education Association, 1968). See also her *Some Correlates of Stimulus-Bound Versus Stimulus-Free Verbal Responses to Pictures by Young Negro Boys* (unpublished Ph.D. dissertation, Los Angeles: University of California 1967).

ing process and of new experimental approaches. For children from deprived backgrounds, therapeutic methods may be legitimate. Even in such situations, there are alternatives. One is to increase the verbal communication between adults and children and in particular to accept as important the communication of the underprivileged child. This suggestion coincides with what good nursery school teachers should do for all children.

CHAPTER ELEVEN

Skills and Insight in the Kindergarten

James Herndon cites a revealing incident near the end of his book *The Way It Spozed to Be*.[1] The story concerns his own son. The summer before the boy entered kindergarten the family had taken a vacation in Mexico. While there the young lad played with some Mexican children. He did not understand that his playmates were speaking their native language and had a right to do so, and that it was he who was speaking a "foreign" language. He refused to make any attempt to pick up even a smattering of Spanish. To the boy there was simply something wrong with these children who did not speak English.

On his return from Mexico, the youngster entered kindergarten. The Herndons were naturally curious about the boy's reaction to it. With a little prodding his father learned that as part of the opening exercises in kindergarten, the children stood at attention when a flag was held up and then the children "spoke to the flag." "What," he inquired, "did the children say to the flag?" "How do I know," replied the boy, "they're talking to it in Spanish."

As with the young Herndon boy, many things happen to children in school that have little meaning to them. One might point out, even from Herndon's story, that what is done may be well intended and may do some good. The

[1] James Herndon, *The Way It Spozed To Be* (New York: Bantam, 1969), p. 192.

155

child who "pledges allegiance" to the flag without realizing what he is doing or what the words mean may pick up some of the symbolism of the occasion. With a little help he will eventually learn the meaning of what he is doing. There is the strong possibility, however, that in the overall process he will have developed an indifference to the ritual. It is this indifference because a "learning" has no meaning that concerns educators.

Activities in all levels of school should be given present meaning or be postponed. The purpose behind the pledge to the flag need not be omitted from the curriculum, even in kindergarten. For example, an appropriate march to music, a flag carried by one or all the children, a patriotic song that kindergarten children can understand could be tried to achieve the desired goal.

Kindergarten Is School

The basic premise from which this chapter starts is that kindergarten is school, but school that is appropriate to the needs of the five-year-old child.[2] In Chapter 10 we stressed that good nursery schools serve important academic purposes and advance intellectual development of children. Kindergarten has the same goals. In fact, there is much overlap. Some kindergartners need nursery school experience. In other words, every child should have a program of real learning for *him*—learning that he can accept now. Some kindergarten children possess skills and insights far beyond those of the average child entering first grade. Yet, they too can profit from a good kindergarten experience, provided that they receive adequate intellectual stimulation in the process. For many children kindergarten is a new school experience. For all it should be a happy learning experience.

Kindergarten Should Look Like Play

There is an old but still current argument: Is kindergarten school or play? The reasons for the query are understandable and to some extent useful. The saddest answer is that some kindergartens are neither of these—the children have little fun, and they learn less. There are all gradations in-between. The answer that should be positively given is that kindergarten is school, but school geared to the developing needs and abilities of the five-year-old child. To the casual observer, such a kindergarten may resemble a play school. The children are not seated at desks. They are not tracing or coloring dittoed sheets. Generally, they are not all doing the same thing at the same time. Individual children may be painting, or molding clay, or building with blocks, or playing "house" or "store." In appearance and in fact, they are having a good time.

[2] Synva Nicol, "A Good Day for the Fives," *Portfolio for Kindergarten Teachers* (Washington, D. C.: Association for Childhood Education International, 1960).

In Greeley, Colorado, there is an experimental all boy's kindergarten taught by a man, with a college male student as an assistant.[3] The boys are taught to wrestle, climb ropes, do trampoline flips, build an Indian fort. There is noise and sometimes running and banging. At any given moment the classroom might not look like school—at least, like school as most of us knew it. The experiment is intended not only to make school a more attractive place for boys, but to free them to develop their ability to communicate away from the competition of the usually more successful little girls.

The Children Are Working

Close observation of any good kindergarten will reveal that the children, even though doing things they enjoy, are hard at work. The observer who listens carefully will discover that the teacher and children are not talking about what kind of play is permitted. Rather, they are discussing what work project they will engage in. There may be a "play" time and probably a "rest" time. Even during these periods learning may take place. Psychologically it is important that the child feel that in the major activities of the kindergarten program he is doing important work.

The other aspect of the concept of kindergarten as work is what looks like play is an essential learning experience to the children. They are learning by means of tools and materials that are adapted to their needs. They are manipulating, constructing, sculpturing, painting, enacting, interacting, pretending, exploring, creating, solving problems, practicing control, and many other things. As is appropriate to their age, they are more concerned with the process of doing than with the end product, although the product, too, may be important. In kindergarten many processes may be going on at once. What the children are doing is not a matter of mere chance or whim. Materials have been provided and the stage set for numerous purposes. Among these is the opportunity to work on projects that provide training in skills that will form the basis for abilities used in more formal school programs. In kindergarten each child should be exposed to a variety of experiences to increase his grasp of meanings so that insight will couple with skill. In addition, he should have varied opportunities to learn about the world and to practice basic skills.

Kindergarten Is School With a Full Curriculum

The remainder of the chapter will be largely devoted to the ways in which good kindergartens teach the language arts and quantitative skills. Important as they are, they are only a part of the total kindergarten curriculum. Probably any academic area has a place in the kindergarten curriculum.[4] The

[3] Veronica Dolan, "Stag Kindergarten," *Look*, 33 (1969), M.

[4] For a discussion in depth about academic curriculum, see Helen F. Robison and Bernard Spodek, *New Directions in the Kindergarten* (New York: Teachers College, Columbia University, 1965).

language arts and numerical concepts are not treated as separate subjects to be taught at certain designated periods by lecture or demonstration, at least, not usually. In one college laboratory kindergarten a Spanish teacher volunteered to visit when she was able to do so and introduce the children to Spanish. No announcement was made that a Spanish lesson was to be given. The children were not asked to stop what they were doing when she arrived. The professor visited with the children as individuals and small groups, speaking slowly and carefully in Spanish. She uttered no word of English. Without any pressure the children not only became familiar with the sound and structure of the language, but over the year were able to call many things by their Spanish names and to speak in simple sentences in Spanish.

Other plans may be formulated to provide for special learning experiences, such as in science.[5] The teacher may wish to take her class to the zoo, the fire station, the airport, or on a field trip through the school yard to look for colored leaves or a variety of things that might be collected and studied on such an expedition. It may also include a cage with a pet hamster to be observed and cared for. The possibilities are endless just in the area of science. Usually the concepts involved in such subjects as biology, chemistry, economics, psychology, health, and geography will be *the normal ingredients of a balanced kindergarten program*. The children will be taught by the experiences of the classroom and the excursions of the class. The teacher need not lecture, nor will she usually demonstrate. She will provide the means for discovery by the children.

After a stimulating learning experience, the teacher may want to help the children analyze what they have learned. It may be more effective learning for the children to tell their parents what they learned from the study of magnets, for example, than to have them take home a sample of "arts and crafts" every day.

The emphasis in most academic subjects on the kindergarten level is on insight rather than skill. However, skill is involved. The child who observes the emergence of the butterfly from the cocoon, as many kindergartners do every year, is practicing his skills of observation and reporting. So in almost any subject that might enter into the kindergarten curriculum, there is some form of skill development involved. The emphasis, however, is on insight: "What happens?" "How does it work?" Although the skills are developing, the purpose in the broad academic areas is usually *insight*.

The Language Arts

Kindergartens have a major contribution to make in the development of the language arts area[6]—an area that has many subdivisions: listening, expressing, communicating, appreciating, reading, writing, and so forth.

[5] Association for Childhood Education International, *Young Children and Science* (Washington, D.C.: ACEI, 1964).

[6] Association for Childhood Education International, *Reading in the Kindergarten??* (Washington, D. C.: ACEI, 1962).

We have already discussed that the skills involved had their beginnings long before kindergarten and their full development will continue far beyond the kindergarten. Kindergarten, however, is a crucial period in the development of many children. It is a year that should make extremely important contributions to the growth of all children in their developing skills in the language arts.

Two things are to be avoided: (1) turning the kindergarten into an imitation of the poorly designed first grade, and (2) failing to use the resources of the kindergarten to cooperate with the children in their endeavors to improve in all the language art areas. Involved in this is the need to emphasize to the public what the kindergarten does teach, while at the same time resisting pressures to teach in ways that are not helpful to the child.

An illustration may explain in part what is meant. A good kindergarten teacher was asked "Do you teach the children to read?" She made a series of mistakes in about thirty seconds. Her basic one was to recoil in horror and say, "No! We do not teach reading in the kindergarten." By that time it was too late to explain that she taught many things essential to reading and sometimes reading itself, for as soon as she had completed her first statement, the father who had asked the question had decided to put his child in a different kindergarten where reading was "taught." The father was wrong. The kindergarten that he chose could not compare with the one taught by the teacher he rejected.

Many kindergarten teachers react essentially the same way to similar queries from other people—parents, principals, superintendents, and fellow teachers. They do it because so many people want to turn kindergarten into a copy of a poorly taught first grade. They do it because they want it to be clear that they do not march kindergartners into the classroom, seat them at desks, keep them there, and drill them on the alphabet.

When confronted with such an inquiry, there are several answers and explanations that a kindergarten teacher can give. She can explain that many important things are taught in the kindergarten, including all the language arts, although not in the same sense as they are taught in the primary grades. In the present context reading is used in a broad sense. There are many phases of reading. All kinds of "reading" are explored in kindergarten. The kindergarten teacher will take each child just as far down the road toward "formal" reading as he can go easily.

The qualifier "easily" is important. Schools lose many pupils because they try to teach things to children who are not at the time able to grasp the concepts. As a result, they teach children that they cannot learn. If schools teach this one idea well, children eventually become dropouts, whether or not they continue to be physically present in school. Whatever is done, the process should not start in kindergarten. It is better that the child move into first grade feeling himself a successful learner, even if he could have been pressured a little further along certain lines to achieve certain standards set up by the school. Much more can be said. Part of the "more" involves putting reading into the broader perspective of the language arts.

Kindergartens Teach the Language Arts All the Time

Reading never stands alone. Too many teachers and parents seem to think that if the child can call out the sounds of a word, he knows how to read. One teacher visited in the home of a kindergarten child. The mother was very enthusiastic about her son's progress. He was learning to read beautifully. This was news to the teacher since no effort had been made to teach the boy to read and he had shown no interest in learning. The mother had the boy get a book—one that belonged to an older child in the home. The boy read the story perfectly. However, the teacher turned several pages at one time, and the child "read" the page that should have followed instead of the page that the teacher had turned to. In a sense both the child who can call out the sounds of words and the child who has memorized a story have learned something about reading. In their different ways they both are reading.

There is much more to reading, however, than either kind of memorization. Reading is a part of the broad area of communication. One can only communicate with someone when there is some understood meaning to communicate and some understood means of communication. Much of the work of the kindergarten is directed toward the development of concepts. For example, the building of vocabulary began long before kindergarten, but it continues apace. The use of vocabulary in understanding and expressing ideas is central. The expression, itself, takes the form of telling, talking, dramatizing, and picturing. Reception at this level is chiefly in the forms of watching and listening and manipulating. Formal reading and writing are of vital importance in life, but not the first item of business in the kindergarten year.

A child of five defines things through action. He thinks in terms of function and use. Blocks are for building. If, for example, the child uses them to build a road, the road is for traveling. It is for traveling in cars and buses, for hauling sand, gravel, building materials, and food, for getting to many places— churches, homes, stores, schools, zoos, and any place the children may think of. Whatever other learnings may be taking place, language is always involved. *Materials convey meanings, meanings involve concepts, and concepts involve words.*

Every kindergarten child has been reading some things for years. It is an open question as to just when a child begins to learn to read. Certainly in the early weeks of the newborn infant there is the beginning of response to outside stimulation.[7] It is suggested that the advantage that the middle-class child has over the impoverished child may be in part, not that there is more stimulation of the middle-class child, but that there is more distinctive stimulation. The mother has more time to interact with her child with fewer distracting influences. Very early mother and child learn to understand each other, and they do it before the development of language response.

[7] H. Rheingold, J. L. Gewirtz, and H. Ross, "Social Conditioning of Vocalizations in the Infant," *Journal of Comparative Physiological Psychology*, 52 (1969), 68–73.

Children come to kindergarten with much more ability. Occasionally, perhaps much more often in future years, children may come into kindergarten already able to read. Some children learn to read at three and four. Even so, there is still much to learn in kindergarten. Reading is just one of the tools of learning—a very important tool, but just a tool. There is a whole universe of learning with and without reading.

Every kindergarten child has already learned much that is basic to reading. At four he has covered the neighborhood, learned who everyone is, and what he does. He uses a comparatively large vocabulary and knows many meanings; he probably knows that red means "stop" and green means "go." He "reads" people—especially his parents; he knows not only what words mean, but whether or not people mean what they say. Kindergarten carries this on. The teacher communicates; she listens. The children talk to each other and learn from each other. In part, the teacher just keeps up the good work. She feeds the child's curiosity. She builds on it.

This kind of learning goes on inside and outside the school room. A kindergarten child came to her teacher one day and almost dragged her to a window. Was there a fight? an accident? a parade? No, none of these. The little girl was saying over and over, "They meet! They meet!" She had discovered the *horizon*. She had looked at this many times before, but now there was a flash of insight. To this extent, her background for meaningful reading was improved.

Reading in Kindergarten

Kindergartens teach reading at special times and in special ways. Exactly what the teacher plans, her materials, and her resources will depend in part on the time of the year, the interest of the children, the children's background of experiences in and out of school. Most kindergartens do plan for some class involvement in experiences related to reading. There will not be a formal reading lesson unless it is a very exceptional class, and probably not then until close to the end of the school year. An illustration of the more informal type of learning related to reading occurs during the relatively short periods of time when most of the group will get together. It may be a "sharing" time, which provides practice in listening and communication.[8] The same children should not do all the sharing every day.

There are also times for reading to children and for story telling. The teacher may have a book in her hand—not primarily to read the story, but to impress the children that stories are found in books. The teacher builds toward a love for books and an interest in reading.[9] The good teacher will dramatize the story and make it come alive. This is building toward formal reading.

[8] Marion Monroe and Bernice Rogers, *Foundations for Reading* (Glenview, Ill.: Scott, Foresman, 1964), Chapter 4.
[9] Roach Van Allen, *Attitudes and the Art of Teaching Reading* (Washington, D. C.: National Education Association, 1965).

Sometimes during the large group time there will be nursery rhymes and poems of interest to the children. These can be learned and said together as a choral group. Children enjoy the feel and the sound of words. They may enjoy the experience even more if they can act out the poems and rhymes. Some children may even gain insight to life through the theme of a poem or story. Thus an appreciation and depth of understanding in the language arts and reading in its fullest sense are increased. When the children begin to make up their own rhymes, there is a different type of growth. It is a start toward literary production. In these and other ways the kindergarten is providing language arts instruction for all children; it is being done easily, gently, and without pressure.

Children are constantly exposed to reading stimuli. There are many things to read in almost any kindergarten. Most teachers put a name tag on each child when he first enters school. Names will appear at other times and various articles will be labeled with the child's name, such as individual storage shelves. Children will soon recognize their own names and even the names of the other children. Children learn to recognize words with special meaning to them. For example, they seem to have little trouble with such words as candy, ice cream, Halloween, and Christmas. There are usually alphabet blocks around if the children want to use them in forming words. Even if they do not put words together, they become familiar with the shapes and sometimes the names of the various letters. Through picture books the children learn to understand the meanings implied by the pictures. The teacher may also write on a large chart the children's words and ideas about a trip that they have taken. She should write these in manuscript since it is similar to the print in books that the children will later read. Most of the class will be interested in reading their own story of their trip. The teacher should use only the ideas and words of the children. If she does so, the children are usually able to read the account that she has written for them. They may memorize the sentences, but it gives them the feeling of success in reading.

The kindergarten teacher is sensitive to the feelings, interests, and aptitudes of her children. With a sensitive teacher and an atmosphere in which the pressure to learn comes from the eagerness of the children, it is the children who will let the teacher know when they are ready for more formal instruction. They will communicate their readiness by what they say, by what they do, by what they make, by what they paint, by attempts to write, by attempts to read. The teacher will soon learn the extent of the child's interest in reading and his ability in it. Then, as she is "tuned in" by the child, she will lead him on from where he is.

Learning is contagious under such conditions. If one child learns to read a little, there will probably be a few who want to try. If one child likes to read labels or special words, others may become interested. The teacher helps the individual because he is important. She helps the individual because all learning is individual. But she also helps the individual because he can help other children. Almost always there is some child that can teach some other child better than the teacher can.

The kindergarten teacher may legitimately experiment with small, select groups of children to lead them toward a more formal reading experience. This experience will be built on all that has gone before. Many informal activities in the building of meanings, concepts, speech sounds should precede more formal instruction. The teacher will have watched, listened to, and interpreted individual children. She will have spotted those who seem ready to move on.

The teacher will guard against possible harm in two or three ways. *Her small group will be open-ended—children can join or drop out freely.* The children's reactions will show whether the teacher is on the right, or at least, a possible track. She should begin with very short lessons—three to five minutes—lengthening them as time goes on. To hold their interest, she will make whatever she does into an interesting game.

It will be necessary to test and re-test constantly her tentative conclusions about the children's interest and maturity. If the game does not go over well, it can be put aside and a different technique tried. The teacher may experiment with a short lesson on associating symbols with speech sounds. She may find that some children may be able to read simple words and may enjoy reading to others. No one is sure how much the mature kindergartner can learn if he is given appropriate help. Where he ventures, the teacher can let him go. Where he follows easily, the teacher can take him. His world of learning should continue to be exciting to him, however far the path may lead.

Mathematics In Kindergarten

A parent may ask a kindergarten teacher, "Do you teach arithmetic?" The answer could be both of the following: "Yes, and so do you," and "We both teach even more than arithmetic."[10] Almost every child is constantly interacting to a world of sizes, shapes, numbers, and relationships. No one is sure as to how far back this learning goes—perhaps as far back in life as the beginning of the learning of verbal communication. However vague the baby's understanding of what he sees, however faulty his reach for any object, there is growth toward quantitative understanding.

It is more than arithmetic, though in a formal sense, it may not be what parents and teachers think of as arithmetic. Today much thought is being given to what constitutes arithmetic. Many psychologists ascribe the beginnings of geometric design to the "scribblings" of very young children.[11] Before he enters kindergarten, the child may be drawing circles and more difficult forms. Do children learn these shapes on their own? Do they absorb them from the environment? These are interesting speculations. The essential is that mathematical learnings begin much earlier than kindergarten.

[10] Louise Ellison, "Mathematics for the Very Young," *Parents'*, 44 (1969), 48, 77, 79–81.
[11] See Rhoda Kellogg with Scott O'Dell, *The Psychology of Children's Art* (New York: Random House, 1967), pp. 27–29.

Children come to kindergarten with various quantitative concepts. Although they may be limited and faulty, nevertheless, they form a foundation upon which the kindergarten can build with a flexible, realistic, appropriate, and informal program. Some kindergartners are able to tell their street address, telephone number, and other numerically related facts—how old they are in years, and sometimes, months; how many people in their families. They may have been taught to count to ten, or one hundred, or even a thousand. Sometimes they can count by twos, by fives, and by tens. The artful kindergarten teacher is aware and makes use of this knowledge. She will not, however, be falsely impressed by these achievements. Some children can do all of these things from memory without really understanding any of it. Still, there is something of value here. The parents are pleased, and the child is proud of his achievement. At a minimum he is demonstrating a good memory. To the parent the teacher says, "Good," and suggests additional ways of helping the child develop toward competence in arithmetic. Parents can put meaning into numbers by helping the child count objects, use money, and notice forms, shapes, and sizes.

The kindergarten teacher needs to emphasize meaning. She will do so in many ways. In part, she simply takes advantage of the mathematical implications of everything that is done. The list can be endless. There are mathematical concepts in work with blocks, in art, at lunch, in supplies for the store, in groups of children working together.

Special emphasis to numbers can be given in some large-group activities. There are songs, games, and stories that emphasize numbers. None of these activities call for lectures by the teacher, but the numerical emphasis is present. Emphasizing the number of days remaining until Christmas and other items related to the calendar may hold little meaning to the class; the nature of the group of children and their related experience will be important factors. One teacher may do this with all her children; others may restrict such matters to children who show an interest in dates and time.

The effective kindergarten teacher teaches mathematics, chiefly, by *setting the stage and then involving the children in situations in which mathematical concepts are needed.* When teaching arithmetic in kindergarten, the teacher will seldom have a lesson devoted only to arithmetic. Sometimes it is design and mathematics. Perhaps it is music and mathematics. Other times it is language and mathematics or any multiple combination of these and others. It can be problem solving using mathematics. There can be creative thinking involving mathematics and decisions based on mathematics. It is difficult to teach anything that has no relationship to arithmetic.

Certain materials do give a special emphasis to mathematics. Most are the kinds of materials that the teacher will not emphasize or even introduce until well into the school year. For example, a large set of dominoes could be placed on a shelf or a table in the kindergarten. A child whose older siblings play dominoes will recognize them and be interested. A very bright child from such a home may know how to play the game. They may be ignored for awhile. Then a child may use them as building blocks to build a fence. In time he may be able to match the number of dots on the ends of the dominoes. The watching teacher may offer a suggestion now and then about how to use them. The child will understand if he is "ready."

About a month after school starts one abacus, or several, can be set out for the children to handle. They will have a good time manipulating one long before they use it for mathematics. In due time the teacher may find a child ready and able to make use of the abacus as a meaningful tool. If the youngster does learn to use it properly, he may with a little help teach other children. Without pressure from anyone, very interesting developments may result.

There are many other instruments and games that help with the use of numbers, but most of them belong on some other level. However, when the teacher finds one that may work in her kindergarten, she should not be afraid to try it. There is no harm in trying something that does not work if the teacher takes it in stride. The purpose is to discover ways of helping children, not to force anything on them. If one project does not succeed, the teacher learns something from the experience, but she should feel neither frustration nor defeat.

"Formal" Mathematics

Is mathematics ever taught formally in kindergarten? "Never" is a word one almost never uses. Perhaps the answer is that almost never is mathematics taught in even a semiformal way to a whole kindergarten class. The teacher will be aware, however, that many kindergartners before the end of the year are more mature than many children entering first grade, and in this group some may be ready to experiment with the relatively informal aspects of a slightly more structured program. Such a program does not usually involve pencil, paper, and written numerals. A flannel board, pictures, and manipulation of objects of different shapes and sizes may be more appropriate. So may the manipulation and counting of play or real money. The teacher should remember the safety valve suggested for first steps in formal reading. Work can be attempted with a small group for short intervals. Group members should be free to drop out at any time.

Is the mathematics taught the "new math"? Kindergarten mathematics is foundational. The teacher is concerned in kindergarten with the discovery of relationships and meanings, and that is essentially what the "new math" is all about. Even some of the terminology and concepts of math may have a place (as in the small open-ended groups), provided the teacher knows that she does not lecture the children. One can picture the disaster if a kindergarten teacher attempted to explain to a whole kindergarten class the basic adult concepts of "set" theory. Nevertheless, the ideas are an integral part of the total program. In a group of twenty-five children, some of them are boys and some of them are girls. Kindergartners understand that they are all kindergartners and all children, but they know very well that individually they are either boys or girls. They soon learn to group according to various criteria.

Kindergarten Teaches Individual Children

That the kindergarten teaches individual children is not, in itself, a striking statement nor a revelation. However, it is a concept that is more honored on all levels of education in theory than in practice. We wish to stress its practice and point out that it underlies the program of every good kindergarten.

Kindergarten as Part of a Nongraded Program

For most schools the only sense in which the kindergarten is graded is that it is the first official public *school* experience of most children. Although both the general public and educators have tended to speak of kindergarten as preschool experience, kindergarten *is school*—not preschool. It is, however, usually a part of school that is kept as free as possible from the fear of failure, which is not only good from the standpoint of the self-concept of the child, but also is good educational practice. Kindergarten children learn best without pressure. For most children both their attitude toward school and involvement in learning experience are highest in kindergarten.

The danger is that children will move from this relatively free experience into an overstructured program of the usual first grade. Such an abrupt change involves a new and strikingly different "beginning." To expect that the kindergarten (almost by definition a place in which children develop at their own unique speed) will automatically prepare all children for exactly the same experience a few months later is unrealistic. Such rigid expectation is also disastrous to the child (and eventually to society), and frustrating to primary teachers.

Several solutions are possible, any one of which is an improvement over the situation as it too often exists. The one that seems the most sensible and in keeping with the thesis of educating the individual *is an ungraded primary that begins with the kindergarten experience.* Edith King and August Kerber have reported on programs in several American cities.[12] In Detroit in 1964–1965, following preliminary pilot projects, an ungraded elementary program was established beginning that year in the kindergarten. The next year the program was enlarged to include the first grade and the year after, the second grade. Numerous school systems have instituted ungraded programs beginning with the first grade. The first approach has a psychological and educational advantage. Not all five-year-olds are ready for kindergarten experience. It may take a year or more in what is essentially nursery school

[12] Edith W. King and August Kerber, *The Sociology of Early Childhood Education* (New York: American Book, 1968), p. 83.

training before they are truly kindergartners. Furthermore, some kindergarten children are ready for much more advanced work than the kindergarten may offer. Overall, it may not matter which approach is used provided the kindergarten program is flexible, and the ungraded primary accepts the children on the level at which they can operate effectively.

Other possibilities include a two-year experience in kindergarten for some children or a *transitional grade*[13] for children who need more time to prepare for more formal instruction. This text agrees with the James Hymes' complaint:[14] Too many existing classrooms for young children have as their primary goal preparing children for first grade. The goal is unworthy of true educators. It is harmful: it causes kindergartens to be merely the handmaidens of first grade; as a result kindergarten teachers cannot plan for the present needs of the particular children in their classes. Hymes adds, "More and more kindergartens are like bad first grades; first grades are not becoming like good kindergartens!" Mario D. Fantini states it differently: "The advocates of compensatory education seem to hold 'constant' the traditional educational process and expect the learner to be somehow 'readied' to fit it. In reality, the learners are being asked to adjust to an obsolete process."[15]

Regardless of this the kindergarten teacher must view her own situation *realistically* and consider what is best for her children in their particular set of circumstances. The children may have no alternative other than a rigidly structured first-grade program. To help the class make the transition toward the end of the year the teacher can introduce "The First-Grade Game." For brief periods on most days the class program can be more structured and the children pretend that they are in first grade. During the "game" they may be expected to raise their hand before asking a question and expected to request permission to visit the rest room. They are encouraged to gather more promptly and uniformly for whole class activities. Brief periods of drill may be included too. Although the children consider the structured activity a game, it does prepare them for the reality ahead.

Chapter 10 discussed some of the advantages and disadvantages of the Bereiter Model in preparing children for the primary grade experience. It is the basic view of this text that the prescription offered should only be used in extreme circumstances. Often some less drastic preventive measure is possible. There is no harm in bringing into the kindergarten high school young people, for example, who could give individual attention to disadvantaged children. With a minimum of training, future teachers can be helpful while they, themselves, gain valuable experience. Such attention is good for almost any child. A free language exchange is helpful. Short games in learning to recognize words, in counting objects, and in telling and reading stories

[13] Joseph Baldwin, "The Transition Grade," *Young Children*, 24 (1968), 90–93.

[14] James L. Hymes, Jr., *Teaching the Child Under Six* (Columbus, Ohio: Merrill, 1968), pp. 11–12.

[15] Mario D. Fantini, "Beyond Cultural Deprivation and Compensatory Education," *Psychiatry and Social Science Review*, 3 (1969), p. 7.

would benefit some children and also prepare them for the conventional first grade.

The Attitudes and Abilities of the Teacher

Experiments with the Bereiter Model, nongrading, and other modifications of the traditional kindergarten program must not lead the teacher to abandon the basic attitude that her normal occupation is the exalted one of assisting the child in his adventure in learning. The kindergarten teacher needs to be a child development specialist. She will not only learn to listen to children, she will also learn how to understand the meaning behind what they are saying. She will learn to observe children and to become an expert in interpreting the language of behavior. The kindergarten teacher should look on the child with a calm understanding and nonpossessive interest. This never means coldness or indifference. The teacher is concerned for and fond of her children, but she maintains a measure of realism in her appraisal of them. She is also realistic with herself. Hers is a temporary relationship.

Two words are pertinent—*sensitivity and empathy*. The good teacher is sensitive to the feelings and needs of her children. She feels with each one the problems he faces and the triumphs he achieves. With such a teacher, the child has no problem in letting her know when he wants to reach out toward a new skill. In such a relationship the teacher has no problem in the timing of a suggestion as to the trial of new experiences. Both the teacher and the child can venture down the paths of learning without fear of failure or of the future.

Flexibility of materials and plans that expand upward as well as downward is essential. Some of the skill subjects pose severe problems for some children. Both reading and arithmetic are much more difficult skills to master in English-speaking countries than in Russia, for example. Children in many other countries can be taught more easily the sounds of their alphabet. Measurement in many other lands is more completely built on uniform concepts. But teachers of young children in our country have found or invented ways to help children with both reading and arithmetic. More recently, companies have marketed various teaching and learning aids—good and otherwise. At a minimum the good kindergarten teacher can have suitable materials available and help in children's exploration as she finds them interested.

If the teacher discovers that she has misunderstood or over estimated a child's present interests or abilities, she will not use pressure. She will adapt her methods to the present situation. No child learns to read in just the same way as any other child. Every kindergarten child learns something about reading. Formal reading may or may not be appropriate. The meaning of words and things, the joy of learning, the confidence to solve problems and make decisions—these the teacher can help each child achieve. They are of even greater importance than the skills at this time. If the children can achieve *more*, they should have the opportunity to do so. Kindergarten should be a time of meaningful activity, of essential learning experience even without the "more." Whatever a kindergarten teacher does, *she should not sacrifice this year of joyous work experience to the false gods of pressure, ritual, and rote.*

Neither should she sacrifice a year to the *equally false god of fear to experiment.* In an earlier chapter a kindergarten boy was mentioned who took so much time in deciding which activity to join that the teacher thought he might be in need of psychiatric help. An illuminating observation suggested something very different. One day, a group of children were building a wagon from construction materials available. They put together a good wagon, but it had one defect. The wheels would not turn. The observer was a visitor and felt that she should not step in; besides, she did not have a ready suggestion. The boy mentioned above was also standing by, as usual. He did have a suggestion. He put his suggestion to action—and 'it worked.

The teacher in that kindergarten had noted that this boy was different. She had then reached the conclusion that there was something wrong with the boy. It did not occur to her that possibly this boy was simply bored by activities that may have been helpful for the other children. Before concluding that the youngster needed psychiatric help, she should have offered him materials that were more challenging. His reaction in all probability would have changed from passive observation to active participation. By his behavior the boy probably had been trying to tell the teacher something. Part of that something may have been that he was fully capable of learning to read, to do arithmetic, to seek out kinds of information that the other children were not yet ready for.

We are not suggesting that the whole group of children in kindergarten be led on into the more formal aspects of academic learning. The kindergarten should remain a kindergarten and a place for all kinds of informal learnings. Even the brightest child should enjoy this year of working at his own pace and in his own way. Such a child, however, should be encouraged to progress as far as he can. He should be given all the assistance he needs.

Summary

Kindergarten is school. It provides a variety of learning experiences related to various academic areas. In the language arts and mathematical areas it helps to bridge the gap between the earlier learning of home or nursery school and the more formal learning of the primary years. How far any child will progress in these academic skills depends on several factors including the skill of the teacher in interpreting correctly his readiness for various learnings. The kindergarten child should not be pressured. He is normally an eager learner. A free learning experience which includes much manipulation of learning equipment, use of a variety of art media, opportunity to experiment, and much opportunity to interchange ideas with other children and adults will benefit him the most.

Many forms of language art instruction and opportunities for discovering numerical and related concepts develop in the program. The observant and sensitive teacher will know when individuals and small groups of children are ready to move beyond the usual limits of kindergarten instruction.

Transition to primary grades may be made relatively easy for many kindergarten children. A small amount of orientation that may take the form of a game may be helpful. Transition for all children is eased when either the primary grades are ungraded or the kindergarten is included in such an ungraded program. Without such an approach, it is unrealistic to expect the kindergarten to prevent the tragedy of first-grade failure for some children.

CHAPTER TWELVE

Skills and Insight in the Primary School

A phone call from a reading specialist suggested a possible visit the next day. The caller mentioned that his children would especially like to see us again. Evidently an earlier visit in the home had been significant. On that occasion, at the close of the meal, the eight-year-old propounded a riddle. The authors were appropriately puzzled but evidently showed enjoyment. Soon the girl brought in a Bennett Cerf book of children's riddles. With some prompting from her younger brother as to which one to ask next she gave riddle after riddle. In the context of this chapter it is to be noted that reading is a skill but this skill always serves some additional purpose. One of these purposes is to provide entertainment. One of our purposes in this chapter is to emphasize that skills in the basic subjects always are a means to further ends.

It has been stressed that no dramatic change takes place when the child enters primary school. Whether or not the child has been in school, he has been developing since conception and learning for almost as long. The task of the primary school is to accept the entering child *where he is* in his development of skill and insight and to lead him on from there. What is needed is not a new start but a *continuation of learning*.

In some school districts this concept is recognized by including the kindergarten in the primary block. This is not a new idea. For example, in 1952 in the

Mount Diablo Unified School District of Concord, California, there was in the Pleasant Hill Elementary School an ungraded block beginning with kindergarten and ending when the child was ready to enter the fourth grade. And even in 1952 it was not a new policy for the school. It had been inaugurated years earlier, and although not working perfectly, it was functioning to the benefit of most children very effectively. Throughout the country there were other schools (not many, though) with similar programs.

There seems to be a growing consensus that the schools of the United States will continue to move in this direction.[1] The "battle" to involve all children in at least kindergarten experience is in the process of a final drive to victory. The Census Bureau estimated that in the fall of 1969 about 66 percent of kindergarten-age children were in school. The estimate included children in private and parochial schools and in federally funded projects. Figures compiled by the National Education Association reveal that as recently as the 1967–1968 school year only 46 percent of the nation's school districts provided kindergarten experience.[2] The percentage of large school districts providing kindergartens was much greater than the percentages shown for very small school districts: 65.7 percent for districts with 25,000 or more pupils; 30.3 percent for districts with fewer than 300 pupils. The drive for public kindergartens for all still has a distance to travel.

The teacher in first grade should know whether or not her children have been to kindergarten. Even if they have, she should not assume too much. At least two generalizations can be made. *One is that no six-year-old should be placed into an overly structured program.* The six-year-old child is not ready to sit still for protracted periods of time; he still needs freedom to explore and manipulate. He cannot follow lengthy instruction. The other generalization is that *every child enters the first grade or its equivalent with varying degrees of skills and insights that differ from those of every other child.* It is the task of the primary teacher to take the child on from the learning he brings into the classroom. There are types of organization, attitudes on the part of the educators, developing teacher competencies that help make this possible. Before these are discussed, it may be noted that there is a degree of "method" in the present "madness" of school organization.

Formal Skills in the Primary Grades

Most children learn to read, write, and perform simple arithmetic operations during the primary years of school. In the primary years the school child's skill in these areas usually becomes evident to others. A few children will show competence in some skills before entering first grade. No one knows

---

[1] Joe L. Frost and G. Thomas Rowland, "The Seventies: A Time for Giant Steps," *Childhood Education,* 46 (1969), 4–13.

[2] "Kindergarten Education, 1967–68," National Education Association *Bulletin,* 47 (1969), 10.

for sure how helpful it is to the child to be able to read, for example, before the child enters first grade.[3] Some reports indicate that in at least some instances it can be frustrating to both child and teacher. The first-grade teacher who has it firmly implanted in her mind that her duty is to teach every child to read may not know what to do with the child who already reads. This, however, is an indictment of rigidity in teaching, not of early reading. Even in kindergarten some children have been "reading" some types of materials for years. It was suggested in the last chapter that if the children showed ability to move into formal reading, this was good and they should be both encouraged and assisted. Nevertheless, most first graders come to school either with no formal reading instruction or such a limited vocabulary that they would not be classified as readers.

For a variety of reasons, some children do not learn to read in the accepted sense during the age span normally covered by the primary school. The latter group is almost as exceptional as the early readers, and is a group that needs special attention.

The major problem that the primary school teacher faces is neither the extremely advanced nor the very slow students. Most children enter the primary grades unable to read, and most complete the primary grades as readers. However, every child will not be able to plunge into formal reading instruction the day that he enters the first grade. The necessity to make such an obvious statement seems ridiculous, except that numerous first-grade teachers and school systems have not yet adapted to this fact of life. Most first-grade teachers, school systems, and textbook publishers have, fortunately. Reading instruction does not even begin with formal reading in most first grades. Instead there is a "readiness" program employing many materials to provide background for more formal instruction. Because of differences in the actual ages of children, because of differences in basic abilities, because of differences in environmental background, because of physical differences, children differ in their readiness for even prereading experience. These factors will affect the rates of progress. Some children will have been in school for a full year before they can begin to attempt a formal reading program—a matter that should not cause undue concern, especially for those children who at the beginning of second grade are only a few days older than some of the children just entering the first grade. What is of concern is that every child in school be given a worthwhile and successful learning experience.

There will be children in the third year of primary school who have made little progress in formal reading. If the child has been learning up to his capacity, even this is not necessarily bad. There will be children in the third year of school whose mental age is only then surpassing that of the average six-year-old. Such children are enrolled in the regular school program—not in special education. Research lends at least limited support to the concept that almost all eight-year-olds can be taught to read. E. Gibson, for example,

[3] Eda J. LeShan, *The Conspiracy Against Childhood* (New York: Atheneum, 1967).

in a study of perception, closely related to reading readiness, found great differences among younger children, but fewer differences among eight-year-olds.[4] Almost all eight-year-olds can be taught to read if they have not been taught too thoroughly that they cannot and if the teacher (or teachers) has not given up. Under skilled instruction such children might be able to make a beginning in reading earlier. S. Alan Cohen may be right when he points out that if we simply wait for children to automatically reach the stage where they are "ready" for reading, some may never be ready.[5] Children who do not seem to be ready for reading by the time are eight may need "expert" help. Whatever else happens, they must not be considered unteachable by the time they are in their third year—which sometimes happens.

Third-grade teachers have been known to give up on children who have not learned to read by then. The prevalent attitude of such teachers is similar to that of the two intelligent English teachers who were asked what they were able to do for high school students who could not read. Their answer was at least honest. Both said, "Nothing! No one ever taught us how to teach reading." In theory almost every third-grade teacher has had some training in teaching reading, and she should put the training to work when necessary. The tragedy in traditionally organized schools may not be that a certain child is slow in learning to read, but that all too soon teachers give up on him. Probably even before the teacher has admitted to herself what her attitude is, the child has sensed it and written himself off as a school failure.

The Development of Skills in the Primary Years

Reading, here, is used to represent all academic skills. The same principles apply to arithmetic and writing. The basic skills are important, but there should not be an overemphasis on them in the school program. Normal children learn the basic skill subjects with the help of the teacher and have an abundance of time and energy left over for a wide range of curriculum interests. As in the kindergarten, the primary school teaches all the academic subjects. There may be a slight narrowing of interests as children concentrate on the acquisition of skills. But any truly professional teacher when teaching reading is bringing in other areas of life and learning. Every story worth publishing has some merit other than the words that appear in print. There is something of beauty, information, understanding, moral sensitivity to be found in the content. Aside from this, not all the child's time should be spent in the formal learning of reading. Science and social studies projects will involve reading as well as observation of life and the use of materials. For that matter, the skill subjects should be undergirded through the primary-age range with a variety of sensory experiences. One advantage to both science and the social studies is that sometimes the poor reader can make very

[4] E. Gibson, "Development of Perception: Discrimination of Depth Compared with Discrimination of Graphic Symbols," in J. C. Wright and J. Kagan (eds.), "Basic Cognitive Processes in Children," *Monogr. Soc. Res. Child Develpm,* 28 (1963), 5–32.

[5] S. Alan Cohen, *Teach Them All To Read* (New York: Random House, 1969), p. 11.

worthwhile contributions. Children who may not be able to read may be competent in other ways. For example, they may be able to paint murals, construct models, manipulate puppets, and participate in discussions. It is important that any slowness in the skill subjects not blind the teacher to other areas of strength.

Keeping in mind, then, that any discussion of reading is intended for illustrative purposes and that very little can be said in an introductory text about the teaching of reading, the fact to be remembered at all times is that primary children *can* be taught to read. Exactly what goes wrong in any individual case cannot be stated without a thorough knowledge of the individual and the situation. There is reason to be suspicious of anyone who thinks that he has the one final answer to the problems of reading. These problems can take any number of forms. A few of them will require the help of specialists. Sometimes these situations can be corrected, but usually not by the classroom teacher unaided.

Numerous children have not enjoyed the wealth of experience in manipulating and discriminating forms or in communicating in standard English to the extent that most middle-class children do. These children can be taught, but the teacher may have to start from a different basis. One teacher of a first-grade girl discovered that she was trying to teach the little girl to write "this" when the girl was actually saying "dis." Wisely, she decided to teach the girl to write "dis" and then after the child had developed greater auditory discrimination to teach her to write the standard "this." The teacher did not give up in her effort to teach the girl. She modified her method, taught the girl to write what she was saying, worked on the auditory discrimination aspect of the situation, and in due time had the girl reading and writing "this."

We wish to emphasize again that probably 98 percent of the children in the primary grades can be taught to read, write, and understand numbers. Most will do so if given even a minimal opportunity. The majority of the remainder can be helped if the teacher will take the time to find out what the stumbling block is, and then work through or around it. If the child learns best by feeling, the teacher can explore teaching through kinesthetic methods. If he visualizes, the child can write his word in the air or close his eyes and see it. If he learns by sounding out words, he can be helped to relate the written symbol with the speech sound. If various teaching machines can be used profitably, particularly for drill purposes, they should be used. There are two things the teacher must *not* do. (1) She should not give up on the child, and (2) she should not conclude that if one method does not work, nothing will.

Necessity of Teaching the Skill Subjects

There are two reasons that the skill subjects must be taught to every child in the primary school. The first is the child's own self-concept. It is fatal to the child's prospects in school if he becomes thoroughly convinced that he cannot achieve.[6] This can happen much earlier than the third grade. One of the authors was asked to work with a first-grade "repeater." The child's first words were, "I failed."

The second is that teachers beyond the primary-age range either do not know how to work with nonreaders or feel that they do not have the time to do so. Such teachers make no effort to help the nonreaders and usually categorize them in their minds—and frequently verbally too—as unteachable. Consequently, they just "make" work for these students that will keep them out of mischief; some have even allowed a student to read comic books while the rest of the class is engaged in the regular lesson. Not only is the student then aware that the teacher considers him a "hopeless case," but also the pupil's peers. A child so "condemned" has little choice other than to become a dropout.

To remedy the attitudes and actions of teachers beyond the third grade perhaps what is needed most is a well-organized and prestigious remedial reading program. William Glasser claims that such a program should involve the most important people in the school—the principal and his assistants, the supervisors, and the most highly regarded teachers.[7] With or without such a program every teacher on the upper level should be able to give the poor reader practical and psychological support.

Reading is a process. Under the best of circumstances it will not be completed by the end of the first, or the second, or the third year in school. Nor will it have begun for anyone the moment the child enters the first grade —reading involves the combining of many subskills to translate written symbols into verbal symbols representing concepts already understood by the child. But for most children the process will have gone far enough before the end of the first grade that teachers and fond parents can proudly state that "Johnny now reads."

It is hoped that if this goal has not been attained by the end of the first year in school that the child will be neither pushed on nor held back. Both alternatives are inconceivable to the concerned educator—both tend to make a child a failure. It is an open question as to which does most harm—to tell a first grader that he has failed or to have him continue to a higher grade, always finding himself the slowest student in the class.

If the child can be kept from feeling himself to be a failure, there is almost always a way to teach him or her to read in the second year. If the second year is not successful, more intensive methods are called for, if they have not been instituted long before. A team that includes the school counselor and/or psychologist, the classroom teacher, and hopefully, a reading specialist should work on the problem. Perhaps it is already two years late. The problem must be located, and the child must find success. School is too long and life too short for all of school to be a series of failures.

---

[6] For an interesting article on the subject, see John Holt, "School Is Bad for Children," *The Saturday Evening Post*, 242 (February 1969), 12–15.

[7] William Glasser, *Schools Without Failure* (New York: Harper & Row, 1969), p. 92.

We Must Teach All—The Advantaged and the Disadvantaged

The advantaged and the disadvantaged are not clearly differentiated groups. An occasional "advantaged" pupil from an upper-middle-class home may be disadvantaged in a variety of ways. Even if this is not true, he should not be neglected. The brightest, best-cared for children come to school knowing many things that some other children do not know. They may have potential that cannot be met by one teacher alone. Many advantaged children can profit from a nongraded, team-teaching approach. In the authors' experience and research, it has seemed to be the brightest children who have been freed by a breakdown of traditional grade barriers to achieve beyond the goals one would predict for them.[8] At the same time this achievement does not prevent the brighter student from associating and many times helping the less gifted child. The bright child can function with his peers on a social and physical level. In this way he can be taught the importance of both academic achievement and social involvement. The approach suggested offers the possibility of added help for both the advantaged and disadvantaged. It certainly does no harm to the child who is neither.

The Many Forms of "Disadvantage"

When one speaks of the "disadvantaged" child, it is taken for granted that one is alluding to a child from a culturally deprived or culturally different background. However, there are "disadvantaged" children who come from backgrounds regarded as "advantaged." Almost every teacher will recognize the category. Limited consultation service in an upper-middle-class neighborhood indicated a surprising number of these children. Even though their physical needs were more than adequately provided for, they had many problems. In one family the mother had committed suicide; in another the father was arrested for fraud. The grandparents in another controlled the money and the parents; the parents did not have sufficient independence or self respect to serve as models for the children. One pyromaniac had plenty of money but rarely saw his father, and the mother had more engrossing interests than a first-grade boy. In one class the teacher estimated that about one fourth of her first graders were on tranquilizers primarily because of pressures on or from the parents. Children may need help in spite of an abundance of the so-called "good things of life." It is not pertinent to point out that parents should be different, but it *is* pertinent to note that schools could, if they would, begin a quiet but massive counterattack against undue pressure on children. Though many teachers and school systems need to begin such a counterattack by honestly considering how their actions have

[8] Ruth H. and Clifford L. Nixon, "A Closer Look at Team Teaching," *Spearhead*, 2 (1966), 10, 11.

contributed to this pressure. And constructive action to relieve such pressure must follow.

Many physically handicapped children are "disadvantaged" as the term is used in the text. All people with physical handicaps function with a disadvantage. For many there are provisions for schooling and treatment geared for their particular disability so that they can learn to function better. However, the degree of the disability is generally the criterion for admission to such programs. Those who suffer from an impairment but not sufficiently to qualify for special schooling, for example, most certainly qualify as "disadvantaged" in the present discussion. A teacher may have a child in her classroom whose vision is seriously impaired. She may, also, have children with hearing problems. Some states provide special schools for the severely disabled, but there may be children who are capable of attending the regular public school who cannot hope to be successful in games or the usual physical activities of the school. Sometimes the physical disability is of a nature that it interferes with accomplishment in the skills. There may be children with mild brain damage in the classroom. There are often children with defective hearts or other equally serious conditions. Sometimes a teacher will even discover that there is a child in the classroom whose life expectancy is a matter of a few months or years. There are many more children in the long-term process of recovery from conditions that contribute to restlessness, or listlessness or who suffer from other physical symptoms that run counter to the best learning situation. Generally such children need some form of special assistance.

The list of "disadvantaged" children could continue almost endlessly. The ordinary classroom will have many children who are below normal in intelligence as well as many above. These average out, although the situation will differ in every classroom. From the teacher's standpoint the age-old question of heredity or environment as the basis for the I.Q. test scores is of minor importance. Her responsibility is to provide the best possible environment for learning in her classroom for the child placed there.

All children suffer from emotional upsets at some time during their school years. These may result from something as minor as a scolding at home or from a chronic home condition that most certainly will mark the child for life. There are children in school who come from homes that serve as "small time" bootleg establishments, or minor gambling dens, or "small time" houses of prostitution. Many such children hear and witness many disturbing things, and regular hours of sleep and prepared meals are unknown. Some children suffer cruel abuse in the home—mental, physical, and even sexual. The school should avoid adding to the problems of the home. Instead school can be a refuge from home for some children.

That such is not always the case is known by those who are familiar with public schools—particularly those which "serve" the disadvantaged. Running through Jonathan Kozol's *Death at an Early Age* are references to incidents of gross mistreatment of students, particularly of a boy named

Stephen, a small, emotionally disturbed fourth grader who was a ward of the State of Massachusetts. This mistreatment of Stephen was partially verbal. The one thing Stephen could do well was draw, but his drawing did not please the art teacher. Kozol reports the kind of incident he witnessed:

She would go to his desk with something truly like a vengeance and would shriek at him in a way that carried terror. "Give me that! Your paints are all muddy! You've made it a mess. Look at what he's done! He's mixed up the colors! I don't know why we waste good paper on this child!" Then: "Garbage! Junk!"[9]

Other treatment included expulsion of Stephen from school and beatings. Of the latter Kozol writes:

But when you hear of a sixty-pound mentally ill Fourth Grader being guarded by two men and whipped by a third for acts that are manifestly crazy, and when the teacher who prepares the punishment is not only gleaming with excitement but has, not ten days before, been speaking calmly of the niggers Down South or the little bastards causing trouble up there in room four, then it seems to me that anyone . . . is going to have to admit that something has gone wrong.[10]

By no means have we exhausted the list of possible disadvantages that may affect children from any level of society. All disadvantaged children need special consideration and help. In total number of children involved, in interest generated at long last, and in terms of the national interests, everything said thus far is dwarfed by the problems of the disadvantaged city and country slum children. White or black, city slum or country poor, help is desperately required. What has been done so far has been largely good, but it has also been totally inadequate.

From the education viewpoint, while all profess concern, few of the most qualified people are willing to teach the disadvantaged on a full-time basis. In addition, comparatively few good teachers are assigned to work with needy children. When they are, they receive very little praise or recognition. Throughout the nation it is the young teacher without adequate professional training and experience who is assigned to teach in school districts serving socioeconomically disadvantaged children. A few communities are attempting to man their schools with qualified personnel, but little is likely to happen until the challenge is emphasized and backed, if possible, by both public recognition and financial reward.

If people who are capable are to work with the educationally disadvantaged, they must be freed from the pressure of a timetable for achievement. The educationally disadvantaged can be taught successfully by the understanding, capable teacher. The teacher will soon become discouraged, however, if the disadvantaged child is expected to make up for lost time and to

---

[9] Jonathan Kozol, *Death at an Early Age* (Boston: Houghton Mifflin, 1967), pp. 3–4.
[10] *Ibid.*, p. 18.

achieve almost immediately on a par with his advantaged peers. To attain this goal requires not equal, but greater learning in the same length of time. There are culturally different children who will make up for their differences and achieve with the best. For most, this should not be considered as a goal. If children start out with handicaps, they should be encouraged and rewarded for achievement no matter how small or how slow the progress. They need real success, not pretense. That success should be measured in terms of each child's increased understanding, not by comparison with the advantaged child.

The neglect of years is seldom made up in a few months. Children must learn the basic skills if they are to become self-sufficient and self-supporting. If they are to learn these basic skills, they should be neither pressured nor held back in moving on just as far as they can, over whatever length of time it takes, and in any acceptable direction. Obviously, more than the basic skills is needed. Both specific skills and attitudes are necessary. The small child, however disadvantaged, can be helped to develop positive attitudes toward work and toward life while he is learning the basic skills. Deficiencies call for special effort, but remedies used must never crowd out all other learning.

Provisions for the Disadvantaged

Every school district has the obligation to do all that it can for every child, either in his advantaged situation or in spite of his disadvantage. To fulfill their obligation to their school children, some smaller school districts will have to join with other districts either through consolidation or cooperation. Whichever happens, all those concerned need to have clear objectives in mind and must constantly work toward the goals. Consolidation makes certain activities possible; it does not guarantee that they will be effectively carried out.

One of the provisions large districts or cooperating districts can provide is "special education" classes. In the broad meaning of this term such classes may be set up to meet any of a variety of needs—physical, emotional, or intellectual. There may be, for example, classes for the unusually gifted students. Too often, the expression is used to refer only to the classes for children who fall below an arbitrary level on certain well known, individually administered intelligence tests. Such classes are helpful if certain precautions are observed. Any such class should have a fully qualified teacher. That teacher should have appropriate materials and setting. Very careful supervision should make certain that the child is in the class he needs.

Some programs have expert teachers; others do not. There are also programs that are extremely repressive. In certain districts school administrators have hired "teachers" who are not only not qualified specialists, but also not qualified teachers. One teacher who did not belong in a special education class because of lack of training and personal background did attempt to provide a classroom conducive to learning for her particular students. The school authorities had not provided suitable equipment with which to work. Her pleas for materials were disregarded. Instead she received only increasingly demanding orders to produce a quiet, orderly classroom. The school, apparently, was only interested in removing certain children from the classes where their presence was not desired, not in the actual needs of these children.

Special problems and dangers prevail in carelessly formed special education classes. One pupil known to be of superior intelligence was placed in a special education classroom at a time of emotional stress. He needed help, but not this kind of help. Other children are placed in classes for mentally retarded on the basis of intelligence tests designed for a different class of children. Some of these children may have been borderline in intelligence, but the borderline foreign-born child or whose parents are foreign-born, or from a family with an even slightly different dialect, or even from a different cultural background falls below cutoff points on accepted intelligence tests. Often, such children need special help, but they are not, and should not be labeled as, mentally retarded.

Even the name "special education" needs refurbishing. One of the unique situations that came to the attention of the writers concerned a college student and a college instructor who had by coincidence attended the same high school. The college student had been in special education. In his school, special education meant what it should always mean, some form of special provision for special needs. The college student was very bright but he had extremely poor vision. He was not blind. He could function with help in the public school and he had received this help. To the college instructor, in spite of this background, the fact that the student had been in "special education" was proof that he could not do college work. The high school had done a good job in making provisions for a special need, but had failed to make clear even to its own students what its purposes were.

Special provision must be made for some children; insofar as possible, it should be done in a framework of concern, acceptance of, and provision for all kinds of individual differences. Honor and reward must be given to both the child who learns in spite of his handicap and the teacher who helps him learn from whatever his level and whatever his rate of progress. None of these things happen automatically, nor do they happen easily. They will not necessarily be carried out even when adopted as official school policy. The remarks in the teacher's lounge are frequently more indicative of the basic attitudes of a school.

Such special provisions find a more congenial environment where they are part of a totally nongraded, team-teaching approach. Remedial reading, speech correction, group work in problem areas, and enrichment resources can easily be woven into such a program. The type of program envisioned, as John Goodlad points out,[11] is not easily obtained. A fully effective nongraded, team-teaching program requires dedication, flexibility, and much work.

[11] John I. Goodlad, "Meeting Children Where They Are," *Saturday Review*, 48 (1965), 57–59, 72–74.

Nongradedness involves adherence to several principles. The basic one for a program dedicated to the child is that the child moves toward a general level of competency as rapidly as he can without harmful pressures and without being labeled a failure. Many complications arise, though they are basically trivial compared to the overall need. By normative standards, no child is equally good at everything. This is where grouping, made possible by flexible team teaching, can help most. The more interesting complication is that the child who matches the work of another child on any test will not have made the same score by doing the same items and processes with equal proficiency. A teacher who takes time, and any teacher can take time for at least a few pupils, will discover the specific difficulties. To the alert teacher such discoveries also make life exciting and teaching more effective. Whatever the organization, the teacher must be a detective who not only finds out what the child cannot do but *why* he cannot.

It is easier to ferret out "what" and "why" if there is a truly nongraded approach. Then some of the pressure is off the teacher to produce certain specified results in the school year. She can take more time to see that the child discovers the reasons and meaning of his operations. As noted earlier, the skills are basically impossible without insight. When team teaching is also employed, a variety of grouping combinations—heterogeneous and homogeneous—can be employed with benefit to the child. If and when the concept of nongradedness and team teaching is accepted, and teachers become proficient in it, children can work at various levels in different subject areas, and children with similar problems in some subjects can be grouped for part of a day. A child's strengths will also be recognized, and the child can be placed with advanced groups whenever this is advisable.

It takes bright, flexible, congenial people to form a team. The fearful, incompetent, arrogant, do not fit; they do not fit anywhere in teaching, and a team-teaching situation makes this even more evident. It takes much planning, replanning, shifting of children, and confidence in other team members to make a team function well as a team. Although the process of teaming is not easy, it is rewarding. Teachers get a new sense of importance and their morale is heightened by the experience. There can be other compensations. Opportunities may be provided for professional improvement, such as visits to demonstration schools with expenses paid, workshops and consultation service on school time, planning time within the school day, and incentive pay for team leaders.

But what of the teacher who must work with an individual or with a group of disadvantaged within the traditional one teacher classroom and with comparatively little recognition or support. Such a teacher, particularly a beginning teacher, needs some basic philosophy and method from which to operate. It is the conviction of the authors that the suggestions made as general principles can be applied, albeit with all the insight and common sense the teacher can bring to the situation. All children learn to make responsible choices, but as noted earlier, this freedom may have to be introduced very gradually. Chapters on this subject pointed out that some freedom existed when the teacher, without openly offering a choice, selected activities appropriate to the interest and needs of her children. The teacher of the disadvantaged may have to begin on this level. Similar comments could be offered with reference to problem solving and creativity.

The teacher of the disadvantaged of any kind must find a balance between concern and realism. Unthinking sentimentality is not a helpful reaction in the "ghetto" or anyplace else. The need is for concerned action and creative insight to do what is possible. Not all can find such a balance. Some teachers who may be wonderful in the suburbs may be dismal failures in the slums. It would be particularly dangerous to be overly dependent on the favorable response of children. The good teacher of the disadvantaged can be fully involved in the effort to improve conditions without expecting that her attitude will always be understood and appreciated. It is basic that she respect herself and her children. She will find their strengths and build on these. Some will love her and this is an added reward. In no educational situation should this be the primary goal of the teacher.

It is particularly important to the teacher of the culturally disadvantaged that teaching and methods be relevant. The chapter has already referred to Jonathan Kozol's experience as a teacher in the Boston public schools. One of Kozol's discoveries was the utter disregard by the authors of the texts he used of anything relevant to the experiences of the disadvantaged children with whom he worked.[12] Almost all of them belonged to a minority group, which, if mentioned at all, was spoken of in derogatory terms. In attempting to bring something more relevant into the classroom he tried out, among other things, a book of poetry by Langston Hughes. *The Ballad of the Landlord* in particular, caught the interest of the class.[13] At their request he mimeographed it. Contrary to his own view of the unimportance of memorization, the children memorized the poem. Here was something relevant to them. Complications followed. This and other activities of Mr. Kozol were not appreciated by some interested parties. The use of unauthorized material was made the excuse for Mr. Kozol's summary dismissal.

Such a result would certainly not follow in every school. Further, there is a growing body of teaching material which is relatively more appropriate to some of the situations the teacher of the culturally disadvantaged faces. At least, some schools are using supplementary materials different from standard, "old-time," strictly white, middle-class-oriented texts of the past. There are other ways to get at the problem. Children can almost always read what they have written. The book of writings of disadvantaged children, edited by Stephen Joseph, is a clear evidence that these writings can be graphic and pertinent.[14]

[12] Kozol, *op. cit.*, Chapter 8.
[13] *Ibid.*, pp. 174, 225, and 231–232.
[14] Stephen M. Joseph (ed.), *The Me Nobody Knows* (New York: Avon, 1969).

William Glasser has experimented with the use of free classroom discussion groups. He finds that culturally disadvantaged children can make valuable contributions.[15] Another idea is to provide times within the classroom when children can talk with their friends, or work together in groups of two or three on reading, arithmetic, or almost any academic area. In this, peers can work together and help each other. A later chapter will discuss the use of resource people, parents, people from the community, and older children. There are possible problems in all of these ideas, but there is also the possibility of tying in the work of the classroom to the life of the community.

There will be differences in working with the culturally disadvantaged. These differences must not be magnified or stereotyped. Fritz Redl, the child psychiatrist, writes in one collection on the topic, "Disadvantaged, and What Else?"[16] His point is that the cultural disadvantage is never "the whole story." A child's cultural disadvantage is never his only problem. Further, the disadvantaged children differ from each other in countless ways. Generalizations may have value if one remembers that they are always oversimplifications. If, as a group, they have known much violence, most of them will be in even greater need than others of safe ways to "let off steam." And further, not every disadvantaged child will react in this way. The Stephen, mentioned earlier, was basically timid, frightened, and withdrawn. Culturally deprived children may, also, be especially in need of activities with materials that can be handled and manipulated. These children may not be highly motivated by the grading system and it may be necessary to find other ways of rewarding effort.

To sum up, the teacher of the disadvantaged needs a keener awareness than others that children must be taken on from where they are, not from an artificially imposed level. They must be guided through relevant learnings as fast as it is feasible. Some will surpass most middle class children but this is not the goal. Their own culture must not be rejected. It can be used as a platform on which to build further learnings. The teacher must have a deep concern and respect for children as individuals that will let her seek ways of helping them whether or not that help is appreciated by everyone involved. It takes dedication and some degree of toughness. But that toughness cannot be the kind that enjoys domination or cruelty, or ever grows calloused to the problems of the children within or without the school.

The Teacher as the Key

In reemphasizing here the vital importance of the work of the teacher of young children, the authors have one basic and two supplementary facts in mind. The first is that the education of young children is of vital

---

[15] Glasser, *op. cit.*, Chapters 10 and 11.
[16] Fritz Redl, *When We Deal with Children* (New York: Free Press, 1966), pp. 467–487.

importance. This has been emphasized with respect to nursery school and kindergarten. From some standpoints the primary teacher is an even more important person. She is the one who is, in our society, expected to induct the child into the intricacies of formal learning. There are fallacies and dangers in this concept. This is one reason the primary teacher needs to be a very knowledgeable person. There is also truth in the concept. This job is much more complex than is generally realized.

It follows, then, that the teacher, herself, must have an attitude of respect for her position as a teacher of the young child. Unless she is alive and alert in this and in her other relationships, she does not belong in this field. Only the enthusiastic teacher can encourage each child to learn. Sometimes, this attitude is made relatively easy by the cooperation of understanding and enthusiastic administrators and fellow teachers. Usually the situation will be somewhat less than ideal. When this is true, she will need special dedication to "keep the vision," without giving up to frustration or disillusionment.

The second supplementary point is that others involved must understand the importance of the work of the teacher of young children. There are still too many in the general population who think that anyone can teach on this level. The colleges of the land are "infected" with this belief. Over the years hundreds of students in preparation for teaching in the primary field have reported slurs from not only fellow students but from college professors. Sometimes this general attitude is evident even in education departments. One college professor of Education almost demanded that a certain young woman prepare to teach on the first grade level. Her reason was that the young woman was small in stature!

The colleges face a problem that is seldom recognized. It is a difficult problem unless it is worked out on a college-wide basis. The pressure for more and more work is even more prevalent in the college than in the high school. There are two additional problems for education departments in the training of teachers. Unless students give more concern to professional courses in education than they do to the so-called academic subjects (there is a high academic content to most professional courses in Education), the students will neglect education from the sheer pressure in other directions. The problem that is seldom recognized, but comes to light far too often in student teaching, is that the students sent out usually teach the way that they have been taught for sixteen years—including the way that they have been taught in courses in education. Some who are most vociferous on removing pressure from small children are most oblivious of the fact that by their way of teaching they are denying everything that has been said.

Every primary child can and must learn to read, however long it takes him. Not every student that enters professional education can or should become a teacher. With sufficient thought and many years of effort, colleges may (and a few have) develop more effective programs. However, far too often colleges and teachers are honored by the percentage of students they fail, not the percentage they succeed in teaching.

Let us assume that a college graduate has secured a credential as a teacher and a job. His or her attitude toward teaching and the students determines whether he or she will be an effective teacher. The teacher's attitude cannot be emphasized too much. This attitude includes some degree of self-confidence and some resistance to untried innovations. But it also includes a concern and delight in the nature of children and in the child as an individual. It includes a purpose and a plan to grow with the increasing knowledge and improved methods that are developing. It includes a plan not only to continue to study various types of methods through classes and reading, but, also, to have an insatiable curiosity about children and what makes them "tick." Knowledge about each pupil may or may not have been stressed in the college training program. Herbert Kohl reports that he took a fifth year in preparation for teaching in one of the most prestigious of the nation's universities. He states that to the best of his recollection, no one even suggested that there was any point in observing the children he would teach.[17]

The good teacher observes, develops a theory as to what may work, tries it out, then observes some more. The dedicated teacher with skill and insight never leads a dull life. She, too, increases in both skill and insight as she helps her children to these dual goals.

Summary

The primary school continues to build on the skills and insights that the six-year-old child brings into the program, whatever the background of the child and whatever the nature of the school program. The teacher should recognize these skills, whatever their nature. She will not hold back a child who has already achieved the goals of the ordinary first grade. She will also recognize that many children may need to learn many subskills before a major encounter with the complexities of formal reading. She will label no child, wherever he is in his progress, either a nuisance or a failure. This will be easier for the teacher if she is in a nongraded, team-teaching situation. Then she will be in a better position to help each child progress from where he is without the usual frustration of the traditional classroom and without undue pressure. In a nongraded, team-teaching set-up several teachers will cooperate to the end that no child will fail to acquire the basic skills in the primary grades, whether a major breakthrough occurs in a first, second, or third year of schooling.

Various administration provisions may be made to help with those children who face special handicaps. All should be part of a total effort that recognizes the uniqueness of each child. Many handicaps exist in clusters. A child may be culturally deprived, deficient in language background, and physically

[17] Herbert Kohl, *36 Children* (New York: New American Library, 1967), p. 13.

handicapped. With some such cluster of handicaps there is increased probability of emotional problems. One may be poor, but proud, athletically skilled, and very bright. The facts, and the combinations, are important.

The teacher is the most important aspect of any educational program. It is not surprising that many less than perfect people teach classes in primary schools. Their profession has not been honored. Their training programs have often been conducted very differently from the way they are expected to conduct their own classes. The bright, competent teacher can become increasingly effective if she makes her teaching career a life-long goal through the study of both books and children.

goals and perspectives

Value and corresponding insight constitute the very essence of human mental life. Take any major human problem, and you will find that it contains this factor.

Wolfgang Kohler, *The Place of Value in a World of Facts*

1 2 3
4 5 6

INTRODUCTION

Goals and Perspectives

This introduction differs from the introductions to the preceding four sections. It is not a general statement to be followed by application to specific levels. The application will focus on early childhood education but will not attempt to deal with the differences between nursery school, kindergarten, and the primary-age range. The section deals with the goals of education in relation to reality and future possibilities.

Most educators share a "dream," one that is more than an American dream. It can be traced back at least as far as Socrates and has been shared by such unlikely people as Charlemagne.[1] It found eloquent expression in the writings of Comenius and in the practices of Pestalozzi. Insofar as the dream has involved the practical concept of universal literacy, it has become a dream that is approaching reality for much of the world. In America we trace the dream back to very early beginnings in Massachusetts, but in some states the acceptance and the implementation of the dream for all children has come in comparatively recent times.[2]

The "dream" in America has been of something more than literacy, even when the accomplishment has been even less. The concepts embodied in

[1] H. G. Good, *A History of Western Education* (New York: Macmillan, 1949), pp. 75–76.
[2] Adolphe E. Meyer, *An Educational History of the American People* (New York: McGraw-Hill, 1957), p. 218.

such great national documents as the Declaration of Independence were neither new nor distinctly American. They are a clear expression of a dream that sees men as equal before the law and in their relationships with their fellowmen. Equality has never become a reality, but the dream has never died. This text was written soon after the issuance of two important statements in 1969. One is a unanimous ruling by the United States Supreme Court stating that the time is past for delay in the implementation of full integration in the schools. The other is a report by the National Commission on Violence. Whatever the merits of the arguments in the case before the Supreme Court, the judgment is an attempt to implement more completely one phase of the American dream. The report of the President's Commission is even more pertinent. It, too, is a statement of the American dream, but in reverse. It calls attention to the vast gaps between the dream and the actual treatment of large segments of American society. There is less than perfect equality before the law, or equality of treatment by fellow citizens and by public servants.

Neither has there been perfect equality in the schools of America. Documentation of this goes back at least to the time of the sociological classic, *Elmtown's Youth*.[3] The problem is as ancient as human life. It has probably never been better expressed than it was by the apostle James of the first-century church. The following is from Phillips' translation:

Suppose one man comes into your meeting well-dressed and with a gold ring on his finger, and another man, obviously poor, arrives in shabby clothes. If you pay special attention to the well-dressed man by saying, "Please sit here—it's an excellent seat," and say to the poor man, "You stand over there, please, or if you must sit, sit on the floor," doesn't that prove that you are making class distinctions in your mind, and setting yourself up to assess a man's quality?[4]

The Goal in Perspective

Even dreams are subject to analysis, but this is somewhat too ambitious a project for the present purpose. Instead several self-evident facts about the goal of universal, free, full, public education for all children will be explored.

The goal, as we have stated it, has never been unanimously accepted. And too often its advocates have been ignored by their contemporaries. Early educational theorists and practitioners were honored by succeeding generations, not necessarily by their own. Socrates had no opportunity to institute proposed reforms for early childhood education, but he gave his life for concepts related to those of this text. Comenius lost wife, children, and all worldly possessions in part because he stood for freedom—religious

[3] August B. Hollingshead, *Elmtown's Youth* (New York: Wiley, 1949), Chapter 8.
[4] J. B. Phillips, *The New Testament in Modern English* (New York: Macmillan, 1962), James 2:2–4.

and educational. Pestalozzi was one of the world's great teachers, but judged in terms of financial success, he was a "born loser."[5]

The acceptance of the idea of education for all young children is relatively recent and not complete. The percentage of American children assisted through public nursery schools of any kind is minute. One third of the age group who would normally attend kindergarten are unable to do so, chiefly, for lack of provision by the states. Difficulties in the primary-age range are more failures in the reality than in the goal. Though even in the goals there are defects.

The ultimate goal itself is not clearly understood. The goal is to provide equal educational opportunity for all. Society has many other obligations to people. The obligation of the school is to see that the varied opportunities it offers are equally available to all. This does not mean exactly the same kind of treatment for all. On the level of early childhood education, the same expectation from each student can in effect mean very unequal opportunity. What must be equal is the chance to succeed. To have equal opportunity, the schools must provide equally competent teachers for all. It means a goal of education that aims to offer the kind of education that is equally suited to the needs of each individual. It means adequate housing, surroundings, and equipment for all. It means a deep concern and respect for all. It means an open door to advanced training for all.

Educational goals constantly compete with other goals in life. They compete in the market place with national, regional, and personal interests. Much of the competition is in terms of money. The United States has more money and spends more of it on education than any people ever have before. But the supply of money is not unlimited and there are compelling claims from other sources. Educational goals also compete on a different level. In theory most Americans want the best for all children, but they may also have a variety of reservations. Some still accept the myth of the superiority of certain classes or races. Some apply outmoded concepts of rugged individualistic competition to young children. Some dismiss the problem of educational needs with, "Certain people simply do not want to learn." Some may seek ways to see that those who pay the most in taxes get the most in services.[6]

The Reality in Perspective

It is not surprising that the reality in much of education falls short of even the generally accepted goals.[7] This is almost in the nature of an inevitable fact of life. For an occasional teacher working with a certain individual,

[5] S. J. Curtis and M. E. A. Boultwood, *A Short History of Educational Ideas* (London: University Tutorial Press, 1953).

[6] Joseph S. Roucek, "Milestones in the History of the Education of the Negro in the United States," *International Review of Education,* 10 (1964), 162–175.

[7] John I. Goodlad, "The Schools vs. Education," *Saturday Review,* 52 (1969), 59–61, 80–82.

success beyond the highest dreams may sometimes be evident. It has even been known to happen that an educational leader who had proposed a new approach with faint hopes of support and less hope of success found an enthusiastic response and a competent achievement. More often there is a lag in both time and achievement between goals and results.

Education for young children may have deteriorated in the middle-class American suburb because of perverted goals. When the goal of the best possible education for everyone turns into pressure to quick success, the actual result in terms of the development of thinking, purposeful children may be thwarted. It has been noted that the American school system has produced a nation of grade achievers, not of learners. Today the school, the home, and even peers constantly exert pressure on a child to get grades, regardless of the level of education. Two first-grade teachers mentioned in one week that they were leaving the profession. They felt forced to apply too much pressure on children to attain artificial objectives.

Even greater deterioration in education seems apparent in the impoverished city and depressed country areas. This is more evident in the city because there are more children clustered in one place. The plight of the children in Appalachia and many other depressed country areas may not be significantly better. Areas with a low tax base and few attractions tend to "make do" with the teachers they can secure. It is reported unofficially that in one small town in the South, there is no teacher in the school who is not there because of family connections or because of inability to find employment elsewhere. The child in a poorer area even in rural America has little probability of interaction with superior teachers.

The inner-city school tends to have the same problems, compounded. There are few good teachers who will serve in such areas. Where tax base, housing, environment, morale have all deteriorated, the child's opportunities for equal education are almost nonexistent. The federal government, private agencies, and to a lesser extent, local and state agencies are working on the problems. The opportunity for equally good education is far from equal to all.

There are many other factors involved. One is the simple matter of inertia. School districts sometimes find greater difficulty in securing the cooperation of their teaching staffs than of anyone else when they consider innovations.[8] Teachers are human with all the possibilities and difficulties that this implies. Teachers need to be responsive human beings, but more alive, concerned, and intelligent than the average. To the present, most school systems have not found sufficient means to attract many outstanding individuals. Neither have they been too successful in stimulating those who enter the profession to the continued growth required. With a high probability that the child will be exposed to people who are getting by as best they can on limited abilities and more limited zeal, the reality for most children will be far below the dream of maximum opportunity.

[8] Ray Halpern, "Tactics for Integration," *Saturday Review*, 51 (1968), 47–49, 66.

The Future in Perspective

The growing volume of discussion of the problems faced and an increasing attempt to meet these problems would seem to indicate the probability of success in attaining educational objectives. The discussion has included suggestions for radical changes in the training of teachers.[9] It has indicated a near unanimity on the need to change the goal from grades to learning. It has stressed the growing number of educational innovations which have proven superior to the standard graded school situation. One can say, hopefully, that anyone entering teaching with the expectation that teaching in the years ahead will remain substantially that of the past, should change his occupational goal.

With this background three related topics will be considered. The first two are more closely related. The first is the more specific: *Success of What Kind and at What Cost?* The second is more general: *A Perspective on Values.* Tied in to these topics is one that concerns means more than ends: *Guidance, Direct and Indirect.*

Summary

Part V differs from those immediately preceding it in that it does not consider a specific topic as applied to levels of early childhood education. It speaks of three major topics pertinent to the twin concepts of *Goals and Perspectives.* The Introduction suggests that while the American dream of equal opportunity in education has had to compete for acceptance, the major problems now lie in the reality of the educational situation rather than the goals. It adds that the future will probably not be utopian, but should be both different and better.

---

[9] James Bryan Conant, *The Education of American Teachers* (New York: McGraw-Hill, 1963).

CHAPTER THIRTEEN

Success! What and at What Cost?

Throughout the text there has been an emphasis on the importance of providing successful experiences for the young child. The term "success" has several meanings in the English language. The first two definitions given in the *Random House Dictionary of the English Language* are the ones most relevant for the discussion:

1. a favorable or prosperous termination of attempts or endeavors.
2. the attainment of wealth, position, honors, or the like.[1]

Since the topic is early childhood education, success must be defined in terms appropriate to young children. Thus the first definition is most applicable in the text.

The second definition, in at least its broadest terms, has a somewhat more distant relationship. Ultimate goals are of concern to individuals and groups. Society in general has a rightful concern with the future of its members. These goals are constantly subject to reevaluation and change. Young people who are questioning such goals as security, prominence, and prosperity have

[1] *The Random House Dictionary of the English Language*, unabridged edition (New York: Random House, 1966), p. 1419.

every right and reason to question. Communism has questioned the capitalistic system though it has failed to produce a society free from equivalent drives. Most of the great religious faiths would question the emphasis on success in terms of wealth and prestige. Even the man in the street will probably suggest that other factors go into a successful life.

One of the chains of thought running through the previous pages is that it is possible to so organize a program of learning experiences that every child will achieve success in terms of what he is able to accomplish. This does not mean low aspiration or easy achievement. Success implies effort in the meeting of personal goals. It is possible to prevent the bright pupil from achieving success by confining his efforts. The emphasis of the book is not on easy successes through rewarding mediocre achievement—it is on *success in terms of* the *present abilities* of the child. By and large, the best of teachers cannot take anyone beyond what he is able to learn.

Society, schools, and parents have a rightful concern for the future as well as the present. In the field of education, in particular, the goal in the forefront must be to make possible the growth of children into "successful persons" and "effective citizens." If this is true, the product and processes of education must be examined in this light. In part, such criticism as this chapter offers is based on the possibility that some present practices may interfere with the attainment of legitimate long-range goals. The problem is largely a matter of *perspective,* for one can focus so completely on desired outcomes that the picture of the child is distorted.

Success—in Whose Terms?

"Success—in whose terms?" is not an easy question to answer. A great many people have some stake in what happens to any child. It is the child, however, who has the most to gain or lose. Stating the truism is not enough, however, because young children cannot define their goals. Whatever goals they ultimately achieve, furthermore, will require adult support and guidance. In practice most teachers and parents work through this apparent confusion. Part of their success lies in putting major emphasis on the immediate goals. These goals are not entirely the child's, but they are relevant to his outlook. Both parents and teachers sometimes miss this perspective.

Parental Pressures

There have always been parents who mistakenly hoped to find the fulfillment through their children that they had failed to achieve in their own lives. What they had not succeeded in accomplishing, the child must do at all costs. Other parents have simply expected more than was possible. Whether from selfish or the best of motives, imposed and unrealistic goals are usually damaging and self-defeating.

Some parents in the past and present with "normal" goals for some reason use abnormal tactics. Two college students known in the past illustrate two rather common mistakes among parents. For one student the results were probably only moderately harmful. She sought counseling because of a personal problem. She was an attractive and capable young woman with nearly a straight "A" average. At the beginning of any course that offered any difficulty, however, she became excessively anxious, suffered psychosomatic difficulties, and could hardly go on. Discussion brought out the fact that the young woman had grown up in a small town and had been in the same class with a relative. As far back as she could remember, whenever she brought home a grade or report, the father's first question had been, "And what did Mary make?" The student responded favorably to counseling. She continued to make good grades and with reduced anxiety. But, she will probably carry some psychological scars for life.

The second was more tragic and probably more complicated. At least two kinds of comparison were involved. The college student was a boy from a minister's family. He was the middle boy in the family and both brothers were more successful. Apparently, this boy's mother compounded this already existing and discouraging competition by a negative attitude toward what should have been a successful school experience. As related, whatever grade the boy brought home, the mother wondered why it was not better. If the boy made an "A −," the mother never said, "Wonderful." She always asked, "Why didn't you make an 'A'?" This kind of comparison can be fatal to both present and future success. The boy gave up the attempt to succeed in school.

School Pressures

Ronald Doll speaks of October 1957 as "a fateful month in the recent history of American education." It was the month in which Russia launched its first Sputnik. This event intensified criticism of American education. Some of the resulting efforts to improve education were wholesome, as, for example, federal financial support for the improvement of guidance services. Other results have been more questionable. In Doll's words:

Soon, large numbers of American teachers became alarmed by the complaints they were hearing and reading. Like most of us when we are afraid, these teachers proved unable to think clearly about what to do to overcome their difficulties; so they simply did more of what they were already doing.[2]

Not all the changes were simply a loading on of more of the same work; different and more difficult work was added. Pressures on the students to

[2] Ronald C. Doll, "The Heat is On," in Ronald C. Doll and Robert S. Fleming (eds.), *Children Under Pressure* (Columbus, Ohio: Merrill, 1966), Chapter 1.

perform were intensified. Concepts formerly reserved for college were moved down into high school. Some concepts that had been taught in high school became part of primary education. There were good elements to some of these moves. It is possible that kindergarten children can learn some things more easily than college students. The pressure that accompanied the moves was not good, though. Before we discuss the latter more fully, there is a further aspect of the judging of success we should examine.

Success—by What Standards?

Success is not only judged too often in terms of external pressures, but also too often is measured by inappropriate standards.

Speed *vs.* Power

Success is most easily measured by how fast a given task is accomplished. Even the manuals of standardized "power" tests explain that each test is designed so that all but some 10 percent of the students will be able to finish most of the work that they are capable of doing. Little thought seems to be given to the 10 percent who may be even more capable, but work more deliberately. This attitude is not confined to tests. Even the learning games—flash cards, teacher-pupil interaction—seem most often geared to recognition of the student who is quick. The concept is not as applicable to life. Almost any job in which speed is the essence can be done by a machine many times more efficiently than by a human.

Surface *vs.* Depth

The pressures of the past several years, including the emphasis on speed, have tended to increase the learning of surface details in order to provide quick answers. If books are to be "covered" in the traditional sense, there can be little time for exploration of meanings. Facts are memorized, usually in order to pass the next test. Something is learned in all of this but usually not enough to provide much depth of meaning and understanding.

On the level of early childhood education the problem is not so much that of tests as the hurrying-over of experiences that might make symbols more meaningful. All students need time to think and organize learnings. The young child is eager to learn; he is not geared to speed for the sake of speed in that learning. The standard of speed is false. Some things in life may only be worth a surface skimming, but the important aspects deserve exploration in depth. For the young child the exploration must be done not by abstract thinking as much as by being able to *take time* to explore, to experiment, to try out ideas. It is more important that he have time to learn well rather than that he "skim over" much learning.

Conformity *vs.* Creativity

All will agree that the child who conforms is much easier to deal with than the child who is different. It is certainly easier to test him. A teacher on almost any level can make up questions to which, supposedly, there is one right answer. The basic problem is that in the process children are taught not to think of other possible answers, not to make use of their creative abilities, not to consider alternatives. The tragedy is that these abilities are the ones that society needs most. Alice Keliher correctly asserts:

We have a moral obligation to acquaint ourselves with the new research material on IQ and creativity. There is some indication that IQ and creativity are not synonymous. Indeed there is suspicion that IQ is a measure of schoolish mental abilities and that creativity often calls for a broader and less-conforming range of intellectual pursuits. It seems possible that children who are able in the non-conforming areas find themselves placed in the slower-moving groups and so their potential is not realized. We cannot afford to lose one iota of creative ability in our society today.[3]

Success—at What Cost?

As judged by various standards and in various terms, there have been successes in recent educational efforts. Most young people are learning a great many facts. More of them are remaining in school. Some are not only remaining in school, but also are demonstrating remarkable talent. However, the complete picture is not all this encouraging. Earlier chapters have called attention to John Holt's conclusions that the schools are turning eager learners into passive recipients and thinkers into guessers.[4] William Glasser holds the schools accountable for convincing the inner-city child that he is a failure.[5] Both Gladys Gardner Jenkins[6] and Bernard Spodek[7] point out that pressure that comes from within the child will usually be helpful; the kindliest of pressures from others may not be.

A stronger statement against pressure, however, appears in *Children Under Pressure*, edited by Ronald Doll and Robert Fleming. In this book Robert Fleming discusses in detail some of the apparent results of pressures on

---

[3] Alice V. Keliher, "Do We Push Children?" *Don't Push Me!* (Washington, D. C.: Association for Childhood Education International, 1960), pp. 6–7.

[4] John Holt, *How Children Fail* (New York: Pitman, 1964).

[5] William Glasser, *Schools Without Failure* (New York: Harper & Row, 1969).

[6] Gladys Gardner Jenkins, "What Price Pressures?" *Don't Push Me!* (Washington, D. C.: Association for Childhood Education International, 1960), pp. 9–14.

[7] Bernard Spodek, "Motivation in Early Education," *Motivation* (Washington, D. C.: National Education Association, 1968), pp. 7–13.

children.[8] He reports that one sampling of male psychiatric out-patients, aged thirteen to twenty-four, revealed that a primary reason for seeking psychiatric help was the *stress of educational endeavor*. From the 1953–1955 period to the 1960–1961 period the percentage designating such stress as *the* reason increased from 34 percent to 74 percent.[9] A report of a survey of age incidence in a physician's office indicated that emotionally based difficulties resulting from pressures concerning school were most prevalent in the age groups, five to seven and eleven to seventeen.[10] Fleming also gives statistics from the New Jersey State Department of Education indicating that the rate of suicide among school-age individuals is rising. He concludes with the statement, "The report is clear that the victims were lonely children who had limited success in school."[11]

In the same book Geoffrey Esty makes additional observations of merit.[12] He suggests that the increased pressures of school have added to overuse of tranquilizers for children, to psychosomatic illnesses, to failures, to the use of alcohol and drugs, and to sexual promiscuity. He is not placing the blame on the school alone. Other factors besides pressure in school are at work in society. The broader implication is indicated in one summary statement: "In general, indiscriminate sex activity becomes a substitute for satisfying relationships in family, school, and community."[13] Success sought through pressure on children and young people not only can fail to achieve the desired goals, but also can help to produce undesirable results.

Johnny was a first-grade pupil whose school records indicated good health and normal intelligence. He did have a specific and disturbing problem. His teacher, an experienced and competent person, could take in stride the "accidents" that sometimes happen on this level. She soon discovered that Johnny's pants were wet all the time. Conferences were held with the parents and the psychologist. Through these and through individual conferences with the boy it came to light that Johnny's eight-year-old sister could be the cause of the problem. She was the miniature and distorted image of a compulsive, driving, and dominating mother. Apart from those times when circumstances forced a separation, she regulated every second of Johnny's life. She pushed, bullied, and ridiculed him. It could never be proven completely that she was Johnny's problem. Nevertheless, when the parents provided separate bedrooms for the children and found ways to interest the sister in other things, Johnny's problem cleared up.[14]

---

[8] Robert S. Fleming, "Spilling Over: A Further Look at Pressures," in Doll and Fleming, *op. cit.*, pp. 64–68.

[9] *Ibid.*, p. 65.

[10] *Ibid.*, p. 66.

[11] *Ibid.*, p. 68.

[12] Geoffrey Esty, "Children in Trouble," in Doll and Fleming, *op. cit.*, pp. 71–83.

[13] *Ibid.*, p. 81.

[14] Ruth H. Nixon, "How Busy Should the Young Child Be?" *The Christian Home*, 1 (1969), 4–6, 63.

Summary

Children need successful experience. Such success is primarily a present success that consists of solving problems that challenge but do not defeat the child. Ultimate goals are important and have value if they are normal and normally applied without the loss of focus on the child and his current situation. Adults and their goals are vital to the development of a child, but the adults cannot learn for a child. Learning takes place within the child and because of his desire to learn. A false emphasis, an emphasis for distorted purposes, any constant comparison with others is defeating. Evaluations that are established on the basis of speed, surface learning, and conformity are not conducive to important learning. Too much pressure is not only self-defeating, but destructive.

CHAPTER FOURTEEN

A Perspective on Values

A four-year-old boy ran away from home with a neighbor of the same age. The two made their way from their residential district into the heart of the small city in which they lived. In the process they crossed a number of busy streets. They not only reached their destination safely—downtown—but eventually returned without a bruise. To the mothers who had been frantically searching for them, the first boy explained calmly that they had been perfectly safe, "We held hands all the way!" Evidently and quite understandably, the little boy had mistakenly assumed that he could cross any thoroughfare safely, just as long as he held on to someone's hand. In early childhood education values are important but not easily taught. Neither do teachers always teach the values that they think they are emphasizing.

Values and Early Childhood Education

Moral Values

Earlier chapters have mentioned Comenius, Pestalozzi, Froebel, and Montessori as outstanding educators. Each of these individuals was a deeply dedicated, religious, and highly moral person. They seemed to share in common not only faith in a Divine Being but a feeling akin to a religious devotion in their attitude toward children. That combination of devotion to both children and principle is still very much alive. It can be found in the classrooms in most of the schools in America. It is found in increasing volunteer service on many fronts. For example, in 1969 a reported 250,000 college students served voluntarily in such community services as tutoring programs for ghetto children, working with delinquent young people, and helping retarded children.[1]

Theoretically, there is a relationship between belief and behavior. A psychologist will recognize that many other factors enter into the actual behavior of children and adults. He might, also, point out the dangers to mental health involved in too rigid moral standards or in any standards too remote from the reality of behavior. There is reason to accept the general concept that the basic values of individuals and of societies are important. There is a sense in which the chief purpose of any educational program is to perpetuate such values.

Apart from theory, there are practical reasons for finding ways to teach some form of values. Dramatic evidence that the inner-city child hopes for a life with higher values and greater safety is found in Stephen Joseph's book *The Me Nobody Knows*.[2] Societies cannot survive where there is no mutual trust.

Problems in the Teaching of Values

What values can be taught involve some difficulty in a democracy. One reason the question must be faced in a text on education, in particular, is that the teacher is constantly by word, action, and attitude teaching her own values. Difficulties arise when values are discussed in terms of religious beliefs regardless of the attitude of the teacher toward religion. David Mallery quotes a high school student, "One thing I'll never forget is when Miss X, who always puts her foot in her mouth, came into class and said, 'When I come in here I leave my religion outside and discuss the truth!' "[3] There have been a series of Supreme Court decisions upholding the objection to the direct teaching of religious views. These decisions are based on the concept of the separation of church and state and the need for fairness in a democracy to children from families representing minority faiths. There is nothing in any of these decisions to prevent a teacher from making clear his beliefs through activities outside the school. Some aspects of "religious" principles are legitimate in the classroom. At the early childhood education level the teacher should accept with genuine interest the expressions of faith by young children. A considerable body of research indicates that very few young children doubt the existence of God.[4] On any level, discussion and contribution by children and young people about God and religion can

---

[1] *U. S. News and World Report,* October 27, 1969, 32.

[2] Stephen M. Joseph, *The Me Nobody Knows* (New York: Avon, 1969).

[3] David Mallery, *High School Students Speak Out* (New York: Harper & Row, 1962), p. 55.

[4] Ruth H. Nixon, "Reactions of Children to Pictures and Questions Related to God" (unpublished Ed. D. dissertation, University of California, Berkeley, 1957).

be accepted with respect. There is a growing conviction that the beliefs of the great religions can be discussed respectfully and fairly.

The problem in teaching generally accepted values is less difficult. There is, however, discrepancy if values are presented as though they are practiced when to the child's knowledge they are not. Honesty as to the failures of individuals, classes, schools, and nations to live up fully to assumed values seems to be the only method by which values will be accepted and practiced in the long run. There is a false sense of security in pretending that all is well. Several reactions are possible, most of them bad. For example, the child may learn to shun reality or he may shun both the pretense and the values assumed.

How openly some subjects should be discussed is a matter for serious consideration. In discussions of teaching the underprivileged someone observed that children had no great interest in reading, "See Jane run," when they had already seen Jane raped. There is some way to bring values into the classroom in an honest way and on a practical level.

John F. Wharton considers problems related to those being discussed.[5] In particular, he speaks of leaders of young dissidents who see the failures and hypocrites in business, education, and politics. These young people express the inclination to throw out all present standards, to tear the fabric of society apart, and to start again from nothing. Wharton suggests that not this but positive leadership with an affirmative morality is needed. As a beginning, he would ask all leaders in politics, industry and education to repeat every night a part of the prayer of St. Francis of Assisi:

Lord, make me an instrument of Thy peace. Where there is hatred, let me sow love; where there is injury, pardon; where there is doubt, faith; where there is despair, hope; where there is sadness, joy; where there is darkness, light.

The idea is worthy of consideration. It is hoped that most teachers in early childhood education would approve the purpose, and some, at least in principle, implement the practice.

Teaching Values in Early Childhood Education

It is the authors' firm conviction that one of the accepted purposes of early childhood education is to teach values. Below we shall suggest how this can be best achieved.

Gradual Development

Value generalizations develop gradually. Piaget made this assertion years ago.[6] In one of his early studies he found that small children tend to base

---

[5] John F. Wharton, "Toward An Affirmative Morality," *Saturday Review*, 52 (1969), 11–13, 46.
[6] See Jean Piaget, *The Moral Judgment of the Child* (London: Free Press, 1932).

their judgments on specific rules and are able only gradually to move to more general concepts. He also concluded that there is a shift of control from external demands to internal standards and from judgment based on the act alone to evaluation that includes the circumstances. More recent studies support these findings.[7]

Piaget's conclusions are logical. We know that children in early childhood education are not ready to understand fully the meaning of Alexander's conquest or the difference between Idealism and Existentialism—nor are many college sophomores. Even for the college student a gradual introduction seems necessary. Children build up generalizations from many experiences. None of their beliefs are necessarily fully consistent. It is to be expected that their concepts of moral conduct are sometimes faulty. Hugh Hartshorne and Mark May learned years ago that children's conduct is not altered dramatically by a few hours of exposure to religious instruction (such as Sunday school).[8] The Russians are right in believing that the foundations of morality are laid in the nursery school. It has been reported that the official position of the Soviet Union with respect to nursery school education contains the statement, "Children's moral traits and the character of their personality should be formed while they are in nursery school."[9] In Russia this may include the two-year-old.

What the teacher in early childhood education says and does is an important part of the moral development of children. The beginnings of this training in values go back even earlier in life. The culmination, to whatever extent it comes, is later. Even in early childhood education the school does not claim exclusive right to engage in the teaching of values. The cumulative effect of the total time spent by children in school should have a major impact.

Through the Situation

Children learn values as they learn other concepts, chiefly through ongoing experiences of life. Lectures on abstract concepts are least helpful. Brief, positive explanations and patient reminders are useful on any level, but the utilization of situations carries deeper meaning. The teacher of young children does not usually develop a structured lesson for the sole purpose of teaching morals. Questions of "value" tend to arise normally and frequently in the activities of the day.

Some situations for learning are deliberately designed. Mention has been made of the nursery school that was so well designed that children could

[7] See Nixon, *op. cit.*, as well as an earlier study by Nixon, *A Survey of Results of Sunday School Experiences of Young Children as Shown by Reactions to Structured Pictures* (unpublished seminar paper, University of California, Berkeley, 1953).

[8] Hugh Hartshorne and Mark A. May, "Studies in the Nature of Character," *Studies in Deceit*, 1 (New York: Macmillan, 1928).

[9] Michael and Sheila Cole, "Russian Nursery Schools," *Psychology Today*, 2 (1968), 23–28.

play freely without harming themselves or the equipment. When it was discovered that children were reacting the same way to everything in the home with ensuing damage and parental unhappiness, inexpensive objects were purchased and the children taught that these were not for their use. Children, themselves, as they interact with each other develop rules and regulations. The young child may want to change the rules to his own advantage, but he is still learning the advantage of rules. George Dennison writes, "Children are capable of positively curative effects on one another when their relationships are allowed to evolve naturally."[10]

Spontaneously or contrived, it is possible to develop value concepts as children interact in "dramatic play" situations. One kindergartner is remembered saying very clearly (his voice ringing across the room) "That's not fair! That's not fair!" The boy was role playing a part in the sale of goods in a classroom store. Some children were helping themselves to the play money. He knew that was not right.

Most of the suggestions in Chapter 15, which is concerned with the guidance role of teachers, have equal application to the present topic. If children are helped toward a developing understanding of themselves and their relationships to others, they will at the same time develop concepts of value.

Through Exposure

Joseph D. Lohman speaks primarily of the teacher's "middle-class" values and "lower-class" children in his article, "Expose—Don't Impose."[11] He makes several worthy observations. His contention that changes in values come gradually seems so obvious that it should not warrant special mention. The same could apply to his observation that the teacher who is respected has more of an impact as a model than as a teacher. Too frequently the obvious is overlooked. Lohman goes on to suggest, as this text has in other connections, that the teacher show respect for the children's values, including speech forms and dress. As to the latter, his suggestion is that "many of the students we call culturally disadvantaged have weak or strongly negative self-images and bolster their self-esteem in ways that are alien to the middle class. The more flamboyant their dress, the greater their sense of belonging."[12] He includes the concept of learning something of the child's present value system, of understanding the meaning of his speech, and of listening with an intent to learn not only about the child but about life as he knows it. Then Lohman presents the idea of exposing children to values rather than attempting to impose values on them.

---

[10] George Dennison, "An Environment To Grow In," *Saturday Review,* 52, (1969), 74.

[11] Joseph D. Lohman, "Expose–Don't Impose," *National Education Association Journal,* 55, (1966), 23–26.

[12] *Ibid.,* p. 25.

While there seems to be general agreement that the adoption of certain values of the dominant middle-class culture is necessary for survival in this society, such adoption cannot be forced. . . .

If school personnel can open the doors for their students without attempting to push them through, if they can sincerely convey to these students that there are different values which may be of practical help to them without intimating that their present values are worthless, if the school can allow the student to take what he wants without insisting that he take everything, then the student may be able to accept some of the school's values.[13]

Lohman's statements would seem to apply in early childhood education to all children. But even here, there is special need of consideration for the culturally different. Good primary teachers sometimes may show great concern for pupils with such a background but at the same time exhibit great condescension. A recognition that there is legitimate value in the speech and manner of any child's culture is important, a thought that relates to the principle that values are acquired gradually. Earlier in the text the same wording as Lohman's title (expose—but do not impose) was used with reference to teaching skills to young children. Value concepts are even more difficult and elusive to teach. Children need to be exposed to them gradually and a little at a time.

In the Child's Terms of Reference

The words, "My father is a can stacker," were spoken proudly by an eight-year-old boy. The boy, a third-grade student in a low-income area, was reporting to the class for a unit of work devoted to the occupations of the father or mother (or both) of the children in the class. Had any of the parents not been working, the project would have been inappropriate. In this case it seemed to be a successful project. The emphasis in the unit was on the value of work to the community. Each child made a picture of a parent at work. A chart was developed using the children's drawings. The boy quoted described vividly his father's work. The cans had to be stacked just right or many problems might develop. In the boy's words, the father's job entailed "being careful, always being there, and not goofing off."

Insofar as discussion of values enters the classroom directly, it must be in terms of what the children understand. They gradually, but early, understand what it is to be fair. They learn something about generosity. An illustration was used earlier of a Head Start nursery school age child who was willing to share her precious but already well-masticated gum. It was pointed out then how easily most of us might have permitted our strong middle-class emphasis on the danger of contagion to blot out the beauty of something more significant.

Respect for self and others is taught in many ways, but most importantly it is taught as the teacher shows by word and action that she respects each

[13] *Ibid.*, p. 25–26.

child. Involvement and responsibility have been discussed at length. It has been noted that both are best taught not by lengthy discussion but by providing the setting in which the child can become involved in something of importance to him and in his acceptance of the responsibility for the activity.

The Value of Early Childhood Education

The basic premise of the text is the value of early childhood education. There is an increasingly recognized potential in the education of young children. We know more than was ever known before about how young children learn. Today educators are experimenting widely with better and more effective methods. The public is spending more in the effort to discover how the work can be done better. The potential includes a more effective introduction not only to the skills and academic areas of learning, but also to a meaningful life of responsible choice, creative problem solving, and effective skills founded in insightful understanding. This chapter adds the even more important concept that early childhood education can make a major contribution to the child's developing sense of personal and interpersonal values.

The potential is there. The actuality is probably closer to the potential in more of early childhood education than on any other level. How far the mark is actually missed, no one can say for sure. Many factors contribute to the present problems in America. As John Holt has pointed out so eloquently, schools are not necessarily good for children.[14] When the assumption is made that early childhood education is automatically good, it is a tragedy. Dullness drives children within themselves or to escape in the street. Pressure can lead to even greater disaster. It will take the best efforts of many if the actuality is to approach the potential.

Summary

Schools do not bear the sole responsibility for transmitting and refining the values of a society. Nevertheless, they cannot escape a major responsibility for the lives of children. Other learnings without a basically sound value system may lead to brighter criminals, not to a better society. On the early childhood level the transmission and development of values grow out of the problems of classroom living, but this involves a teacher who is concerned about her personal value system, respects other views, and is alert to opportunities to support children in their search for meaning in life. Children may be exposed to values, but values cannot be imposed on them. They are better exemplified by a teacher who respects children than taught by precept. They can only be understood and accepted gradually—and in the child's terms of reference.

[14] John Holt, "School Is Bad for Children," *The Saturday Evening Post,* 242 (February 1969), 12–15.

CHAPTER FIFTEEN

Guidance: Direct and Indirect

Jean E. Mizer has written a valuable article for the beginning teacher in the format of an interchange of letters between a beginning teacher and the author. The teacher is concerned about a boy in her class who was disruptive.[1] Mizer gives the usual "good advice" about studying the student's records, and the teacher writes back that although all the records indicate a normal youngster, the trouble persists and grows worse. Mizer replies with the further suggestion that the teacher find an appropriate time and place and ask the student why he is acting as he is. Then he relates a story that is pertinent to our chapter.

One time in our school we had a little boy who refused to leave the first grade. He had done well, seemed mature, had adjusted well, and all the rest. But the first day of his second year he ran back to the first-grade room, clung frantically to a desk, and howled defiance at being removed. For a week we held parent conferences. The school counselor called in the school psychologist. We had much hushed discussion in the hall. Finally I blundered out on the playground and stopped one of the child's buddies. "What do you think is wrong with Jimmie that he won't go on into the second grade with you?"

"Why don't you ask him?" he queried levelly.

I did. Jimmie looked at me wide-eyed. "I have to stay here," he explained in the patient tone one uses in talking with someone not so bright. "My little sister

[1] Jean E. Mizer, "Special Feature on the Beginning Teacher: Dear JM . . . ," *Today's Education*, 57 (1968), 21–25.

is starting the first grade and I have to take care of her. That little kid couldn't even find the bathroom by herself unless I was here to show her."[2]

The story stands by itself though this chapter does not reflect merely the implications of the above account. The possibilities involved in the cooperation with a school counselor are indicated, but the focus is on the work of the teacher. The title of this chapter, "Guidance: Direct and Indirect," reflects a philosophy of guidance that in working with young children one is concerned about the child and how best to help him—not with a technique or theory of counseling. Sometimes this is best accomplished by working directly with a child. Sometimes consulting with parents may be more profitable. Often a counselor, or other individual acting in this capacity, works both directly with the child and with others who are in a position to influence behaviors in ways not available to the counselor.

The chapter belongs in this section of the book for guidance is concerned with *goals and perspectives*. It also relates to the chapters following, in particular, Chapter 16, *Working With and Through Parents*.

The Teacher and the Guidance Program

Guidance for the young child is not simply good teaching. Good teaching includes a guidance function, but this does not imply that good teaching alone will meet every need of even a well-adjusted child.

Helen Heffernan in her book *Guiding the Young Child*[3] published in 1959 simply wrote of good teaching for young children, not of specific guidance procedures. It is only recently that educators of young children have advocated specific guidance for young children by trained specialists. Previously almost the only guidance provided on the level of the young child was by the teacher. At the end of the 1960s a change not only in attitude but also in practice is evident. June and Harold Shane point out:

As recently as 1965 one could find almost no "new guidance" programs in primary and middle schools. Now, however, with governmental funds to lubricate the machinery of expansion, and with incandescent new interest in childhood (especially early childhood), the emphasis on providing guidance services at an early age has become little short of spectacular.[4]

This does not mean that the full range of possible guidance services are provided for every school or even that a counselor of any kind is as yet available in every school—or even most schools. Nor does it mean that where such a program is available, it is fully functional or adequate. The

[2] *Ibid.*, pp. 21–22.
[3] Helen Heffernan, *Guiding the Young Child* (Lexington, Mass.: Heath, 1959).
[4] June Grant Shane and Harold G. Shane, "Guidance at an Early Age," *Today's Education*, 58 (1969), 37–38.

concept of elementary guidance is not new, but the emphasis is. George Hill and Eleanore Luckey have written an illuminating book on guidance in elementary schools.[5] One of their concerns is the title for the guidance person who serves on the elementary level. They assume that the recommendation of the joint committee of the Association for Counselor Education and Supervision and the American School Counselor Association that the elementary guidance person be called School Counselor will gain acceptance.[6] It is of more concern that the literature of the past several years has abounded with discussion of what the counselor should do. At a minimum, the new emphasis has made clear that teaching is not the whole of guidance. Though it may remain true for some time that the teacher will provide most of the guidance available in some schools.

Whatever the circumstances, no teacher is expected to play the role of a trained therapist; neither is the school counselor. Both, in their own sphere and on the levels of their competencies, serve the developing needs of children. Both sometimes provide services that may be considered therapeutic, but neither is expected to be a psychiatrist or, for that matter, a fully qualified psychologist. There are, however, differences in the work of the teacher and the counselor, and these differences can make the competent counselor of significant help to teachers and pupils.

How the Program Helps the Teacher

The counselor can serve children in a number of ways, but some of his functions appear to overlap the guidance functions of a good teacher. Both may listen to, seek to understand, and confer with individual pupils. Here the counselor is not competing but supplementing the work of the teacher. In this and in the other services of the counselor there are many possibilities of helping the teacher to accomplish her purposes for the academic and personal growth of her students.

For the sake of both counselor and teacher it is important to correct two possible misunderstandings. The counselor's office is not a place in which a child is "straightened out." The counselor is not the disciplinarian of the school. To be placed in this role reduces his potential as an agent of change. If "discipline" simply meant punishment, almost anyone else could do the job more effectively than the trained counselor. Counselors are needed because discipline in this limited sense has not been effective in meeting the needs of children. The other misunderstanding pictures the counselor as a miracle worker. Sometimes miracles do happen when a counselor is called in, but counseling is usually an involved process and one that does not necessarily give immediate results.

[5] George E. Hill and Eleanore Braun Luckey, *Guidance for Children in Elementary Schools* (New York: Appleton-Century-Crofts, 1969), p. 101.

[6] ACES-ASCA Joint Committee on the Elementary School Counselor, *Report,* April 2, 1966 (Washington, D. C.: American Personnel and Guidance Association). Mimeographed.

A counselor was the recipient of both misunderstandings with reference to one small boy. George was not doing well in school work and was proving a disruptive influence. The teacher sent him to the counselor and then reported that "George was better for fifteen minutes" and a little later that George was as "bad as ever today!" The counselor, knowing something of the causes for George's behavior, had a conference with the mother and also arranged for both mother and father to talk with a psychologist. George's parents were separated, in the process of getting a divorce, and using George as the tool against each other. This story has a happy conclusion, but it did not come about in the time the teacher seemed willing to allocate. Over the months the parents did reach an understanding and reconciliation, and George's behavior and interest changed.

Perhaps, this illustrates what is meant by the title of the chapter. Sometimes a teacher can help a child herself; this would be classified as direct guidance. Sometimes she helps by referring to a counselor or other appropriate person; she then is giving indirect guidance. The counselor, himself, may find it necessary to refer to more highly trained specialists. He may also find it advantageous to work with a child by indirect means. Sometimes parents can be helped by a suggestion.

Sometimes the counselor can assist teachers who in their closeness to a situation have overlooked a possible course of action. Still another avenue of help by the counselor for the teacher is possible. When the teacher is troubled about a child, talk with the counselor even when he can offer no satisfactory solution can be of much value. One counselor remembers a teacher who regularly stopped by his office to pour out her concern for various students. Time always ran out before any suggestions could have been offered if the counselor had so desired. Still, the teacher seemed to go away strengthened for another week. Other situations have arisen over the years in which teachers have found themselves involved in serious difficulties and have found help in talking with a concerned counselor who could be trusted to maintain confidence.

No teacher should expect more of herself than it is possible to give, nor should she assume burdens and responsibilities beyond her capacities. A teacher can be very effective in "guiding" the young child. In so doing she makes as full use as possible of such guidance services as are available. The most enlightened and capable classroom teachers will be the ones who make effective use of the services of the counselor. They will use the available program, support it, and seek to strengthen it if it is adequate.

Even with a fully effective, organized guidance program, there will be need for the teacher to use all her own resources. For most children the teacher remains the most important guidance person in the school.

What follows in no wise contradicts anything previously stated. It is an attempt to emphasize those activities in guidance that especially concern the teacher.

Guidance as Part of Teaching

In this section we shall examine some of the suggestions made in other chapters with regard to teaching the young child and indicate the relationship between the suggested teaching practices and guidance.

Providing Successful Experiences

It is basic to the present and future happiness of an individual that he develop a concept of himself as a successful person. This should be a realistic concept. It is harmful when the child feels he must be better than other children in everything. Sooner or later he will find himself in a situation in which he is not the best. Much of success and all of failure should be related to what can realistically be expected. Failure should never, for the young child, be emphasized as failure to perform as well as or better than another child.

The personal relationship of the teacher to each pupil can never be entirely separated from the total classroom experience and should not be. The emphasis here, however, is on the more general attitudes and actions of the teacher of young children. For even in the midst of an ongoing class program, the teacher should maintain attitudes that are in harmony with a guidance perspective.

There are certain basic attitudes that show through in the work of the guidance-oriented teacher. One is an acceptance of the nature and needs of children. There is the further concern to make activities—class, group, or individual—meaningful and within the range of interest and competency of the children. In a sense, the entire group is provided with successful experience. There is an emphasis on both how much the group is learning and on how much individuals within the group are gaining. Part of this concern shows through in providing for group activities in which children of varied abilities can make worthwhile contribution. Thus the teacher organizes the classroom activities in such a way that the children can experience success much of the time. In addition, she sets up the organization of the class program so that each child will have the opportunity to show his own special ability.

The foregoing must be within the realm of reality. Pretense has its place in the life of a child, but only when all involved are pretending for the fun and stimulus of imaginative effort. One does not pretend that children are better than they are. The emphasis, the tone of the class, is on present and potential success, not on the lacks and failures. The counselor is primarily concerned with building from strength.[7] So, also, is the "counseling-oriented" classroom teacher as she functions in the classroom activities.

[7] See Oscar C. Christensen, "Education: A Model for Counseling in the Elementary School," *Elementary School Guidance and Counseling*, 4 (1969), 13.

Expression

A child develops as a self-reliant person as he is permitted and encouraged to make choices and to accept responsibility for those choices. Choice should always be within limits, and it always carries some measure of responsibility. Helping children become aware of the limits and responsibilities of choice is guidance too. Chiefly, however, the teacher contributes to development of self-esteem and self-determination as she permits meaningful decisions in the classroom.

Creative activities, in the broad meaning of the term, and the solution of problems are conducive to growing skills and confidence. They perform another valuable function if through them the child comes to realize that life usually contains alternatives. The neurotic individual tends to see either only one possibility or two extreme possibilities—both bad. The creative problem solver finds numerous possible approaches; thus his chances of success with both present and future problems are enhanced. Much of counseling consists in assisting individuals to evaluate their alternatives. The teacher of young children has a tremendous opportunity to make such evaluation habitual.

A person may obtain release from his anxieties, fears, anger, and other emotions through creative activities. Children from the nursery school age on can find some form of artistic experience that permits them to express their fears and other emotions. The child who is inhibited may be the one who most enjoys and seems to profit the most from the freedom of finger painting, for example. Depending on the level of developing abilities, children can find a safe outlet for emotions in free expressive movement, as in music, in dance, in making rhymes, in drawing "something funny," in writing a story, or in acting out a role. In encouraging such activities the teacher does not assume any role not rightfully her's as a teacher. She may in her observation of any of these activities, gather hints of the nature of children's needs. The emphasis here is that there is release and sometimes a kind of learning "to feel free" in the expression of emotions through creative activities. This is one of the goals counselors and therapists often seek in working with individuals. The teacher without stepping out of her rightful position may sometimes encourage this attitude. She accomplishes much earlier in the child's life that which might later require extensive professional help.

Identification

Feelings are involved in all kinds of identification. Many forms of identification—with teacher, with friend, with group, with class—enter into the normal development of wholesome children. Any one of these forms of identification can go beyond the normal, but such is not usually the case.

Identification is not only normal, but necessary to development. Here we are concerned with the identification of children with the characters in stories in their literature. To so identify possibly begins even earlier than nursery school—and should never end. All of us need some safe escape techniques, and the escape of losing oneself in a story is usually wholesome. For the young child there is almost always identification with a character in the story: man, animal, or object. Very frequently the child will see a relationship between his own problem and the character's problem in the story. "That," children will say, "happened to me, too." The stories offer possible solutions, and given the chance, a child may see an application to some of his "unvoiced" problems. Insight into problems and solutions is a purpose in many counseling relationships. In the work of the competent teacher this insight is permitted to develop naturally and easily.

Discussion

Given an opportunity, children will talk to the teacher and to each other. They will often talk freely about things that are important to them. Adults have to learn to do this. Realistically, the adult knows that he cannot talk about everything with everybody. The young child must learn this, but the lesson should not be stressed too early or too rigorously. While the child is in the process of learning whatever he needs to learn about necessary cautions, he can also learn that there are people who will listen with respect to what he has to say. Children, with little help, learn the equivalent of adult "brain storming." As they develop in maturity, they learn to contribute what they can to problem solving. Group counseling, which requires much skill with adolescents, may come with relative ease and naturalness when young children trust their teacher. The teacher is a part of the discussion group, but not a dominant part. She is permitting the children to help each other with the questions and problems they face.

Relaxation

Teachers of young children have known and used techniques to relax their classes over the years. With the pressures of recent times, the principle "Easy does it" has sometimes been forgotten. There come times in teaching when either excitement or weariness makes learning difficult or impossible. Something to change the pace is called for. The child who has come up against a block in learning is in special need of change from whatever tension may be preventing perception. Whenever any child passes beyond the stage of eagerness to the stage of pressure and nervousness, he is more likely to respond poorly in all situations.

The following is taken from a mimeographed booklet provided for the teachers of Contra Costa County, California, in 1949.

There is no child, and no teacher, who could not work more effectively and more happily with greater relaxation. There is no lesson that would not be more effective, more fun, and remembered longer with greater relaxation. There is no difficult day that might not have been more productive and less tiring, and happier, with more relaxation.

Quiet body—Quiet thinking—Quiet speaking

That is the order of relaxation and the motto for any nervous person who desires to be less nervous in speech and in manner and more effective in living. It is the essential "must" for quieting the disorganized, jittery minds and bodies of difficult children. Obviously, it is most important for those children—and grown-ups—who need it most, but there is no person who cannot profit by its wisdom. And the teacher who sees in relaxation an essential educational tool, has within her hands a boundless treasure of strength in directing her own energies and the energies of the children who are in her care.[8]

These seem strong words, but there is much truth in them. A light touch works best with small children in almost all situations. A time to quiet down and relax is especially good for children who have gone out of control. A period of rest with soft music is essential as a counterbalance for more active endeavors.

The booklet quoted speaks of relaxation as an overall attitude toward life and problems that the children can "catch" from the teacher. It also suggests that being relaxed is relative rather than absolute. It is not something that happens automatically. Teachers may have to teach themselves and their children how to relax. They may have to search for techniques that will work with a particular group of children. Included in the booklet are the kinds of poems and songs that most teachers collect over the years. One that is fun and highly "suggestive" follows:

The Quiet Time

Your feet have done so much for you—
(Jumped and skipped and run for you!)
Give them a chance to rest for you!
Play that they are sleeping. . . .
(Quiet feet are sleeping. . . .)

Your hands have done so much for you—
(Carried and lifted and thrown for you!)
Give them a chance to rest for you!
Play that they are sleeping. . . .
(Quiet hands are sleeping. . . .)

Your eyes have done so much for you—
(Looked and looked and looked for you!)

[8] B. O. Wilson, *On Relaxation* (Martinez, Calif.: Contra Costa Community Schools, 1949). Mimeographed, p. 1.

Give them a chance to rest for you!
Play that they are sleeping. . . .
(Quiet eyes are sleeping. . . .)

Your body does so much for you—
(Lives and sings and shouts for you!)
Give it a chance to rest for you!
Play that it is sleeping. . . .
(All your body sleeping. . . .)[9]

Any child who responds to such a poem, or the many like it, will not only be more likely to continue into the next minutes under adequate self-control, but while he is resting may be open to a few words of encouragement and direction. The relaxed adult or child can accept ideas that he might not consider when too wrapped up in other matters.

Meaningful Fun

One afternoon a third-grade boy shocked his mother with the statement, "You know, Mrs. Smith is the sneakiest teacher I know!" The mother knew that Mrs. Smith had a good reputation because of her innovative teaching. She also thought that the boy liked her. As a matter of fact, he did, as his explanation made clear. The enlightening statement was, "You know, we play and play and play all day. Then when you think about it, you realize you've worked yourself to death."

Meaningful fun is part of a broader concept than fun and games. It may include the inherent drive in the normal child that leads him to seek learning and may also include the excitement that can accompany even very directive school work. The whole range of activities that makes learning something to be desired and achieved is related to guidance. Realistically, not all learning will be enjoyable. Eventually, the individual must discover that some things he would prefer not to do must be done, but early childhood education need not be of this nature.

Even tasks that could be dull can sometimes be turned into an interesting "game." One might paraphrase Longfellow and say that into each life some drill must come, but add that much of the drill can be made entertaining. Purposeful drill may increase learning; children learning skills may enjoy practicing them. When they do not, the teacher can frequently turn the dull into exciting fun. Learning is most effective when it is enjoyed. If a teacher can turn what might be an unpleasant experience into a happy one, she has performed an important guidance function. If she imbues her class with the attitude that what appears dull or unpleasant when approached constructively can become challenging and exciting, there has been very effective guidance. The teacher has armed her pupils with a means to overcome the monotony of some phases of life.

[9] *Ibid.*, p. 12.

Guidance as Personal Concern

There is no clear-cut distinction between the guidance functions of the teacher in relation to the entire class and to individual pupils. All will need her personal attention many times during the course of a school year. With some this concern need be little more than an acceptance of the child as a unique human being of worth and importance. The child will usually make satisfactory progress and adjustment within the security of a wholesome classroom atmosphere. No child should be lost in the crowd, but neither will every child be cause for detailed study.

Acceptance and Concern

To speak of acceptance and concern on the part of the teacher seems trite in this "enlightened" age. However, a considerable body of literature in education indicates that these attitudes are not universal. More direct testimony could be produced both from personal contact and from reports. An advanced class of undergraduate education majors witnessed a film depicting a teacher's understanding of individual differences. Many of these college students had spent several days at the opening of the school year observing classroom procedures in schools in their hometowns. "Why," they asked, "isn't it like this in the schools?" "Go to the teacher's lounge," they added, "and listen to the teachers. Not one of them seems to be concerned to understand why students act as they do. What they do is 'cut down' their students." Not a single college student dissented from this report of teacher reactions.

Perhaps, it is not surprising that all teachers do not exhibit the traits that are taken for granted. Much study in counselor education is devoted to the concept of accepting the individual as he is. The objective is to help the counselor distinguish between behavior that may be objectionable and the individual as a person. The teacher has less training in acceptance and tolerance. Furthermore, she is in more direct and annoying contact with certain behaviors. She may feel threatened if she admits that the pupil could be helped while at the same time realizing that she does not appear to be successful. Acceptance is not routine or easy. In the classroom it is important.

Understanding

Acceptance and concern are sometimes enough. Years ago in a western suburban school there was one black boy in a kindergarten class. The children in the class came from the immediate neighborhood. One afternoon two white girls lingered for a while and asked to kiss the teacher good-bye. In the background was the little black boy. "Teacher," he asked, "could I kiss you, too?" The teacher accepted the kiss with appreciation. The boy, then, ran off toward home as fast as his legs could carry him. He never made the request again, but his attitude in the class was different. He became a happy, involved group member. Seemingly, a simple demonstration of acceptance gave added confidence and security.

More often, acceptance must be balanced by a search for better understanding. Understanding does not replace acceptance; the two go on at the same time. Parents and teachers need to observe their children through "rose-colored" glasses—looking for good, emphasizing the best, and seeing the potential. But sometimes both parents and teachers need to take a look through very clear glasses at the child as he is with his needs and problems. The acceptance and concern remain, but they can become more effective through more complete understanding.

This chapter will not go into detail about the study of records, though these can be of value. Information about family and health, for example, may be important clues to causes of behavior. Test results may be helpful. No single item of information should be considered as more than a possible clue. It is too easy to use test results, family background, or other information as an excuse for giving up on a child.

A teacher should not jump to conclusions on the basis of limited observation. It is important that she learn to watch for hints as to possible causes of behavior. Art, writing, stories, dramatic play, free play, construction, and most other forms of behavior give clues as to the fears, problems, and hopes of children. Listening to children is an invaluable source of information. Sometimes a solution may be disclosed as directly as that in the opening illustration of this chapter. Children often speak very frankly in the hearing of teachers and directly to teachers. They can seldom give explanations. The teacher must combine these clues with those already at her disposal. A teacher once asked a six-year-old boy, "Why did you do that?" He looked up startled and puzzled. In all honesty he replied, "I don't know, teacher. I don't know!"

Probably it is best that anyone working with other individuals keep in mind the limits of knowledge and the complexities of people. Within all the limits of the situation and within her limits, the teacher seeks as clear a picture as she can obtain. She keeps her mind open to new insights. Her vision is never perfect and is always colored by her own background and experience. Knowing this and accepting it reduces distortion. Knowledge is never complete. Knowledge about changing children can never be fixed. But the teacher can come to understand much about a child if she studies, observes, checks with others, and thinks about the clues discovered.

Possibilities

As acceptance is sometimes all that may be needed, so understanding may be almost all that is needed. Understanding is never quite enough, but sometimes it indicates a simple change in techniques that will help. Usually, the good teacher will arrive at one or a series of "hunches"—hypotheses. Where there is a functioning guidance program, the teacher may seek consultation. Children can, also, be given the privilege of talking with the counselor, to whom they have long before been introduced. He may work with the child, suggest other approaches, or support the teacher in her work with the child.

The teacher may decide that the problem is one that she can work with best in the classroom. If she does, it will again be on the basis of what might be of possible help and safe to attempt. She will want to give her theory a chance to work, but will not "be stuck" with it. If one idea does not prove effective, others may.

The Teacher as an Agent of Change

Indirectly, the title for this section comes from the work of two behavioral therapists, E. Lakin Phillips and Daniel Wiener.[10] Their book is not recommended to the teacher who has had only an introduction to counseling and advanced psychology. It is addressed to professional therapists in training. One of the ideas presented, however, can be effectively employed in the classroom. Phillips and Wiener contend that help very often can best be provided, not by long-range counseling sessions, but by finding an individual who is in daily contact with the child and working through him.

The teacher is one such possible person. She is in contact with a child for many hours each week. She cannot give her whole attention to one child, but she may be in a position to keep more of the child's behavior under observation than anyone else, including the parent. What she does can be very important.

Depending on what is involved, the teacher will either have sought assistance or will have acted on her own. Which she does should depend on the nature of the problem. For example, cleanliness can be a problem. Bruno Bettelheim points out that he would be more concerned about a four-year-old who felt compelled to stay clean or compelled to get dirty than the child who was simply indifferent to dirt.[11] Essential cleanliness for the normal youngster is handled with tact, good nature, but effectively in the nursery school as in the home. It is not considered a problem. The problem may come with the child who is afraid to get dirty. The teacher may help the child break through some repressions if he sees her get her own hands dirty in finger paint or modeling clay. Sometimes a longer-range program is needed. A child may need to watch other children for a time. A word of explanation as to when it is right to get one's hands dirty may help. Smocks that keep

[10] E. Lakin Phillips and Daniel N. Wiener, *Short-Term Psychotherapy and Structured Behavior Change* (New York: McGraw-Hill, 1966).

[11] Bruno Bettelheim, "Reading the Signs of Mental Health," in Michael S. Auleta (ed.), *Foundations of Early Childhood Education: Readings* (New York: Random House, 1969), pp. 78–79.

clothes clean make a transition easier for the child. Perhaps the child and teacher will need to work gradually toward solutions.

Many child development specialists, including L. Joseph Stone and Joseph Church, point out that many children when they are seven or eight years of age take things from the mother's purse.[12] This is not behavior to be encouraged, but neither is it usually, at this age, behavior indicating deep emotional disturbance. When such behavior is exhibited in the classroom, the teacher does not label the child a thief or conclude that a psychiatrist is needed. Long-range effective growth in behavior is called for—the teacher's problem is how can she assist in this.

The teacher accepts, observes, listens to, and communicates with the children. Sometimes she suggests and reminds them to practice alternative behaviors. Other times she simply rewards more appropriate behavior and so far as is possible ignores the undesirable, or she may plan a long-range attack that rewards slight changes in behavior that may eventually build toward major change. Sometimes she studies cycles of behavior trying to find the point at which intervention can be most effective. And then, she may simply change her own behavior in some respect. Always, she wonders if change is required and if it is, how can she assist the child in meeting the problems that he is facing.

Summary

Help for the teacher in her efforts to meet the guidance needs of children is increasingly being provided. As they become available, the teacher will support and use guidance personnel. With or without help the teacher of young children is engaged in guidance. She organizes her classroom activities to provide the support and encouragement children need in developing as competent, confident individuals. She listens to and observes all children, but may give particular study and attention to certain pupils. Acceptance and concern for children are always appropriate, but objectivity and strategies to help may also be necessary. The latter may include simple changes in procedures, discussions, or even long-range planning for gradual change in behavior patterns.

---

[12] L. Joseph Stone and Joseph Church, *Childhood and Adolescence: A Psychology of the Growing Person* (New York: Random House, 1968), pp. 543–544.

materials and resources

Nature wants children to be children before they are men.
If we deliberately pervert this order, we shall get premature
fruits which are neither ripe nor well flavored
and which soon decay. . . .
Childhood has ways of seeing, thinking, and feeling,
peculiar to itself, nothing can be more foolish
than to substitute our ways for them.
Jean Jacques Rousseau, The New Heloise

1 2 3
4 5 6

Materials and Resources: Principles and Practices

The final section in the text differents from the preceding sections in at least one way. Each of the preceding sections deals with concepts that appear to be in contrast. A major purpose underlying the discussions in these sections was to attempt to find a meeting ground between the concepts stated. No such contrast is intended in the final section. Insofar as there is any form of contrast, it is that in discussing resources the emphasis is on people; the materials are equipment and supplies.

In a sense the difference between this section and those which precede it is more in the title than in the content. Each of the other sections dealt with concepts that were primarily philosophic, but they also considered the practical outworkings of the philosophy suggested. In this section the basic philosophy remains that presented throughout the text. Materials and resources are important, not to make a good impression, but to provide opportunity for choice, problem solving, and creative experience, and to make possible the acquisition of skills and insight. Such a philosophy lends itself to a climate in which the child is more likely to clarify his goals and develop wholesome perspectives on life's problems.

Practical Considerations

The purposes of this section are practical. This is true in spite of the fact that there are many complications in the present social situation. The polarization within American society, the long delayed but still difficult problems of integration, the very practical problems of poverty, sometimes accompanied by filth, disease, crime, and associated evils, make some of the high flown rhetoric about home-school cooperation appear unrealistic. Schools exist in a rapidly changing world and society. In some places these changes involve desperate need for the most basic of school equipment: decent housing. Even this may appear impossible to achieve because of related conditions and attitudes.

The authors are well aware of the limitations under which many teachers work. Some ideas are in open conflict with other widely held concepts. If these are skirted in the text, it is because there is no certain remedy that can be suggested. Other ideas may be practical and relevant but beyond the scope of this text.

The School

Nothing, however, is more practical than the fact that every teacher works within a school setting. Even so, she is never fully limited by this setting. The teacher who is to continue teaching, however, must maintain at least a nominal working relationship with administration and with fellow teachers. In the school of the future,[1] it will be imperative that the teacher be able to work effectively as an educator-executive[2] in close association with equals, assistants, and superiors.

Parents

Too often schoolteachers, particularly new teachers, fear parents. Too often parents are only called into consultation when something is "wrong with Johnny." Too often parents are burdened with helping in their children's school work. Too often parents cause difficulties by creating pressures that work to the disadvantage of their own children. Most of the time teachers and parents can work together in a much happier relationship, each helping the other to understand and assist the child.[3]

---

[1] Harold G. Shane and June Grant Shane, "Forecast for the 70's," *Today's Education*, 58 (1969), 29–32.

[2] Joe L. Frost and G. Thomas Rowland, "The Seventies: A Time For Giant Steps," *Childhood Education*, 46 (1969), 4–13.

[3] Association for Childhood Education International, *Parents-Children-Teachers: Communication* (Washington, D. C.: ACEI, 1969).

The Community

The work of the school under normal conditions is supported by and supplemented by the work of the community. This mutual support is never complete, and neither school nor community are so perfect that they always function to provide the best possible environment for the child. In an imperfect world there is still the possibility of mutual support and of supplementary services. Even in very imperfect communities with far from ideal school conditions, the school and other strengthening agencies can cooperate for the good of children.[4]

Principles Involved

Children and Teachers Need and Deserve the Best

It is basic to the philosophy of the text that all children are important. More than once it has been indicated that if children are important, then early childhood education is the most important field in all of education. Children on this level deserve the best. Teachers need the best materials in order to teach effectively. All the special services of school and community should be available to the young child. Money should be available for the relatively inexpensive supplies. The equivalent of the price of textbooks on the upper levels would go far toward adequately equipping the early grades of school.

Teachers Need to Recognize Their Own Limitations

This is true for all persons; it is the weak man who must claim to be strong in every way. No teacher, alone, is able to do everything for every child. She needs all the resources of school and community. She certainly needs the cooperation of parents. She can improve her work by becoming a part of an effective team of teachers, specialists, and other interested persons. The effective teaching of young children is a big enough job to involve everyone.

Teachers Should Be Willing to Accept and Give Help

In an earlier chapter it was suggested that the new teacher should not enter with too much crusading zeal into a strange situation. She does well to listen, learn, and ask for help when help is needed. In a sense, the previous paragraph is being restated. The teacher should not hesitate to seek the help of superiors and experts as to suggestions for understanding and assisting the child who is not making progress in school. There is an opposite reaction that

[4] Lois V. Edinger, "Schools for the Seventies and Beyond," *Today's Education*, 58 (1969), 74–75.

comes from some teachers. They are heard to say, "I learned the hard way; let him do the same." There is a difference between pushing an idea and being willing to share it. All of us together know far too little to help some children.

Teachers Should Set Examples in Cooperation

Far more than any other person that one can think of, the teacher of young children should set an example in willingness to work with others. Early childhood is a period when children are learning what it means to compromise, to get along, to work together. Some otherwise fine teachers make no contact with fellow teachers or the public. As in all of life, the teacher teaches cooperation by attitude and action more effectively than by "dictate."

The Teacher Should Be Alert to Possibilities

Under the best of circumstances it takes a while to discover what the possibilities in any given school situation are. Some orientation programs are much better than others. Even with the best possible program, however, few teachers can grasp all the intricacies of a program designed to offer help. Printed material is valuable but it explains how things are supposed to work. What actually happens may be different. Perhaps this introduction should have been headed: Materials, Resources, and Resourcefulness. The teacher will keep her eyes and ears open, ask for answers to particular problems of anyone who can help, recognize that methods of operation change even while she is learning the present situation. The teacher keeps alert. If she does and keeps looking, there is almost always some way of finding help for any child's problem.

Summary

This introduces a section that brings together two equally important ideas. One is the value of understanding and using resource people available in the school and community, the most important of whom are the parents of the children. It emphasizes equally the importance of adequate materials for the work at hand.

CHAPTER SIXTEEN

Working With and Through Parents

"Could you come to our house for dinner?" The invitation came as a surprise to the student teacher. Momentarily, she had mixed emotions. Since she had been teaching in the class as a student teacher, she had been concerned for the boy who had invited her. She could not help but notice that he was poorly and carelessly dressed and that he had little interest in his school activities. She had heard about his family and that very morning had been told about the circumstances that probably had prompted the invitation. The meal to which she was invited would not be prepared for the occasion. The night before this "lower-class" family had attempted to celebrate a silver wedding anniversary. They had made extensive preparations and invited neighbors, but almost no one came. The student teacher, who had a deep concern for children, was glad for the opportunity to get to know the boy better. She wanted to see his home and meet his parents, but she had misgivings about going for a meal. Her reply, however, was, "Of course, I'll come, and may I bring a friend?"

She and her friend enjoyed the evening. They accepted their hosts and surroundings on the family's terms. If the rules of etiquette and the English spoken were not theirs, they showed no signs of it. Neither of the young people made any attempt to instruct the parents on any subject or in any way. They simply gave of themselves and their friendship. The results were spectacular. The boy who had invited the student teacher came alive in the days that followed. His attitude toward school improved, and his skills developed. The attitude of the home toward the school changed too. The student teacher changed at least as much. The experience seemed to give her increased assurance and enthusiasm.

Not every home-school contact proves this effective in improving relationships. The optimum school environment is one where insofar as possible parents and teachers know each other, like each other, and cooperate for the best interests of children. In the past the practice of the teacher "boarding around" did establish a personal relationship between the teacher and the community. Times have changed and community and school relations too. Most of the changes have been for the good. But one problem that has developed, probably the major one, is the tendency for the school to become remote from the home. A newer problem is the opposite extreme. Fairly often, now, the teacher's problem may be not how to break through silent barriers, but how to hear what is behind the shouting and the demonstrating. As Lois Edinger mentions, "This is an age of confrontation."[1]

That latter point is made almost continually by the newspapers, the popular magazines, TV and radio, and even by the most scholarly of journals. Underneath the apparent differences the problem is still very much the same. It is that of *finding effective ways of communicating and cooperating in order to combine parent and teacher power on behalf of children.*

Understanding Parents

The present topic is in itself broad enough to involve a chapter, or a book, or a lifetime of study. The suggestions made must be oversimplifications, but they should prove useful.

From years of talking with parents the authors have concluded that almost regardless of who they are—doctor, lawyer, short-order cook, or housewife—most parents fear the teacher. They retain traces of an image of themselves as helpless children under the domination of the all-powerful teacher. This may be true even though their teachers were excellent and their school experience satisfactory. The teacher was someone who was in charge. The parent may have grown larger than the teacher; his position in life may be superior to the teacher's. Still when he walks into the classroom to talk with his child's teacher, some of the old feeling of inferiority tends to surface. This feeling may be exhibited in a wide range of behaviors, from excessive cordiality to verbal attack. Whether or not this is, or remains true, there will undoubtedly be reactions caused by school experiences.

What this means to the teacher is that whatever the nature of the conference with the parent, the first consideration is to put the parent at ease. A quiet spot away from all children is necessary, but even more important is

---

[1] Lois V. Edinger, "Schools for the Seventies and Beyond," *Today's Education,* 58 (1969), 74.

an interest in the parent, an honest attempt to understand what he is saying and why, a sincere respect, and a feeling that somewhere underneath any apparent differences is a mutual concern for the child.

Parents Are People

Most parents are well-meaning. They love, care for, and do the best they can for their children. Consequently, they are ready to cooperate in almost any reasonable way with the school and teacher. Often they feel overly inadequate. They may need reassurance. Sometimes it helps to let them know that the parent who enjoys his children and tries to do the right things for and with them will usually be successful. Such parents may make many mistakes, as may teachers, without stunting the development of the child. Being a parent involves privileges, pleasures, some hardships, many responsibilities. It should make life richer and the parent wiser and more dependable. Probably parents are better people because they are parents.

Parents Are Important

All parents differ, but all are individuals of special importance to the teacher. A bulletin published by the Colorado State Department of Education states:

The teacher needs to feel the importance of parents. To assume that all parents are seeking the best education possible for their child helps a teacher to build a successful relationship with parents. Being a parent is not easy and a teacher must have an appreciation of the job.

The same bulletin goes on to state, however:

Parents are as different as children. There are differences in communities, in socioeconomic status and educational level as well as the myriad of differences in individuals. There is the timid parent, the defensive, the rejecting, the accepting, the adequate, the overprotective and the ambitious. . . . The beginning is the same with all types—a warm accepting approach.[2]

Some Parents Need Special Help

Occasionally every teacher will meet a parent with whom she is not prepared to work. She can maintain a cordial attitude. She may, nevertheless, need to refer some parents to people or other agencies for more help than she can give. Not many parents are brutal, but in any given year there are thousands of cases of child abuse of various kinds reported in the papers. Some people are not equipped emotionally or otherwise to be parents. In some areas of the nation the problems are more frequent and intense. David Wilkerson is a minister who went to New York City to attempt to help a specific group of boys who were charged with murder. The outgrowth was an extensive youth

[2] Colorado State Department of Education, *Kindergarten Guidebook* (Denver: State Department of Education, 1960), pp. 140, 141.

program. He wrote of more recent experiences in *The Little People.*[3] Much of the book deals with the plight of children whose parents are drug addicts. One situation he reports is not necessarily associated with drugs. Wilkerson had gone home with a street gang leader and was leaving the house with the boy when he noticed something.

I had almost overlooked the only occupants who had stayed behind. They were so small, so still, that I walked by them without seeing them. Then I turned back. There on a lumpy sofa in a dingy room sat a little girl and a little boy, following me with their eyes, but not moving a single muscle of their bodies.

"Hello," I said, crouching down. "Who are you?"

They pulled back from me and their eyes narrowed. The little girl lifted her hand to protect her tiny face. I was ashamed. Never in all my life had I frightened a child.

Miguel had come back to me. "C'mon" he said impatiently, not even speaking to the children.

"Who are they, Miguel?"

He laughed. "I guess you could call them my 'brother' and 'sister'—the newest ones."

"But they're scared to death!"

"That's because my mother beats them if they make a move outa this room" he said. . . .

"Who takes care of them?"

"You gotta be kidding, preacher! Who's gonna stay in this dump all day?"[4]

Time magazine had an article on children entitled "The Battering Parent."[5] It reported on studies at the University of Colorado that found that in all cases of child abuse investigated the parent who had inflicted damage on his child had himself suffered similar abuse by his own parent. C. Henry Kempe, chairman of the Colorado Department of Pediatrics, believes that such parents are not basically monsters, but people in extreme need of help. Kempe and those working with him have found that they could best provide help for the child by working with the parents. In some cases this has almost amounted to moving into the home and serving as a surrogate parent for the parent. They report that the treatment is effective. They have found no repeaters among parents treated. Such situations are beyond the capabilities of the classroom teacher.

Understanding the Individual Parent

It has already been implied that understanding means more than understanding about parents.[6] Ideally every teacher should know each parent

[3] David Wilkerson, *The Little People* (New York: Pyramid Books, 1966).

[4] *Ibid.*, p. 180.

[5] *Time*, November 7, 1969, pp. 77, 80.

[6] For an enlightening discussion about understanding parents, consult Gladys Gardner Jenkins, "Understanding Differences in Parents," *Parents-Children-Teachers: Communication* (Washington, D. C.: Association for Childhood Education International, 1969), pp. 35–40.

personally. This does not mean that any one parent will become the special friend of the teacher; dangers are very possible in such a relationship. Such danger as may exist though is minor compared to the danger of a wall of misunderstanding between parent and teacher. The parent rarely desires a close relationship. What he seeks is to be understood as a person. For the teacher this involves a willingness to listen and openness to understand, regardless of differences in outlook and background.

It is not easy to get to know a parent in many instances. There are communities in which parents attend the P.T.A. and come on schedule for parent-teacher conferences. Other parents do not. There are other situations in which the parent does not feel welcome at the P.T.A. or at ease in a parent-teacher conference. Sometimes the gap between parent and teacher can be bridged by a visit of the teacher to the home.[7] Generally, before making a home visit, the teacher should gather information about the home background. A home visit may indicate to some parents that something is wrong. Then a child may be punished, and parents further alienated from the school.

Other approaches may be better than home visits to establish a rapport. For example, Anne Christensen tells of a boy from a Spanish-speaking home who had trouble with English.[8] The teacher discovered that he sang well, and she gave him many opportunities to perform in class. Encouraged by this interest, the boy volunteered the information that his father sang even better. The father, who had never evinced any interest in his son's school, was invited to teach the children Spanish songs. This contact made other contacts possible and enjoyable.

There are other possibilities. In some areas a phone call is more welcome than a home call, and may do as much good. Sometimes a brief stop at the place of the parent's employment may be a partial substitute for or an opening wedge for parent conferences. Sometimes a school faculty can hold an evening "open house" and as occasion permits, develop the beginnings of understanding.

Consulting With Parents

Overall, parents are the best source of information about their own children. As Mildred Sabath says:

Parents are unique, resource persons with their reservoir of information about the child's past and present life. A planned interview where a parent tells a teacher

[7] For one of the helpful books on the subject see Ruth Strang, *Reporting to Parents* (New York: Teachers College, Columbia University, 1947), p. 64.

[8] Anne L. Christensen, "Forces Which Change Perceptions," *Primary Education: Changing Dimensions* (Washington, D. C.: Association for Childhood Education International, 1965), p. 73.

about the child's early life is basic to the teacher's understanding of a child and his parents' aspirations for him.[9]

Possibly a Project Head Start bulletin states the matter even more clearly:

... professionals can gain considerable insight and understanding from association with parents. The latter often have valuable ideas about interests, reactions and attitudes which are essential to working successfully with the child. It is clearly not possible to draw a distinct line between the responsibilities of the professional and the parent. It is quite clear, however, that a maximum of cooperation and interaction between teacher and parent is likely to produce the greatest benefit for the child.[10]

Seeking the aid of parents in understanding the child is valuable. Sometimes the teacher comes away from such a conference with a new perspective on the child. In addition, a conference is a much better approach to mutual understanding. At least two things take place simultaneously. (1) The teacher learns about the child. Even the uncooperative parent may reveal much. Negative attitudes and reaction from parents help explain the child's behavior in school. (2) The parent's attitude is probably changing. If the parent's negative reactions are accepted, the conversation will usually take a more positive tone. Most people tend to alter their positions when they find no need of defending them. At a minimum they are more likely to listen to a teacher who has listened to them first.

The focus of the conference should be on the child and how he can be helped. One helps parents most, not by criticizing them, but by wondering aloud what both teacher and parent might try that would be more effective in accomplishing mutual goals. It is not essential that teacher and parent are in complete agreement on their ideas of child rearing. Parent conferences should usually concentrate on specific needs, but they should not start off with the needs of the child or his problems. There is something in every child that can be commended. Eventually, if there is a problem, it should be faced. Problems may be mentioned only if the teacher hopes the parent will have a constructive idea that she can try, or if the teacher has an idea that she thinks the parent may try. Such suggestions can be offered not as commands but as possibilities to be explored. Few parents are helped by becoming the brunt of the suppressed feelings involving the child that the teacher may have built up over the weeks. They, the parents, are more apt to be helped and to be cooperative if they find that there is someone who shares their concern. The teacher can keep in mind and admit, openly, that her's is the lesser concern. Under normal circumstances the parents' rights in regard to their child's welfare are supreme.

[9] Mildred R. Sabath, "Children, Parents and Teachers," *Toward Better Kindergartens* (Washington, D. C.: Association for Childhood Education International, 1966), p. 26.

[10] Office of Economic Opportunity, *Project Head Start: Parents Are Needed* (Washington, D. C.: OEO, 1967), pp. 8, 9.

The purpose of all conferences is not to prove a point—but to prove helpful. The parents may have many questions. A mother may carry many burdens. Seldom can the teacher do much about these. Sometimes she can be only a helpful listener. A parent conference does not necessarily have to be confined to fifteen minutes, for example. If it does, a teacher can make an appointment for a longer period—if this seems appropriate. Usually, however, any help to parents comes not by direct suggestion, and not necessarily by listening, but by focusing on a special problem. If the parent can assist in solving one specific problem, he will to that extent be strengthened to face some other problems. Never should a parent leave a conference feeling that an additional load has been placed on his shoulders.

Suggestions for Parent Conferences[11]

The suggestions below have been found useful. They do not provide for every possible contingency, but they may make the conference both more pleasant and more effective.

1. Parents are people—usually fine, normal individuals—wonderful to meet and know. Look forward to meeting them.
2. Parents who are more difficult may have their own problems. They need help. Some you can help. Some you can encourage to get help.
3. Working with parents is a vital part of the teacher's task and is sometimes more helpful for the child than anything else the teacher will ever do.
4. A good relationship can usually be established with parents if the teacher can stay relaxed enough to look at the child through the eyes of the parents. Show interest, understanding, acceptance. Be willing to listen. Be tactful but honest.
5. If a teacher has confidence in herself and her program, it will not be necessary to be defensive.
6. Do not expect too much of one conference. Do not try to tell too much. Listen more.
7. A teacher can learn from the parent. At the least, he can learn what kind of parents the child has, but usually he can learn about the child.
8. Be slow in giving advice. When you do, make it as nondirective as possible. Such words and phrases as, "possibly," "Sometimes this helps," "Have you thought of this?" make it easier to accept suggestions.
9. Do not insist on agreement. People sometimes accept suggestions weeks later and think they are their own ideas.
10. Do not talk in front of the child. Do not talk to the parent across a desk.
11. Go along with the parent's plans when feasible.
12. Be alert to the parent's underlying feelings and respond to them.
13. Face the negative, but emphasize the positive.

[11] Clifford L. Nixon, unpublished notes, prepared for Workshop of the North Carolina Kindergarten Association, 1966.

Parental Approval and Involvement

The discussion, of necessity, overlaps somewhat on the chapter that follows. Parents are a major part of the total community resource. The endeavor in this chapter has been to consider the relationship between the teacher and the parent. Even here it must be acknowledged that wider questions related to the nature of the community have bearing on what the teacher can and should do.

Throughout, the focus has been primarily on the work of the individual teacher. It has not been possible even in speaking of learning goals to keep the focus quite so limited. Learning takes place in a total atmosphere involving school, community, region, nation, and even the outside world. In speaking of parental approval and involvement the individual classroom teacher most often is functioning in his individual way as a part of a larger school unit and, as such, is frequently involved in some form of community interaction. Such involvement can become very complex.

On occasion involvement has become confrontation; a confrontation that has come from either side or both. Parental organizations and groups have met, petitioned, marched, picketed, and, on occasion, made use of violence. Teachers have grown more militant and have used sanctions against districts and larger units. Teachers have, also, marched, picketed, and gone on strike. All of this, and more, happened in New York City in the fall of 1968. Central to the issue in New York was the question of local control as against the rights and privileges of teachers.[12]

This chapter can do little more than acknowledge the existence of major problems for education throughout the country. Major news media have raised the question, or at least acknowledged the question, as to whether the central city can even survive, let alone educate its children.[13] Surveys of public attitudes have indicated a nationwide opposition to increased expenditure for public schools.[14] Private schools are on an upsurge.[15] There are very few, if any, national problems that do not have bearing on the total life and educational environment of the children schools seek to educate.

Involvement in Local School Issues

There is hope in the larger scene. Problems are at least being discussed. Both the public and educators are concerned, which is important for it has

---

[12] "A 'Victory' for Teacher Power Over Community Power in New York City?" *Phi Delta Kappan,* 50 (1968), 138.

[13] *Newsweek,* March 17, 1969, pp. 40–42.

[14] "Gallup Measures Attitudes Toward Schools by Public Readiness to Pay—With Grim Results," *Phi Delta Kappan,* 51 (1969), 157, 163.

[15] *U. S. News & World Report,* November 10, 1969, pp. 50–52.

bearing on the local situations that teachers and parents face. Life appears more difficult when problems are out in the open. In working with individuals such people as physicians and psychologists frequently have to ask themselves how much of the truth individuals can accept. Sometimes teachers and often school counselors must face the same question in dealing with students and parents. Questions of local pride, preference for things as they are, unwillingness to face unpleasant facts are involved in many situations. There may need to be a compromise between a too abrupt disclosure of difficulties and a settling for the status quo. Someway, nationally and locally, there is need of honest appraisal by all educators, honest seeking for interchange of ideas with parents and the general public, a continual seeking to involve parents, public, teachers, and students in a search for ways and means to improved learning. Perhaps all that can be said here is that all educators who work with young children should be even more concerned than others.

One additional point that is far from new needs to be stressed. Democratic processes take *time* and often seem inefficient. It is natural to assume that experts in Washington or a local school district can reach conclusions, issue directions, and produce the desired results. Sometimes such methods may be necessary, and sometimes they are successful. The concept of democracy does not deny the necessity of leadership at all levels from the national scene to the nursery school classroom. Overall, more chance of reaching helpful solutions exists when time is taken to present ideas for discussion, when people are given time to understand and consider, and when they have a meaningful voice in the actions taken.

In the 1940s one of the authors was asked to investigate a successful nongraded program in a school district within the general metropolitan area in which she served. The record of the development and inauguration of the program had already been documented. Individuals that were involved, including school officials, were interviewed. She learned that there had been extensive preparation for the new program—information had been sent to parents, parent meetings had been held, parent-teacher conferences had been scheduled. The local P.T.A. was utilized for discussion and promotion. Furthermore, the new program was instituted one grade at a time. But looking back over all that had been done, the principal of the school directly involved stated: "If I were doing it over again, we would lay more groundwork and go more slowly."

What the principal saw in retrospect was that the school had done a good and basically successful job of selling a program—but it had still been an imposed plan. In essence, it was imposed not only on parents and children, but also on the teachers. Educators desperately need to come up with good ideas. They also need to be good salesmen. The even more basic need may be an openness to an interchange of ideas so that the programs developed are much more the product of the thinking of all the people affected.

Involving Parents in the Classroom

The question of involving parents in classroom activities is an old one. In theoretical terms and within strict limits the concept has been accepted for many years. Most schools, particularly most elementary schools, have had Parent-Teacher Associations. They have conducted "open house" with everything "spruced up" and with the best available children's work on display. Parents have been called on to assist with school excursions. Parents have also frequently contributed time, work, and money to provide needed materials and equipment. Good schools have long encouraged parents to visit the classroom on occasion. These activities and others like them are of value. One value to the school is the public relations impact. People who know their school and the teachers of their children are much more likely to support it.

Of even more importance to the concerned educator is that parents involved, even indirectly, in the work of the school influence the learning experiences of their children in worthwhile ways. The attitude of the home is a powerful factor in education, particularly in early childhood education. There seems to be special value in the parents' actual presence in the classroom. A report by Jay Connor that dates back to the late 1940s is still pertinent:

The study involved 2000 elementary school children and their parents in seven elementary schools in San Diego. An experimental and a control group with matched pairs of pupils were used. In the experimental schools, provision was made for parents to spend two hours a week at school. The parents spent one hour observing classroom procedures and one hour for discussion and planning with the teacher and their children. The control group had no planned parental cooperation. On the basis of achievement tests given at the beginning of the 20-week experimental period and, again, at the close, it was found that the experimental group had made significantly greater gains in achievement of regular subject matter. The experimental group consistently exceeded achievements of matched partners in the control schools in other areas, such as: friendship, status, attention, work habits, and class participation.[16]

No doubt other factors in addition to the parents' presence in the classroom played a part. New parental insights through observation and conferences may have been the more important elements in this situation. It still remains true that children were helped by having the parents there.

Over the years situations have been observed in which teachers of particular groups had nearly 100 percent of the parents represented at meetings in which the teachers explained their purposes and programs. Parents evinced enthusiasm and cooperation not only when the school

[16] Jay Davis Connor, "Parent Participation Pays Dividends," *Review of Educational Research* 22 (1952), 321.

personnel explained what they were doing, but also when the staff presented ideas as to how the parents could assist. It is questionable that any parent should be expected to help with homework assigned by the teachers, but in some communities parents have turned out in large numbers to learn what the "new math" was all about. There is much more that most teachers could do in the areas of parent participation that will prove beneficial not only to the child but to the school and community too.

Involving Parents in Management and Operatior

Many schools and related organizations have even involved the parents in the actual management and operation of schools. This may or may not mean more complete parental cooperation in the actual day-by-day operation of the school.

One of the early childhood education programs that has paid particular attention to parental involvement has been the government-funded Head Start Program.[17] The people involved in these programs have been convinced that children can be helped by helping their parents. They have also come to believe that parents are best helped by involving them in the program rather than by simply talking with them. The Head Start Program has by policy looked for all kinds of ways to involve parents and has even used legitimate pressures to draw parents in. All have been expected to make some contribution; some have even been hired to work in the program. Robert Clasen explains that if children are provided schooling and other care not normally a part of the regular public school system, the parents must assume responsibility for assisting with the work of the school and also take part in discussion groups. One of the beneficial aspects of this is that the parents grow as they participate. More interesting is the indication that the mothers almost always are able to make valuable contributions to the program. Those who can, help with the educational part; others perform needed services. All are made to feel that they are doing something important for their children in the school.

The concept of involving parents in school management is more debatable. In practice, the idea has not been invariably successful. Clasen presents the Head Start concept that the parents need to be involved in the actual management of the program. He argues for a strong parent council, with the right to make decisions and question practices.[18]

As Clasen also suggests, there is a tendency for all—teachers, administrators, or other "leaders"—to be concerned when anyone else, particularly from the "outside," becomes too involved in the work being done. Obviously, there is danger of loss of prestige. More important are the possible dangers to the goals of a program. In the Head Start Program the overriding consideration

[17] Office of Economic Opportunity, *Project Head Start: Parent Involvement* (Washington, D. C.: OEO, 1969).

[18] Robert E. Clasen, *On to the Classroom* (Madison, Wis.: Dembar Educational Research Services, 1969), Chapter 9.

has been the possibility of developing the potential of the adults involved.

The teacher in her early childhood education classroom is in no position to organize a parent council with authority to interfere with her work. She may, with the approval of her superiors, and often with their enthusiastic cooperation, think of ways to involve parents in the conduct of the class. One kindergarten teacher regularly invited a policeman to the class—not to lecture, but simply to be present, visit with the children, and answer their questions. Very often parents can be invited to share ideas about their work and experiences. Some adults may need orientation first as to what is possible and practical when visiting young children. Lectures are almost always a disappointment to both the speaker and the children. Things to show and handle, often informally, or activities with the children participating are more practical and enjoyable for the children.

Sometimes parents will volunteer to assist with a class on some understood basis. In helping underprivileged children, in particular, there seems to be a growing consensus of the need of a ratio of one adult to approximately five children. With tact and good judgment volunteers can be used effectively.

Summary

Working with parents is normally a pleasant and rewarding experience. Through the parent the teacher can gain insights into a child's behavior and sometimes helpful ideas as to improving her own effectiveness. Parents are most often helped by focusing on the teacher-parent mutual concern for the child. Some parents need help beyond the capacities of the teacher. Even very impoverished parents can sometimes not only be helped to understand the program of an educational agency, but can also contribute to it in important ways. Both parents and children are helped on any level of society when the parents are involved in meaningful ways in the program of the school. Involvement that includes actual influence on educational procedures carries some measure of risk to teachers and administrators, but may be more than worth that risk. Apart from this, the teacher can give substance to the concept of parental involvement through the options that are open to her.

CHAPTER SEVENTEEN

Additional Resources in School and Community

      "Gina! Gina! Is this a Nine?" The quotation is from an enlightening and delightful motion picture *They Can Do It!* produced in 1968 by the Educational Development Center of Newton, Massachusetts. The film presents extracts taken at various times during the year of a group of first graders, presumably underprivileged, in a Philadelphia experimental project. The major emphasis is the mutual development of the attractive young teacher and her pupils as the teacher changed from traditional methods to more effective small group and individual projects geared to the interest and achievement levels of her children.

No comment is made in the film concerning the following incident: On several occasions a bright, capable child named Gina takes part in a scene. In one scene Gina is working on a project of her own. Near her on the floor is another pupil trying to match the number of beans to the numerals on a board. Again and again she turns to Gina, sometimes reaching to touch her, asking for help: "Is this nine?" "Is this five?" "Is this seven?" Sometimes Gina assures her that it is nine, a five, or a seven, but other times she corrects by saying, "No, that's a two." In another scene Gina is seated by a slow reader giving help, but only when needed and asked. The teacher had an adult assistant, but Gina appeared to be a needed and effective helper.

This chapter deals with the resources available to the teacher within the school itself, the school system, and the wider community. The possibilities in some instances are limitless. The creative teacher will discover many that are not even mentioned in the text. Space permits only a limited number of suggestions.

Resource People Within the Classroom

The teacher, naturally, is the chief resource person within the classroom. Some schools are fortunate enough to have teaching assistants, either full-time or part-time. The possibility of parent assistance has been discussed in the previous chapter. There is another resource that can be profitably used —the children themselves. Children are very effective teachers of each other.

The idea is not new. It has been experimented with successfully and unsuccessfully many times. The monitorial schools, which were devised by the English Quaker Joseph Lancaster, were tried in America as early as 1806. The so-called Lancaster schools were widespread for many years in the first half of the nineteenth century. The basic appeal was twofold. It appeared to offer the possibility of education to those who had not previously been taught, and it did so at a very low cost. According to James Frasier, the annual cost was often less than $2 per pupil.[1]

It is possible that the defects and failures of the plan have had a permanent effect on the concept of education. The defects were many, one of them being that one teacher was expected to teach a selected number of pupils who in turn taught all the students in the school. These students were untrained and virtually unsupervised. In effect the plan did not provide even a minimal level of competent adult support and guidance. It did not supplement the work of the teacher—it attempted to do without the classroom teacher.

Schools have gone to the opposite extreme in the more recent past. It seems assumed, even in some first grades, that one teacher can effectively teach thirty or more children and that any interchange of information or other help between pupils is to be prevented. This is almost as mistaken a concept as the idea that no adult help is needed.

Individual Children as Helpers

There is usually a "Gina" in the classroom. Individual differences being what they are, some children are both bright and popular. There are other children who are not "good" in every thing but who can help in some areas. Many teachers discover ways in which each child can be of help and so enhance his self-esteem, thus paving the way for receptive learning. In one sense,

[1] James E. Frasier, *An Introduction to the Study of Education* (New York: Harper & Row, 1965), pp. 167–168.

every teacher learns from every child. Former Vice-President Hubert Humphrey has said that he has learned more about some things from his delightful, but retarded granddaughter than he has from anyone else. In the same way, every child has something to teach. Even when this is not readily discoverable, every child can be made to feel successful and important.

The very capable children generally make valuable teacher aids and in the meantime these youngsters remain interested participants in the class activities. In the nongraded approach that the text has recommended such children will normally move through a school program more rapidly than other children. There are still problems to be faced, but they are less severe and more easily dealt with than in a strictly graded system. In the latter, the child may become so bored that he learns little himself and disrupts the learning activities of others. In such a situation, high potential may be largely dissipated and misdirected. Besides, the school has failed to teach the potential leader those qualities of compassion and concern that society needs from its brightest people.

Many children can help teach. But how? The solution is not simple and has many facets. Usually some way can be found to permit any child to work with other children on his level at some time in the program. Enrichment activities can also be encouraged. But part of the solution, handled with tact and training, is to use such students to help those who are slower. Most will not be able to do so without guidance. The very bright may have more trouble relating to the slow child than the teacher. The solution may sometimes be a "mini-course" in psychology, or it may be to use the very bright with the moderately bright, these with the average, and the average with the slow. Part of the answer will lie with the nature of the particular children.

Much more common in most classrooms than the child who is bright in all areas is the child who is very good in some areas of achievement but not in all. It has come to be generally accepted that it pays to build from strengths rather than to emphasize weakness. The differences in individuals enable the teacher to use the skills of the beautiful writer, the accomplished reader or story teller, the organizer, the artist, and so forth. If a child can help teach another child, he is needed for this purpose.

Models

It has been found that even in nursery school age-mates were more influential models for other children than teachers.[2] This, on any level, can work in various ways—desirable or otherwise. The alert teacher can make use of the growing identification with other children in many ways. The example earlier in the book of the boy who became the kindergarten story teller of the year is one illustration. It may be remembered that the teacher did not choose him for the role; she simply gave him a chance to show what he could do.

[2] Paul Henry Mussen, John Janeway Conger, and Jerome Kagan, *Child Development and Personality* (New York: Harper & Row, 1969), pp. 399–403.

When the children showed appreciation and enjoyment, she went along with the developing situation. She found that she had an assistant, but the other children had a model of creative and expressive dramatization from someone on their own level.

If children are not involved and used, they will still serve as models. Model is used not in the sense of the "model" child, but in the sense that children and others admire and seek to identify with certain individuals. The children will do so regardless of the teacher's intention. The teacher's task is to use this tendency without misusing it. The concept should never be used to hurt the child who is different. The model should not represent the bias of the teacher. Probably the advice of Haim Ginott to parents is apropos.[3] He warns parents to praise behavior, not character. This, he suggests, is true even in private conversation. A child praised for being a "good" child may feel compelled to prove that the evaluation is incorrect. Commenting on a specific act as helpful carries less risk. The danger of praise for overall excellence is especially inappropriate when offered in the presence of other children. The other children may know the child to be anything but "good" in some situations. They may, also, resent this kind of praise. Some children, even on the primary level, may attack the recipient of such attention verbally, or even physically.

What the teacher does may include praise for work well done, but it is even more a matter of giving the child a chance to "do his thing." This may differ from the usual curricular pattern. It is important that the teacher recognize not only the bright, but the resourceful and creative student. Usable ideas that can be accepted, new and better ways of doing things, ideas for projects and excursions can be given recognition.

In addition to the fact that some children can be used deliberately to help teach other children and that some children help teach in more informal ways there is another aspect of early childhood learning to be mentioned.

Team Learning

The phrase "team learning" is not used as often as "team teaching," but for some it indicates a concept of greater importance. Both in this text and in the practices of good teachers team learning is more a new term than a new concept. Children learn to work together even on the nursery school level. With increased age, there should be a growing capacity to learn from agemates.

Team learning can take a wide variety of forms. The size of learning teams can vary from two to several children. For instance, two children can work together in reading; both children get more practice and probably become more involved than in the usual reading groups. Two children can also work together on arithmetic. This may be especially helpful when they are solving problems or learning concepts by the actual manipulation of objects. Two

[3] Haim G. Ginott, *Between Parent and Child* (New York: Avon, 1965), pp. 43–50.

children can work in one workbook. Groups of three or more can work together in gathering information, working on a project, using learning equipment, playing educational games, and sharing experiences.

One of the values in such a concept of teaching is that it permits the interchange of ideas between children of various aptitudes and levels of ability. Better students will work with those having more difficulty; paired children of relatively equal ability can work together; slightly larger groups with children of various kinds of ability can be utilized. The further value is that the emphasis can be primarily on what each child can contribute to the learning of the group. Children under these circumstances can learn from each other without any child being labeled.

Resources Within the School

While there are normally many resource people within a school, the resource person most closely related to the discussion in the preceding paragraphs is the older student. Many schools, perhaps most schools, make some use of the older students. Although it may be on a "hit or miss" basis, even this may be of some value. The upper-grade student called on to take over a classroom until the substitute teacher arrives probably learns something from the experience, and the children are better off than if left alone. One kindergarten teacher remembers with gratitude the third-grade girl who took on the responsibility of the care of the class hamster. Both having the responsibility and a relationship with the teacher proved helpful to the girl.

There are schools in which more organized programs are undertaken. In one school the problem originally discussed was the fact that there were no male figures with whom the primary boys could identify. Even the consultant and the principal were women. One suggestion made and tried was to involve some of the oldest boys in the school in the physical education activities. No systematic study was made of the results, but the experiment seemed to serve its intended purpose. There was the added benefit of relieving the primary teachers of part of their responsibility. In addition, the older boys seemed to learn from and enjoy the experience.

J. Carl Fleming has reported on a well-organized and successful program that effectively utilizes upper-grade children in the Fernwood Elementary School in Portland, Oregon. He begins his article[4] with a brief dialogue between a seventh-grade student and a second-grade child quoted in part:

Debbie, the seventh-grade student: "What would you like to do today?"
Linda, the second-grade pupil: "I'd like to write a story."
Debbie: "Do you want to close your eyes and think something up?"
Linda: "No, I want to look out the window."

[4] J. Carl Fleming, "Pupil Tutors and Tutees Learn Together," *Today's Education*, 58 (1969), 22–24.

Debbie: "The grass and the bushes are pretty, aren't they?"
Linda: "Yes, let's write about them."
Debbie: "OK. Tell me what to put down."[5]

He adds that this illustrates "Student Team Action, a program that, at no extra cost, helps the Portland, Oregon, school system solve two crucial problems—how to make education relevant and how to individualize instruction."[6]

He goes on to explain that entire classes of upper-grade students prepare lessons that they teach to primary students "usually in a one-to-one relationship that assures each student in the program the undivided attention of another person, a chance to be seen and heard each day, and a feeling of importance."[7]

The Portland school system uses the low achievers as well as the better students. Fleming reports that there is improvement for both the primary and upper-grade students and improvement for both the poor and good upper-grade students. The upper-grade students have a job to do that is important; they become involved with both life and learning. Some who have shown little interest in school work hard to prepare for the experience. The primary children receive the kind of individualized help that they have never known before.

Members of the school staff may be excellent resource people. Of these, the principal is the most important. A kindly principal in a primary school is a resource just by being present. He frequently is both model and counselor. He sets the tone of the school in many ways. One principal found himself in a situation in which he was besieged with pupils sent to him for various infractions of rules. He passed the word to teachers and students for the students to come to his office only when they had something good to report to him. Soon there were children waiting to tell their achievements. The psychology is ancient, but sound. There is greater gain in recognizing what is desired than in punishing the undesirable.

Other possibilities depend in part on the school situation. There are almost always teachers with special interests or abilities. Very informal and limited team teaching goes on in many schools. This may be as simple as all the first grades meeting for a songtime the last period on Friday. One of the teachers will play the piano while another leads the singing. There can sometimes be (apart from a formal team arrangement) an informal interchange among teachers. Occasionally, one teacher may have something that several groups could share. Sometimes teachers can trade classes for specific learning purposes. A group of teachers can provide the means for one teacher to do remedial work with small groups.

---

[5] *Ibid.*, p. 22.
[6] *Ibid.*, p. 22.
[7] *Ibid.*, p. 22.

Numerous elementary schools now employ school counselors. Because the counselor was discussed at length in an earlier chapter, he is only mentioned here as an important resource to keep in mind and utilize. Probably even more elementary schools have full-time librarians, and many have part-time ones. Librarians who both know their materials and love children are generally excellent resource persons. They do more than help individual students select appropriate reading materials. Frequently, they visit classrooms with the new additions to the library and discuss these with the children. Some librarians hold children's story hours during which children can listen to an "expert reader." Some perform effective guidance services by locating stories about characters and events in which the children can find identification and solutions to some of their problems.

Every school has a custodian; many have dieticians and other cafeteria workers. Each has meaning to at least some children. There are custodians who are concerned and helpful in their contacts with children. Some local schools have their own art teacher, music teacher, speech therapist, reading specialist, and audio-visual technician, all of whom provide an additional arm for the teacher, freeing her for more effective teaching.

Resources Within the School System

The variation within school systems makes brief discussion difficult. There are usually one or more supervisors or consultants on call. Curriculum and remedial specialists may divide their time among schools. Psychological services range from those programs in which there is no fully qualified person to major programs including psychiatrist, psychologist, and social psychiatric workers. There may be social workers based in the central office who can furnish information concerning homes and provide consultation services to both teachers and parents. There is usually a school nurse who, if not on call, makes some systematic attempt to counsel with teachers and parents about the physical needs of children.

The resource most neglected is related to what has been said about the use of classmates and older children as teaching aids. Every high school should have an active association of future teachers, and they should be used in some systematic way to assist the elementary teachers. Those with an interest in young children can be of help in countless ways in the classroom. They can tutor individuals, can work with small groups, help with physical activities, assist in the preparation of materials, support children in their group endeavors, help with the playground supervision, and help supervise the organized games on the upper levels of the primary grades. The participation can be an expanding operation, perhaps an hour a week for freshmen to longer periods for upper classmen. In school systems where the junior college is part of the system, the program can include all college students interested in teaching. Such work can be voluntary or it may be a part of credit courses.

On both the high school and college level, the work of the student in tne elementary school can benefit the teacher and the children. It can, also, help the young people involved decide whether they wish to pursue a teaching career.

Resources Within the Community

The School as a Resource for the Community

One of the more exciting aspects in the American educational scene today is the emergence of schools that are almost literally a part of the community. Some are private schools seeking to reach dropout high school students. Jonathan Black reports on several of these schools in, "Street Academies: One Step Off the Sidewalk."[8] His title is taken from the fact that "street academies are storefront schools." Young people are literally persuaded in from the street, talked with, worked with in any kind of a flexible curriculum that will meet their need, counseled, helped in the street academy and in the street, brought up to eighth-grade equivalency, and some taken on through the high school level.[9]

Such schools and related projects[10] offer hope, but point up a tragedy. Luvern L. Cunningham has written with humor and pathos of what he learned when as a college professor he traded places with a junior high school principal in an inner city.[11] The tragedy is national and probably still increasing, though it is not new. America has never provided the full opportunity for the under-privileged that has been part of the American dream.[12] From the standpoint of this text the obvious application is the need to provide all through the school system the flexibility, the creative opportunities, the real chance for successful experience that will lower the loss later on.

Even the street school usually works in harmony with the public school system. Experiments are also being tried by the public schools. One of the more interesting is that in Philadelphia in which approximately 140 high school students are attending a "school without walls."[13] They have no single building for learning purposes, though they do meet in small groups for seminars. The students spend most of the day in two dozen different public

[8] Jonathan Black, "Street Academies: One Step Off the Sidewalk," *Saturday Review*, 52 (1969), 88–89, 100–101.

[9] For a good brief description of their operation, see *U. S. News and World Report*, November 10, 1969, p. 52.

[10] Another approach to reaching the dropout student is presented by George Dennison, *The Lives of Children: The Story of the First Street School* (New York: Random House, 1969).

[11] Luvern L. Cunningham, "Hey, Man, You Our Principal? Urban Education as I Saw It," *Phi Delta Kappan*, 51 (1969), 123–128.

[12] Theodore Brameld, "Illusions and Disillusions in American Education," *Phi Delta Kappan*, 50 (1968), 202–207.

[13] Donald Cox, "Learning on the Road," *Saturday Review*, 52 (1969), 71.

and private institutions. The experiment is part of Philadelphia's attempt to bring drastic changes to its inner-city schools.[14]

The Community as a Resource for the School

There are various kinds of resources in every community. Some of them are so burdened and overwhelmed as to be almost helpless. Some are highly effective. The teacher will need to know as much as she can about these. There should be someone in the school or the school system who is an authority on the resources of the community.

The Official Agencies. Every community either has its own official agencies or is in some way associated with a larger unit, which provides a great many community services. Schools generally work closely with many of these. Every school will sometimes need their services. Such agencies include public welfare organizations, health departments, mental health clinics, police and related agencies, probation services, and others. The teacher of classes in early childhood education will have contact at some time (at least indirectly) with all of these.

Unofficial Agencies and Groups. Most of the service organizations have an interest in the children of a community and, at least indirectly in the schools. All of the churches have contacts with children who are also in the public school. Their interest in, methods, and success with children will vary. Sometimes a local pastor or priest can be an important resource person. Numerous organizations attempt in some way to help children with their problems. The teacher can, at least, appreciate whatever element of good intent there is on the part of all such unofficial organizations, and with judgment, may find some that will be helpful with certain children. In the sense of this paragraph, one of the unofficial agencies in many communities is the four-year college. Students in college need some place of service, and many could be used effectively by the schools.

Individual Help. Most important of all to the classroom teacher is the individual help that she can receive from people in the community. The basic intent is the same as that mentioned in seeking the cooperation of parents and students. The teacher is concerned for adequate provision for the needs of her classroom. Some people are good resource persons to be used on an informal basis. It was mentioned in the last chapter that a father who was a policeman would frequently visit in a kindergarten class. He was there simply to chat with children who were interested. This could be even more helpful in deprived areas. A child who has visited with and touched a policeman might never feel that he was necessarily an enemy.

There are other individuals who are easier for children to identify with— athletes, of course, but also, taxi drivers, beauticians, salespeople, bricklayers, auto mechanics, and so on. When such people are invited to visit, the teacher

---

[14] Wallace Roberts, "Can Urban Schools Be Reformed?" *Saturday Review*, 52 (1969), 70–72, 87–91.

should make it clear that they are not expected to talk to a classroom of children. Most times it is more profitable for the children and the visitor if the latter demonstrates what he does in his work. An auto mechanic, for example, brought his tools to class. Such visits are a connecting link between school and community. Sometimes they serve as preparation for an excursion into the neighborhood.

There is a further resource being tapped by numerous organizations, but very little as yet by public education. The federal government is experimenting in the training of retired people to assist in the care of nursery children and children with physical and emotional problems. One might wonder if there is not a reserve of retired school teachers who could no longer take charge of classes five days a week but might be delighted to share the work of the teacher for a few hours. There may be other highly educated and capable retired people who could help with individuals and small groups. It would help if small salaries supplementing social security benefits could be paid.

Summary

The teacher is urged to look first within her own classroom for assistance. There are always children who can help other children learn. In team learning children work together in pairs or small groups to help and drill each other. Older children from the upper grades, high school, and college can be utilized effectively to work with younger children. Both groups benefit. In this way the children are given individual attention, and the older students become involved in worthwhile projects, which, in turn, may be related to their life work.

In the interrelationship between school and community the school should be a resource for the community and the community a resource for the school. Within the community there are innumerable agencies, official and unofficial, that can help children. The classroom teacher can call upon class parents or other individuals who may enjoy visiting so that the children will become acquainted with them and their work. Many members of the community may be very qualified, such as retired teachers, to assist with the children under the guidance of the teacher. The job of the teacher is to seek these people out.

CHAPTER EIGHTEEN

Materials and Equipment

It is vital that ideas concerning materials fit into a total view of teaching. Materials are important only as they serve the learning needs of children. Teachers everywhere are in a quandary about what to use that would be the most beneficial for their classes. They constantly are seeking appropriate materials and equipment. In this chapter the authors hope to aid the teacher in evaluating the materials available. Practical suggestions will be offered as to the type and sizes needed for the varied activities of early childhood education.

Purposes and Criteria

Although "purpose" and "criteria" have much in common, they are not exactly the same. Purposes are goals. Criteria refers to standards by which one judges whether anything (in this case, a specific item) accomplishes the purpose. The most important criterion in the present context is whether or not the equipment to be secured meets the need of the children in their situation.

Purposes for Materials and Equipment

While almost all equipment and supplies should make life more pleasant for the children, this should seldom be the sole purpose. Sometimes learning and growth fostered by the equipment can be largely incidental. The three-year-old climbing a jungle gym certainly does not need to understand that he is developing his strength and control, let alone that this control will soon make possible the use of more direct learning tools. The teacher should know, however, that there is a connection between this "play" and later work.

Perhaps even the fun part of materials and equipment could be classified as providing for *developmental experiences*. It may depend on how technical one is as to whether this is considered learning. However the experiences are classified, there is equipment that makes possible experiences appropriate to the developmental needs of children. One judges these chiefly by noting what the children enjoy doing. However, almost always in any activity some incidental learning is involved that ties into later more formal learning. At a minimum, there is the learning that school is a good place to go to. There is, also, the possibility of a developing insight by the child that he, himself, is important and capable.

Most material that the teacher on any level will secure has more specific learning purposes. These purposes will vary with the age of the children and their present attainments. In the nursery, kindergarten, first grade, and later, if need be, many materials can be classified as preparatory tools for school-related skills or more complex areas of knowledge, proceeding from the simple to the complex as the child develops. Some materials are preparatory for all the skills. Children must be able to distinguish shape in order to read, write, or use numerals. This does not mean total dependence on any kind of book or worksheet. Manipulation of objects may tie in to both skill and insight. Sequence and exactness can be discovered in most forms of construction. Particular materials are especially relevant for certain purposes. Free drawing and painting, for example, seem to lead naturally to the control and insights involved in reading and writing.

Other materials may be more appropriate for providing insight into the skills being taught. For example, children need many practical experiences with the counting, arranging, manipulating of objects as a basis for the understanding of mathematical concepts. Sometimes these experiences will precede the teaching, and thus children can discover some of the principles. Even when this is not possible, it is vital that children really understand the meaning of what they are doing. It is possible to make the child less competent in the kinds of mathematics required for effective life in our complex world when misunderstood theories or theories that carry no meaning are memorized. In the levels beyond those that the text considers, mathematics needs the undergirding of experimentation with some of the multitude of devices now available.

Similar points can be made for other subject fields. In some instances the child may use the materials both for preparatory experimentation and experiential reinforcement. A simple example would be liquid measuring devices. A child may discover that a half quart is a pint, not more, not less than a pint. After the child understands the concept, he may continue to prove it and related concepts by filling and refilling containers. The child who does not have an adequate command of acceptable language may be engaged in an activity combining readiness, insight, and correction simultaneously when he listens to a record synchronized with the reading of a book. He may move several steps further in his language development if he listens to a tape recording, then records his own speech, and finally compares his delivery with the original tape.

At every level the materials should be such that they can be employed by the teacher to *set the stage for learning*. Houses and stores, whether in kindergarten or the second grade, can provide the means for both social and academic learning.

Criteria

As noted, purposes form the basis for criteria. The one overriding criterion is that in the cooperative interchange of children's choice and teacher planning *the materials should further the learning experience of the children*. It is also part of the same criterion that *the materials must be suitable to the age and developmental level of the children*. Many materials are suitable for a range of age groups; but, even so, there will probably be differences in the specific tools. The third grader can usually use more sophisticated tools in working with clay or wood than the kindergartner. The learning games he enjoys may also be different. Sometimes the problem is similar to the problem of books for the slow reader. Interest may be on one level and ability on a lower one. Materials may be required that are different than those used in nursery and kindergarten, but that are not more difficult.

Detailed lists of criteria can be given, but space does not permit this. One of the manufacturers of materials discusses a list of eleven criteria which are of value.[1] Included in the suggestions are four that all teachers should keep in mind when requesting materials for their class use:

1. The extent to which equipment is versatile is most important.
2. Good equipment should stimulate children to do things
   for themselves.
3. The durability of the equipment is important.
4. Equipment should encourage cooperative play.

The variety of purposes to be served is a basic consideration. All classrooms at the early childhood level should have materials that fulfill nine requirements. However, one item may satisfy more than one requirement. The nine requirements are:

1. Materials that provide for exploration.

[1] *Criteria for Selecting Play Equipment for Early Childhood Education* (Rifton, N. Y.: Community Playthings, 1967). This company furnishes copies of its bulletin on request.

2. Materials that provide for the teaching of specific skills.
3. Materials that serve as props for learning experiences.
4. Materials that provide for safe fun.
5. Materials that are self-corrective devices.
6. Materials that encourage learning of quantitative concepts.
7. Materials that are useful for practice in perceptual and discriminatory skills.
8. Materials that encourage motor control and physical adaptability.
9. Materials that provide practice in the skills themselves.

Supplies Needed

There are many things that, rightly or wrongly, must be taken for granted. It is understood, for example, that no class on any level functions effectively without sufficient space, which is especially true in the whole range of early childhood education. How a teacher utilizes her space can have bearing on the effectiveness of her class program. Two publications in particular present useful ideas as to space, arrangement, and suitable equipment: *Space, Arrangement, Beauty in School* and *Housing for Early Childhood Education.*[2] Both can be obtained from the Association for Childhood Education International, Washington, D. C. A third that also presents constructive suggestions is *Planning Environments for Young Children: Physical Space,*[3] available from the National Association for the Education of Young Children, Washington, D. C.

Many of the same general types of equipment and supplies belong equally in the nursery school, kindergarten, and primary grades. Lillian Logan points out: "There is no longer such a difference between the nursery school, the kindergarten, and the primary rooms as there once was."[4] They all need sturdy chairs—the size increasing with the increasing size of the child. They all need work tables or benches—again adjusted to the size and projects involved—plus learning centers. Basic materials for artistic expression will differ in a number of ways, but their presence and general purpose are the same.

The authors advise all teachers and students to obtain a copy of a booklet entitled *Equipment and Supplies* from the Association for Childhood

[2] Margaret Rasmussen, *Space, Arrangement, Beauty in School* (Washington, D. C.: Association for Childhood Education International, 1958); Association for Childhood Education International, *Housing for Early Childhood Education* (Washington, D. C.: ACEI, 1968). See Appendix A for the association's complete address.

[3] Sybil Kritchevsky, Elizabeth Prescott, and Lee Walling, *Planning Environments for Young Children: Physical Space* (Washington, D. C.: National Association for the Education of Young Children, 1969). See Appendix A for the association's complete address.

[4] Lillian Logan, *Teaching the Young Child* (Boston: Houghton Mifflin, 1969), p. 419.

Education International[5] before making any decisions as to what materials and equipment will be needed in their classrooms. This invaluable bulletin is as complete and helpful a source in the field as one can find. Among other things, it lists supplies of both a general and special nature for children in nursery school through the intermediate grades. The reader is offered a multitude of suggestions as to the kinds of possibilities pertinent at any level of early childhood education. In addition, amounts, sizes, and types of materials are specified.

Catalogs from companies selling the types of equipment suitable to one's needs are another must when deciding what materials to order. A limited number of addresses of distributors will be found in Appendix C of the text; a more complete list appears in *Equipment and Supplies.*

A tentative selection of the most appropriate materials required by the teacher should be compiled before the administration makes its annual query, "What do you need in the way of supplies next year?" Frequently the remark follows, "Be sure and include the prices." The really foresighted individual will list equipment by priorities.

A section could be included in the text of the general equipment valuable at all the age levels under consideration. Instead, a portion of the list of materials suggested for the primary grades in *Equipment and Supplies* is given below. The list has been limited to the primary range for two reasons— to emphasize the types of material that belong in the good primary classroom and to indicate to nursery school and kindergarten teachers that such materials, when adjusted to the size and ages of their groups, are essential to effective instruction. Space does not permit the reprint of all the suggestions found in the bulletin. The list is based on the needs of a primary class of twenty-five children.[6]

Primary Group of 25 Children

ART AND CRAFT
Access to:
Kitchen complete with utensils

Art
Brushes, 12, 1″ bristle, 12″ handles and short handles
Brushes, 18, ¾″ bristle, mixed handles
Chalk, asstd. colors, 1 gross to box. (Avoid oil-based type, makes marks on
    board difficult to erase.)
Clay, 50 lbs., mixed
Containers, ½ pt. or pt., plastic or metal, with covers, for paint, 15

---

[5] Association for Childhood Education International, *Equipment and Supplies,* Bulletin 39 (Washington, D. C.: ACEI, 1968). Cost: $1.50. See Appendix A for the association's complete address.
[6] *Ibid.,* pp. 13–17.

Crayons, big, 8 mixed colors, 25 boxes

Easels, individual, to be used at painting table, 12. (Other standing
easel available.)

Garbage can, plastic, cover and liner, for clay

Glue, white vinyl (Elmer's)

Laundry starch, liquid, for making finger paint or papier-mâché, 5 gals.

Muffin tins (6 places to a tin) for paint

Oilcloth, 6 yds.

Packets of cloth and felt pieces

Paint, finger, 5 qts. asstd. colors

Paint, powdered, 4 lbs. ea., red, green, blue, yellow, magenta;
3 lbs. ea., white, turquoise, black; 2 lbs. ea., orange, brown,
flesh (or 1 qt. ea., tempera, liquid)

Paste, 6 pts.

Poster chalk

Scissors, 25, some blunt, some sharp points

Scissors, lefthanded, 6, blunt and sharp

Soapflakes for making finger paint, 2 boxes

Staplers, 2 or 3, and staples

Wheat paste powder (for making finger paint and papier-mâché)

Yarn, asstd. colors, 12 balls

Paper

Bogus paper

Coated paper, 36" x 10-yd. rolls, asstd. colors

Construction paper, 12" x 18," 100 sheets to pkg., asstd. colors

Corrugated paper, 4' x 25,' asstd. colors

Crepe paper, flameproof, 20" x 7½,' asstd. colors

Finger painting paper, 16" x 22," 100 sheets to pkg., 4 pkgs.

Manila paper, 12" x 15," 500 to pkg., 4 pkgs.

Manila paper, 18" x 24," 1 pkg.

Newsprint paper, 18" x 24," 3 reams

Newsprint paper, colored, 2 reams

Paper sacks, paper plates

Paper tissues for paint rags, 5000 to pkg., 2 boxes

Poster paper, 18" x 24," 500 to pkg., asstd. colors, 1 pkg.

Tissue paper, white and many asstd. colors, 3 pkgs.

Wrapping paper, 36" wide, 1 roll

Sewing, Knitting, and Weaving Materials

Burlap, 6 yds.

Carpet warp, ½ lb. spool

Cloth, coarse unbleached muslin, 10 yds.

Cloth, printed cambric, 6 yds.

Looper looms, 6

Loopers, large, 8 pkgs., 1 ea., red, white, blue, yellow, black; 3 asstd. colors

Mesh cloth (Dixie) for stitching

Needles, 2 pkgs. ea., crewel and embroidery
Needles, weaving, large eyes, pointed, 3″ and 5″
Sanisilk or Silkateen, white and colors for coarse sewing, 4 balls
Table oilcloth, tinted, 47″ wide, 5 yds.
Yarn, Germantown rug

Woodworking
(It is recommended that a central woodworking room be available
 to four classrooms.)
Alcohol, 1 qt.
Beaverboard, 2 pieces 4′ x 12′
Brace, nonratchet, and bits, various sizes, ¼,″ ½,″ ¾,″ 1″
Brads, 1 box
Carpenter's workbench with vise; or 2 or 3 individual sturdy wooden
 tables; or low, broad-topped sawhorse with vises
Clamps, 8, 6″ opening
Claw hammers, 12; 13 oz. to 16 oz.
Dowel rods, 1 doz., various sizes, ¼,″ ½,″ ¾,″ 1″; also
 awning pole, 2½″
Enamel, 1 pt. ea., yellow, red, blue, violet, orange, black, green,
 brown, white
Eye screws, 1 box
File card for cleaning files
Files, wood, 4, half round
Hand drill, ¼″ (file point of nail for smaller size drill)
Linseed oil, 1 qt.
Lumber, white pine, surfaced 4 sides 1″ x 4,″ ½″ x 3,″ ½″ x 1,″
 1″ x 1″ (for axles on vehicles); 1″ x 4″ (for bases on boats,
 cabins, etc.), in 4′ and 6′ lengths
Molds, wooden or button, 1,″ 1½,″ 2½″ for wheels
Monkey wrench
Nail nipper or 6″ plier
Nails, finishing, 1½″; with heads, 1½,″ 2″; blue lath (fine shank,
 head 1″ long); box, smooth wire, 1½″; roofing, with large
 heads (to fasten wheels to axles)
Paint, house, 1 pt. ea., white, yellow, red, blue, black, green,
 violet, brown, orange. (Poster paint can be used.)
Paint remover
Rasps, 2 medium
Sandpaper, #1, #1½, 1 quire
Saws, compass, 2, 10″ long
Saws, crosscut, 6, 18″ long
Screwdrivers, 2
Shellac, white, 1 qt.
Smoothing plane
Try squares, 6

Turpentine, 2 qts.
Wood, 12 pieces, 2" x 2" x 6"
Wood, 12 pieces, 1" x 1" x 6"
Yardsticks, 3

AUDIOVISUAL
Access to:
Microprojector
Projectors: sound, slide, opaque, filmstrip, overhead
Radio
Screen, movie
Tape recorder
Tapes
Television
On Hand:
Books, charts, reproductions of fine paintings; ceramics; carvings; textiles;
     all kinds of good art work for children to respond to
Films
Film strips
Flannel board
Globe, project
Manuscript letters
Maps: state, U. S., world
Pictures
Slides
View Master Stereoscopes, 2

COMPUTING AND MEASURING
Abacus
Bingo game
Cash register
Clock
Counting block, rods, discs
Counting frame
Dominoes, large
Flannel board, kits
Flannel board, magnetic
Flash cards
Measures, plastic: gal., qt., pt., 1, 4, 8 of each respectively
Number board, showing 100
Number line
Peg boards
Place value chart
Place value holder
Ruler, giant
Rulers, 12," 25, with ¼," ½," and 1" markings
Scales

Tape measure
Thermometer
Toy money
Yardstick

LANGUAGE ARTS
Literary Material
Children's books
Recordings of stories and poems
On Hand:
Costumes (and chest to contain them)
Doll carriage or stroller
Dolls (ethnic variety; 2 sets of clothes for each doll)
Doll's high chair
Hats
Materials for constructing puppets
Puppets, hand and finger

Playhouse Equipment
Chest of drawers
Cleaning set
Clothesline, clothespins
Cooking set
Cradle
Dishes, plastic
Dishpan, towels
Dutch cupboard
Iron, ironing board
Kitchen utensils, set
Knives, forks, spoons
Refrigerator
Sink
Stove
Table and chair set
Telephones
Washing set

Table and Floor Equipment
Animals; boats; cars and buses; trucks, trains, planes
Color cubes
Design cubes
Dolls, community workers
Dolls, family
Floor blocks, large, building, 2 sets
Games: Lotto, Old Maid, Parcheesi, anagrams, picture dominoes,
    link letters, checkers, Scrabble
Peg board
Puzzles

Table blocks (smaller than floor blocks), 3 sets
Tinker toys

MUSIC
Access to:
Piano
Radio

Musical Instruments
Autoharp (12-bar)
Chime bells
Chimes
Clappers
Drum
Finger cymbals; 7" brass cymbals with mallet
Hand castanets
Jingle bells
Manipulative staff (with notes)
Maracas
Marimba
Melody bells
Resonator bells
Rhythm sticks
Sand blocks
Song bells
Step bells
Tambourine
Time bells, tuned
Tom-tom, Chinese or Indian
Tone block
Triangle
Xylophone
Phonograph and Records
"Listening post," 4–6 sets of earphones and jack
Singing and rhythm records
Teaching Aid
Chromatic pitch pipe

PLAY

Apparatus—Indoor and Outdoor
Climbing structure
Horizontal bars
Horizontal ladder
Traveling rings
Tumbling mats, 4' x 6' x 2
Turning bar
Wagon

Walking beam or board with cleats on ends

Games and Sports Equipment
Balls, indoor, 2 large
Balls, latex, 18" and 24"
Balls, rubber, 7–12, 7"; 4 balls, 8"
Balls, 4 volley, soccer and kick
Beanbags, 6
Beanbag toss board
Glassguards
Hoop, 8
Jackstraws, 2
Jumping ropes, individual, 8; several long jumping ropes
Puzzles, simple; large pieces interlocked, wood or heavy cardboard
Ring toss, 2
Softballs, 6

SCIENCE
Access to:
Ant farm
Barometer
Bioscope
Cage for visiting pets, removable bottom
Electric bell, wire, dry cells
Hose, 20'
Incubator
Iron filings, 2-mesh
Magnetic compass
Microscope
Preserving fluid for specimens
Prism
Test tubes and beakers
Tuning fork
Weather glass
Weather vane

For Each Room:
Aquarium with glass cover
Flower boxes and containers, various sizes
Insect cage
Jackknife
Magnets, 2
Magnifying glass
Measuring stick
Thermometers, 2, indoor and outdoor

Garden Equipment
Hoes, 6 child-size

Rakes, 6 child-size
Seeds and bulbs
Shovels, 3 child-size
Trowels, 3
Watering cans, 2

In addition to providing a guide to desirable equipment in the classroom, such lists can be helpful for other situations. When setting up a new demonstration program, the fortunate administration that has the means and purpose to provide everything will have to spend little time in research, for all the necessities have been determined for it. In reality, such a comprehensive list makes a worthy "master" list when checking supplies. Teachers who may have to be content with somewhat less than they might wish will still check the list—and request more than they can expect to receive and at the next opportunity put in a further request. Eventually, they may find that they have accumulated all the things that they can use profitably. If a teacher in the past has gotten along wtih almost no supplementary equipment, it will probably do little good to present an overly long list of needs.

A word of caution—before ordering supplies and equipment: make certain that they are not on hand but unused. Frequently, materials are available that could be used if the teacher would go to the trouble of finding out their purpose and use. If the materials are not available, she should begin a gentle but persistent campaign to secure the additional things that are needed.

There are several things the teacher can do, apart from the regular channels of purchase and supply, to obtain materials for her classroom.

Other Sources of Materials and Equipment

Practically every teacher has developed some means of securing additional supplies. Not many of the kinds of materials this chapter suggests fall into the category just below but it may be kept in mind.

Free Material

On every level of education there are suitable materials to be had for the asking. The teacher keeps her eyes open for such materials and a package of cards handy on which to note what can be obtained and where to make the request.

Beautiful Junk is the title of a booklet by Dianne Warner. She explains her meaning:

Educators are often unprepared for the extensive list of equipment and supplies considered necessary for a preschool program. What they are [also] not aware of is the equally long list of program aids that can be added, with relatively low cost, to supplement purchased equipment. This list constitutes what we in the profession call "beautiful junk"....[7]

From this beginning she goes on to explain that with leg work, head work, and hand work, many materials can be secured merely by requesting them. A beneficial by-product is the possible involvement of the children in the class. Often they can assist in the gathering of materials suitable for specific purposes. There are some dangers to keep in mind. Children with good intentions may pressure parents; may bring things from home without permission; and sometimes may pick up things that have not been actually discarded. Still, there are many things that are burned as trash, or otherwise destroyed, that could be used as teaching aids. With caution the children may locate them. Their parents may work as carpenters or grocery clerks, or have access to such things as outdated sample books of wall paper, paints, or pictures. The list of possibilities is endless. Warner makes some valuable suggestions: small, empty telephone cable spools for the outdoor play area; crates for storage space; old tires for playground swings; samples of carpeting, scrap paper, scraps of fabric, discarded clothing and empty food containers. The teacher and her children, or their parents can check the possibilities of the area.

Every teacher of young children becomes something of a scavenger and a hoarder. This can be overdone. One teacher boasts that she never throws anything away. That may be carrying a good idea too far, but the basic attitude is fine. Many teachers show high creativity in seeing some potential for use in almost anything available.

Teacher-Provided Materials

Probably every teacher at sometime puts some of his own money into his own classroom situation. The teacher has already invested thousands of dollars to secure a college education. He will donate much more to various charitable institutions in the course of a life time. This text is not suggesting that money spent in teaching should be taken from contributions to church or other organizations. Still, it is not often these days that an individual has the opportunity to make a direct gift to help a group of children. Besides its helping to make teaching easier, it is, also, under present law, tax deductible.

Quite apart from this, there are emergencies and economies within the province of most teachers. If the school has the means to provide a few dollars but not the much larger expense involved in the purchase of finger paint materials, play dough, paste, and other such materials, teachers will usually have their favorite set of recipes and instructions for these things.

[7] Dianne Warner, *Beautiful Junk* (Washington, D. C.: Office of Economic Opportunity, 1966), p. 12.

If needed, most teachers can afford the small cost of some of the supplies involved.

Parents

What parents can provide in the way of materials depends on many factors. In one kindergarten an individual parent with free time took great pride (and, apparently, found enjoyment and satisfaction) in being able to construct a house and furniture. Sometimes groups of parents can undertake projects in which some contribute labor and others provide materials. Such projects may come through the parent-teacher group, or they may develop out of contacts with interested parents. The parent-teacher association in some schools provides funds directly to the teacher to spend as she pleases to supplement the materials for her room. Individual parents may be able to direct the teacher to sources that would not otherwise be available for needed materials.

Teacher, Parent, Community Cooperation

There are projects that can involve just about everyone. For example, one class has a shortage of rhythm instruments, and funds are not available for the purchase of additional ones. A teacher could take as her own project the making of a drum. This could involve her own work and a little expense for the covering. It could also involve the gift of a nail keg or a round wooden bowl or cardboard carton by a local merchant. Some of the children may have simple musical instruments at home that they can bring to class for their own use. Through the joint efforts of the teacher and various members of the community other instruments could be crafted. Heavy wire bent into the shape of a horseshoe and large nails make acceptable triangles. Ordinary blocks and pieces of wood serve many uses. Sandpaper glued on to blocks of wood gives an interesting sound when rubbed together. Various lengths and sizes of dowelling can be used to illustrate many principles of sound effects. Glasses with various levels of water and different kinds of bells will provide many different kinds of sounds and also illustrate a variety of scientific concepts. The suggestions of the materials needed could come from the teacher, the particular materials could be supplied by the community, and the children could be involved in the "manufacture." The children not only receive enjoyment from the final product, but they also have the opportunity to learn many concepts through their experiences. In particular, they learn that even "ordinary" things have rhythm, tone, and quality of sound.

The search for and construction of equipment must be kept in harmony with the total program. The teacher cannot spend all of her time collecting and building equipment. How much she will do depends partly on the needs, partly on what she personally enjoys, and partly on the cooperation she receives.

The education of the future will call for many types of equipment and materials that neither teachers nor parents should be expected to furnish. If such materials further the learning experiences of children, especially if they make those experiences more pleasant and meaningful, they are probably worth whatever the cost may be. If they free the teacher to work with small groups and individuals more of the time, they are very worthwhile.

In the school program a place and need for the creativity and contributions of parents, friends, and the children themselves will always exist. In this technical age, perhaps more than ever before, all need to feel that they have made some direct and personal contribution to the cause of education. Perhaps, too, there is need to show the taxpayer that the teacher, too, is willing to share by contributing to the program.

Summary

Early childhood education requires materials and equipment. The lack of proper tools may hinder the children's learning experiences. The teacher should have on hand estimates of what may be needed, catalogs of companies from which materials can be secured, an understanding of purposes and criteria, and a plan as to which to secure first or what has priority. She also needs to be resourceful in finding and developing her own materials and in involving the parents, children, and community. Overall, the emphasis must be on suitable and adequate materials. Many of these will come from commercial sources. There will always be a place for the creativity of teachers and the involvement of all interested parties in the provision of education equipment for the best types of learning for young children.

Suggested Readings

Included in the brief lists below are books that have proved especially enjoyable and/or profitable. They are grouped under four headings: (1) General, (2) Nursery School, (3) Kindergarten, and (4) Primary.

General Readings in Early Childhood Education

Auleta, Michael S. *Foundations of Early Childhood Education.* New York: Random House, 1969. Probably the most helpful collection of readings specifically devoted to the field of early childhood education.

Bruner, Jerome S. *The Process of Education.* New York: Vintage Books, 1960. Not specifically on the education of young children, but the concepts are important and pertinent.

Ginott, Haim G. *Between Parent and Child.* New York: Avon, 1965. Addressed to parents, but many of its ideas will help the teacher in her relationship wtih her students. Delightful reading.

Glasser, William. *Schools Without Failure.* New York: Harper & Row, 1969. Glasser, a psychiatrist who has worked successfully with delinquent girls with his Reality Therapy, examines the inner-city school. Although the book is primarily for teachers of slightly older children, the basic ideas deserve thoughtful consideration by all.

Holt, John. *How Children Learn.* New York: Pitman, 1967. All of Holt's books are stimulating and very readable. This volume, however, is the one concerned the

most with the age level considered in this text. If the teacher of young children
could read only one book, this one might well be IT!

Miel, Alice (ed.). *Creativity in Teaching.* Belmont, Calif.: Wadsworth Publishing, 1961.
A collection of essays on the practical aspects of creativity and teaching that has
many applications to early childhood education.

Nursery School

Books that deal with both the nursery school and kindergarten levels have been
placed in this section. They all have bearing on the work of the nursery school
teacher. Some will be equally helpful to the kindergarten teacher.

Association for Childhood Education International. *Nursery School Portfolio.* Washington, D. C.: ACEI, 1961. A collection of brief discussions dealing with various
aspects of the nursery school.

Axline, Virginia M. *Dibs: In Search of Self.* New York: Ballantine, 1964. Paperback.
A book about therapy for a disturbed child. It could be placed under the general
heading, but the story does begin in a nursery school.

Bereiter, Carl, and Siegfried Englemann. *Teaching Disadvantaged Children in the
Preschool.* Englewood Cliffs, N. J.: Prentice-Hall, 1966. If the teacher knows other
views and can keep this in perspective, it is interesting and potentially helpful.
It suggests a directive and therapeutic approach to specific disadvantages of
children.

Bromwich, Rose M. *Developing the Language of Young Disadvantaged Children.*
Washington, D. C.: National Education Association, 1968. A balanced view of
effective but less directive ways of helping the disadvantaged child than those
suggested by Bereiter.

Janis, Marjorie Graham. *A Two-Year-Old Goes to Nursery School.* New York: National
Association for the Education of Young Children, 1965. The story of one little girl
and her year of adjustment to nursery school is presented here chiefly because it
is difficult to find material on this age level in the nursery school.

Landreth, Catherine. *Early Childhood: Behavior and Learning.* New York: Knopf, 1967.
An exceptionally well-written text. It is most helpful in providing an understanding
of the development from conception on through the early months, but covers the
period in life up to the age of six.

National Association for the Education of Young Children. *Montessori in Perspective.*
Washington, D. C.: NAEYC, 1966. A valuable collection of articles that attempt to
do exactly what the title indicates.

Read, Katherine. *The Nursery School: A Human Relations Laboratory.* Philadelphia:
Saunders, 1966. A good text for nursery school teachers that emphasizes the social
rather than the potential intellectual learnings of the nursery school.

Schulman, Anne Shaaker. *Absorbed in Living: Children Learn.* Washington, D. C.:
National Association for the Education of Young Children, 1967. An interesting
account of a parent-sponsored nursery-kindergarten project.

Standing, E. M. *Maria Montessori: Her Life and Work.* New York: New American
Library, 1962. A popular and pro-Montessori book that is particularly helpful in
explaining Montessori's life and concepts.

Kindergarten

Several books listed just above are equally applicable to this section.

Association for Childhood Education International. *Portfolio for Kindergarten Teachers.* Washington, D. C.: ACEI, 1951. Despite its date of publication, still useful.

Heffernan, Helen, and Vivian Edmiston Todd. *The Kindergarten Teacher.* Lexington, Mass.: Heath, 1960. One of the more helpful books dealing with the broad area of kindergarten programs.

Hymes, James L., Jr. *Teaching the Child Under Six.* Columbus, Ohio: Merrill, 1968. Hymes is the author of many books of value to teachers in early childhood education. They tend to be clearly written, easily read, and eloquent presentations of a practical, child developmental approach to education.

Primary Education

There are literally hundreds of books that would prove useful for some phase of teaching on the primary-age level. The specific suggestions are limited, partially because more are given under the heading "General."

Association for Childhood Education International. *Primary Education: Changing Dimensions.* Washington, D. C.: ACEI, 1965. A collection of helpful articles on primary education.

Cohen, S. Alan. *Teach Them All to Read.* New York: Random House, 1969. A book with a wealth of practical suggestions for the teaching of reading.

Goodlad, John I., and Robert H. Anderson. *The Nongraded Elementary School.* New York: Harcourt, Brace Jovanovich, 1963. One of the better books dealing with a concept that appears vital to the improvement of education—advancing each child at the child's own pace rather than the pass-fail system.

Stuart, Jesse. *The Thread That Runs So True.* New York: Scribner, 1949. This could be listed under general. It gives Stuart's experiences and developing insights in teaching, which started in a one-room school in the mountains of Kentucky. In time he moved on to high school teaching, administration, and then to writing. There is abundant application to the work of the primary teacher.

Bibliography

Almy, Millie. *Young Children's Thinking*. New York: Teachers College, Columbia University, 1966.

Anderson, Margaret. *The Children of the South*. New York: Delta, 1958.

Anderson, Robert H. *Teaching in a World of Change*. New York: Harcourt, Brace Jovanovich, 1966.

Anderson, Verna Dieckman. *Reading and Young Children*. New York: Macmillan, 1968.

Arnoff, Frances Webber. *Music and Young Children*. New York: Holt, Rinehart and Winston, 1969.

Association for Childhood Education International. *Art Guide: Let's Make a Picture*. Washington, D. C.: ACEI, 1969.

_____. *Creating with Materials for Work and Play*. 1957.

_____. *Early Childhood: Crucial Years for Learning*. 1966.

_____. *Equipment and Supplies: Tested and Approved for Preschool/School/ Home*.

_____. *Feelings and Learning*. 1965.

_____. *Housing for Early Childhood Education: Centers for Growing and Learning*. 1968.

_____. *New Directions in Mathematics*. 1965.

_____. *Nursery School Portfolio*. 1961.

_____. *Parents-Children-Teachers: Communication*. 1969.

_____. *Portfolio for Kindergarten Teachers*. 1951.

_____. *Primary Education: Changing Dimensions*. 1965.

_____. *Readings from Childhood Education*. 1966.

_____. *Toward Better Kindergartens*. 1965.

————. *Young Children and Science.* 1964.

Association for Counselor Education and American School Counselor Association. Joint Committee on the Elementary School Counselor. *Report,* April 2, 1966. Washington, D. C.: American Personnel and Guidance Association. Mimeographed.

Auleta, Michael S. *Foundations of Early Childhood Education.* New York: Random House, 1969.

Axline, Virginia M. *Dibs: In Search of Self.* New York: Ballantine, 1964.

Baldwin, Joseph. "The Transition Grade," *Young Children,* 24 (1968), 90–93.

Bandura, Albert. *Principles of Behavior Modification.* New York: Holt, Rinehart and Winston, 1969.

Barach, Carol, and Caroline Bird. "How Babies Learn to Talk," *Woman's Day,* 32 (1969), 62–63, 101–102.

Barman, Alicerose S. "Four-Year Old Development," in Joanne Wylie (ed.), *A Creative Guide for Preschool Teachers.* Racine, Wis.: Western Publishing, 1966.

Barron, Frank. *Creative Person and Creative Process.* New York: Holt, Rinehart and Winston, 1969.

Battle, J. A., and Robert L. Shannon. *The New Idea in Education.* New York: Harper & Row, 1968.

Bereiter, Carl, and Siegfried Engelmann. *Teaching Disadvantaged Children in the Preschool.* Englewood Cliffs, N. J.: Prentice-Hall, 1966.

Berson, Minnie Perrin. *Project Head Start: Daily Program III—For a Child Development Center.* Washington, D. C.: Office of Economic Opportunity, 1967.

Bettelheim, Bruno. *Love is Not Enough.* New York: Collier Books, 1965.

————. "Reading the Signs of Mental Health," in Michael S. Auleta (ed.), *Foundations of Early Childhood Education: Readings.* New York: Random House, 1969.

Beyer, Evelyn. *Nursery School Settings—Invitation to What?* Washington, D. C.: National Association for the Education of Young Children, 1958.

————. *Sharing: A New Level in Teacher-Parent Relationships.* Washington, D. C.: Association for Childhood Education International, 1959.

Black, Jonathan. "Street Academies: One Step Off the Sidewalk," *Saturday Review,* 52 (1969), 88–89, 100–101.

Brameld, Theodore. "Illusions and Disillusions in American Education," *Phi Delta Kappan,* 50 (1968), 202–207.

Brandwine, Aliza. "Upbringing of Children in Kibbutzim of Israel," *Young Children,* 24 (1969), 265–272.

Brogan, Peggy. "The Case for Creativity," in Alice Miel (ed.), *Creativity in Teaching.* Belmont, Calif.: Wadsworth Publishing, 1961.

Bromwich, Rose M. *Developing the Language of Young Disadvantaged Children.* Washington, D. C.: National Education Association, 1968.

————. "Some Correlates of Stimulus-Bound Versus Stimulus-Free Verbal Responses to Pictures by Young Negro Boys." Unpublished Ph.D. dissertation. Los Angeles: University of California, 1967.

Bronfenbrenner, Urie. "The Dream of the Kibbutz," *Saturday Review,* 52 (1969), 72–73, 83–85.

Brown, Roger. "Three Processes in the Child's Acquisition of Syntax," *Harvard Educational Review,* 34 (1964), 133–151.

Bruner, Jerome S. *The Process of Education.* New York: Vintage, 1960.

————. *Toward a Theory of Instruction.* New York: Norton, 1966.

————, Rose R. Olver, and Patricia M. Greenfield. *Studies in Cognitive Growth.*

New York: Wiley, 1966.

Burton, William H., and Helen Heffernan. *The Step Beyond: Creativity*. Washington, D. C.: National Education Association, 1964.

Burts, Eleanor, Joan Kennedy, and Jean Lutz. "Self-Selection and Self-Direction," *Toward Better Kindergartens*. Washington, D. C.: Association for Childhood Education International, 1965.

Caldwell, Bettye M. *Project Head Start: Daily Program II—For a Child Development Center*. Washington, D. C.: Office of Economic Opportunity, 1968.

Cass, James. "The Crucial Years Before Six," *Saturday Review*, 51 (1968), 59.

Cherry, Clare. *Creative Movement for the Developing Child—A Nursery School Handbook for Non-Musicians*. Palo Alto, Calif.: Fearon Publishers, 1968.

Cheyney, Arnold B. *Teaching Culturally Disadvantaged in the Elementary School*. Columbus, Ohio: Merrill, 1967.

Christensen, Anne L. "Forces Which Change Perceptions," *Primary Education: Changing Dimensions*. Washington, D. C.: Association for Childhood Education International, 1965.

Christensen, Oscar C. "Education: A Model for Counseling in the Elementary School," *Elementary School Guidance and Counseling*, 4 (1969), 13.

Clasen, Robert E. *On To The Classroom*. Madison, Wis.: Dembar Educational Research Services, 1969.

Cohen, S. Alan. *Teach Them All to Read*. New York: Random House, 1969.

Cole, Michael and Sheila. "Russian Nursery Schools," *Psychology Today*, 2 (1968), 23–28.

Coles, Robert. *Children of Crisis*. New York: Dell, 1967.

Colorado State Department of Education. *Kindergarten Guidebook*. Denver: State Department of Education, 1960.

Community Playthings. *Criteria for Selecting Play Equipment for Early Childhood Education*. Rifton, N. Y.: Community Playthings, 1967.

Conant, James Bryan. *The Education of American Teachers*. New York: McGraw-Hill, 1963.

Connor, Jay Davis. "Parent Participation Pays Dividends," *Review of Educational Research* 22 (1952), p. 321.

Cornelisen, Ann. *Torregreca*. Boston: Little, Brown, 1969.

Cox, Donald. "Learning on the Road," *Saturday Review*, 52 (1969), 71.

Cunningham, Luvern L. "Hey, Man, You Our Principal? Urban Education as I Saw It," *Phi Delta Kappan*, 51 (1969), 123–128.

Curtis, S. J., and M. E. A. Boultwood. *A Short History of Educational Ideas*. London: University Tutorial Press, 1953.

Daniels, Elva S. *Creative Rhythms for Your Class*. Dansville, N. Y.: Owen Publishing, 1960.

Darrow, Helen Fisher, and R. Van Allen. "Independent Activities for Creative Learning," in Alice Miel (ed.), *Practical Suggestions for Teaching*. New York: Teachers College, Columbia University, 1961.

Dennison, George. *The Lives of Children: The Story of the First Street School*. New York: Random House, 1969.

————. "An Environment to Grow In," *Saturday Review*, 52 (1969), 74–76.

Detjen, Ervin Winfred and Mary Ford. *Elementary School Guidance*. New York: McGraw-Hill, 1963.

Dolan, Veronica. "Stag Kindergarten," *Look*, 33 (1969), M.

Doll, Ronald C., and Robert S. Fleming. *Children Under Pressure.* Columbus, Ohio: Merrill, 1966.

Edinger, Lois V. "Schools for the Seventies and Beyond," *Today's Education,* 58 (1969), 74–75.

Edman, Irwin. *Arts and the Man.* New York: Norton, 1949.

Edwards, Esther P. "Kindergarten Is Too Late," *Saturday Review,* 51 (1968), 68–70, 76–79.

Edwards, Morton. *Your Child—Today.* New York: Permabooks, 1960.

Ellison, Louise. "Mathematics for the Very Young," *Parents'* 44 (1969), 48, 77, 79–81.

Estvan, Frank J. "Teaching the Very Young: Procedures for Developing Inquiry Skills," *Phi Delta Kappan,* 50 (1969), 389–393.

Evans, Ellis D. *Children: Readings in Behavior and Development.* New York. Holt, Rinehart and Winston, 1968.

Fagan, Edward R. *English and the Disadvantaged.* Scranton, Penn.: International Textbook, 1967.

Fantini, Mario D. "Beyond Cultural Deprivation and Compensatory Education," *Psychiatry and Social Science Review,* 3 (1969), 6–13.

————, and Gerald Weinstein. *The Disadvantaged: Challenge to Education.* New York: Harper & Row, 1968.

Fleming, J. Carl. "Pupil Tutors and Tutees Learn Together," *Today's Education,* 58 (1969), 22–24.

Flesch, Rudolf. *Why Johnny Can't Read.* New York: Popular Library, 1955.

Foshay, Arthur W. "The Creative Process Described," in Alice Miel (ed.), *Creativity in Teaching.* Belmont, Calif.: Wadsworth Publishing, 1961.

Foster, Josephine, and Neith E. Headley. *Education in the Kindergarten.* New York: American Book, 1966.

Frasier, James E. *An Introduction to the Study of Education.* New York: Harper & Row, 1965.

Frost, Joe L. *Early Childhood Education Rediscovered.* New York: Holt, Rinehart and Winston, 1968.

————, and Glenn R. Hawkes. *The Disadvantaged Child—Issues and Innovations.* Boston: Houghton Mifflin, 1966.

————, and G. Thomas Rowland. "The Seventies: A Time for Giant Steps," *Childhood Education,* 46 (1969), 4–13.

Gardner, John W. "The Ever-Renewing Society," *Saturday Review,* 46 (1963), 92–95.

Getzels, Jacob W., and Philip W. Jackson. *Creativity and Intelligence.* New York: Wiley, 1962.

Gibson, E. "Development of Perception: Discrimination of Depth Compared with Discrimination of Graphic Symbols," in J. C. Wright and J. Kagan (eds.), "Basic Cognitive Processes in Children," *Monogr. Soc. Res. Child Development,* 28 (1963), 5–32.

Ginott, Haim G. *Between Parent and Child.* New York: Avon, 1965.

Glasser, William. *Schools Without Failure.* New York: Harper & Row, 1969.

Good, H. G. *A History of Western Education.* New York: Macmillan, 1949.

Goodlad, John I. "Meeting Children Where They Are," *Saturday Review,* 48 (1965), 57–59, 72–74.

————. *School, Curriculum, and the Individual.* Waltham, Mass.: Blaisdell, 1966.

————. "The Schools vs. Education," *Saturday Review,* 52 (1969), 59–61, 80–82.

————, and Robert H. Anderson. *The Nongraded Elementary School.* New York: Harcourt, Brace Jovanovich, 1963.

Halpern, Ray. "Tactics for Integration," *Saturday Review,* 51 (1968), 47–49, 66.

Hartley, Ruth E., and Robert M. Goldenson. *The Complete Book of Children's Play.* New York: Crowell, 1963.

Hartshorne, Hugh, and Mark A. May, "Studies in the Nature of Character," *Studies in Deceit.* Vol. 1. New York: Macmillan, 1928.

Hartup, Willard W., and Nancy L. Smothergill. *The Young Child: Reviews of Research.* Washington, D. C.: National Association for the Education of Young Children, 1967.

Haupt, Dorothy. *Science Experiences for Nursery School Children.* Washington, D. C.: National Association for the Education of Young Children, no date.

Hechinger, Fred M. *Pre-School Education Today.* Garden City, N. Y.: Doubleday, 1966.

Heffernan, Helen. *Guiding the Young Child.* Lexington, Mass.: Heath, 1959.

————, and Vivian Edmiston Todd. *The Kindergarten Teacher.* Lexington, Mass.: Heath, 1960.

Herndon, James. *The Way It Spozed to Be.* New York: Bantam, 1969.

Hess, R. D., and V. C. Shipman, "Early Experience and the Socialization of Cognitive Modes in Children," *Child Development,* 36 (1965), 869–886.

Hill, George E., and Eleanore Braun Luckey. *Guidance for Children in Elementary Schools.* New York: Appleton-Century-Crofts, 1969.

Hollingshead, August B. *Elmtown's Youth.* New York: Wiley, 1949.

Holt, John. *How Children Fail.* New York: Pitman, 1964.

————. *How Children Learn.* New York: Pitman, 1967.

————. "School is Bad for Children," *Saturday Evening Post,* 242 (1969), 12–15.

————. *The Underachieving School.* New York: Pitman, 1969.

Huey, J. Frances. *Teaching Primary Children.* New York: Holt, Rinehart and Winston, 1965.

Hughes, Marie M. "Integrity in Classroom Relationships," in Alice Miel (ed.), *Creativity in Teaching.* Belmont, Calif.: Wadsworth Publishing, 1961.

Hunt, Paul R., and Elvin I. Rasof. "Discipline: Function or Task?" in Robert D. Strom (ed.), *The Inner City Classroom: Teacher Behaviors.* Columbus, Ohio: Merrill, 1966.

Hymes, James L., Jr. *Before the Child Reads.* White Plains, N. Y.: Row, Peterson, 1958.

————. *Teaching the Child Under Six.* Columbus, Ohio: Merrill, 1968.

Ilg, Frances L., and Louise Bates Ames. *Child Behavior.* New York: Dell, 1955.

————. *School Readiness: Behavior Tests Used at the Gesell Institute.* New York: Harper & Row, 1965.

Inhelder, Barbel, and Jean Piaget. *The Early Growth of Logic in the Child.* New York: Norton, 1964.

Janis, Marjorie Graham. *A Two-Year-Old Goes to Nursery School.* New York: National Association for the Education of Young Children, 1965.

Jenkins, Gladys Gardner, "Understanding Differences in Parents," *Parents-Children-Teachers: Communication.* Washington, D. C.: Association for Childhood Education International, 1969.

————, "What Price Pressures?" *Don't Push Me!* Washington, D. C.: Association for Childhood Education International, 1960.

Jersild, Arthur T. *When Teachers Face Themselves.* New York: Teachers College, Columbia University, 1955.

Joseph, Stephen M. *The Me Nobody Knows.* New York: Avon, 1969.

Kaplan, J. D. *Dialogues of Plato.* New York: Pocket, 1950.

Keliher, Alice V. "Do We Push Children?" *Don't Push Me!* Washington, D. C.: Association for Childhood Education International, 1960.

Kellogg, Rhoda with Scott O'Dell. *The Psychology of Children's Art.* New York: Random House, 1967.

King, Edith W., and August Kerber. *The Sociology of Early Childhood Education.* New York: American Book, 1968.

Kneller, George F. *Foundations of Education.* New York: Wiley, 1967.

Kohl, Herbert. *36 Children.* New York: New American Library, 1967.

Koplitz, Eugene D. *Guidance in the Elementary School: Theory, Research, and Practice.* Dubuque, Iowa: Brown, 1968.

Kozol, Jonathan. *Death at an Early Age.* Boston: Houghton Mifflin, 1967.

Kritchevsky, Sybil, Elizabeth Prescott, and Lee Walling. *Planning Environments for Young Children: Physical Space.* Washington, D. C.: National Association for the Education of Young Children, 1969.

Landreth, Catherine. *Early Childhood: Behavior and Learning.* New York: Knopf, 1967.

Langdon, Grace, and Irving W. Stout. *Teaching in the Primary Grades: Methods and Techniques for Kindergarten Through the First Three Grades.* New York: Macmillan, 1964.

LeShan, Eda J. *The Conspiracy Against Childhood.* New York: Atheneum, 1967.

Lindstrom, Miriam. *Children's Art.* Berkeley: University of California, 1959.

Logan, Lillian M. *Teaching the Young Child.* Boston: Houghton Mifflin, 1960.

Lohman, Joseph D. "Expose—Don't Impose," *National Education Association Journal,* 55 (1966), 23–26.

Loretan, Joseph O., and Shelley Umans. *Teaching the Disadvantaged—New Curriculum Approaches.* New York: Teachers College, Columbia University, 1966.

Luszki, Margaret Barron, and Richard Schmuck, "Pupil Perceptions of Parental Attitudes Toward School," in Jerome M. Seidman (ed.), *The Child: A Book of Readings.* New York: Holt, Rinehart and Winston, 1969.

Mackintosh, Helen K., and Lillian Gore. *Educating Disadvantaged Children Under Six.* Washington, D. C.: U. S. Department of Health, Education, and Welfare, 1965.

Maier, Henry W. *Three Theories of Child Development.* New York: Harper & Row, 1969.

Mallery, David. *High School Students Speak Out.* New York: Harper & Row, 1962.

May, Rollo. "Love and Will," *Psychology Today,* 3 (1969), 17–64.

_____. *Man's Search for Himself.* New York: Signet, 1967.

Mead, Margaret. *Coming of Age in Samoa: A Study of Adolescent Sex in Primitive Society.* New York: Mentor, 1928.

Merritt, Helen. *Guiding Free Expression in Children's Art.* New York: Holt, Rinehart and Winston, 1964.

Meyer, Adolphe E. *An Educational History of the American People.* New York: McGraw-Hill, 1957.

Michener, James A. *America vs. America.* New York: New American Library, 1969.

Miel, Alice. *Creativity in Teaching.* Belmont, Calif.: Wadsworth Publishing, 1961.

Miller, Keith. *The Taste of New Wine.* Waco, Texas: Word Books, 1965.

Mizer, Jean E. "Special Feature on the Beginning Teacher: Dear JM . . ." *Today's Education,* 57 (1968), 21–25.

Monroe, Marian, and Bernice Rogers. *Foundations for Reading: Informal Pre-Reading Procedures.* Glenview, Ill.: Scott, Foresman, 1964.

Montessori, Maria. *The Absorbent Mind.* New York: Dell, 1967.

_____. *The Montessori Method.* New York: Schocken, 1964.

Montgomery, Chandler. *Art for Teachers of Children.* Columbus, Ohio: Merrill, 1968.

Morgenstern, Anne. *Grouping in the Elementary School.* New York: Pitman, 1966.

Mussen, Paul Henry, Jane Janeway Conger, and Jerome Kagan. *Child Development and Personality.* New York: Harper & Row, 1969.

National Association for the Education of Young Children. *Essentials of Nursery Education.* Washington, D.C.: NAEYC, 1966.

_____. *Montessori in Perspective.* 1966.

National Education Association. "If the Shoe Fits," *Today's Education,* 58 (1969), 41–43.

_____. "Kindergarten Education, 1967–68," 47 (1969), 10.

_____. *Those First School Years.* Washington, D.C.: NEA, 1960.

Newbury, Josephine. *Church Kindergarten Resource Book.* Richmond, Va.: Covenant Life Curriculum, 1964.

Newsweek, March 17, 1969, pp. 40–42.

Nichols, Hildred, and Lois Williams. *Learning About Role-Playing for Children and Teachers.* Washington, D.C.: Association for Childhood Education International, 1960.

Nicol, Synva. "A Good Day for the Fives," *Portfolio for Kindergarten Teachers.* Washington, D.C.: Association for Childhood Education International, 1960.

Nixon, Clifford L. (Unpublished notes) prepared for Workshop of the North Carolina Kindergarten Association, 1966.

Nixon, Robert C. *The Art of Growing: A Guide to Psychological Maturity.* New York: Random House, 1962.

Nixon, Ruth H. *Acceptance of a New Curriculum by Parents.* Unpublished report.

_____. "How Busy Should the Young Child Be?" *The Christian Home,* 1 (1969), 4–6 and 63.

_____. *Reactions of Children to Pictures and Questions Related to God.* Unpublished Ed. D. dissertation. Berkeley: University of California.

_____. *A Survey of Results of Sunday School Experience of Young Children as Shown by Reactions to Structured Pictures.* Unpublished Seminar paper. Berkeley: University of California, 1953.

_____, and Clifford L. *The Art of Kindergarten Instruction.* Pembroke, N.C.: Pembroke State, 1969.

_____, _____. "A Closer Look at Team Teaching," *Spearhead,* 2, 1966, 10, 11.

North Carolina State Department of Public Instruction. *Art in the Elementary Classroom: Grades One–Eight.* Raleigh, N.C.: State Department of Public Instruction, 1963.

_____. *Kindergarten Curriculum Guide.* Preliminary draft for discussion purposes only. Raleigh, N.C.: State Department of Public Instruction, 1967.

Office of Economic Opportunity. *Project Head Start: Daily Program I—For a Child Development Center.* Washington, D.C.: OEO, 1967.

_____. *Project Head Start: Equipment and Supplies.* 1967.

_____. *Project Head Start: Parental Involvement.* 1969.

_____. *Project Head Start: Parents Are Needed.* 1967.

Osborn, Alexander. *Your Creative Power.* New York: Dell, 1948.

Otto, Wayne, and Richard A. McMenemy. *Corrective and Remedial Teaching: Principles and Practices.* Boston: Houghton Mifflin, 1966.

Passaw, A. Harry. *Education in Depressed Areas.* New York: Teachers College, Columbia University, 1963.

Phi Delta Kappan. "A 'Victory' for Teacher Power Over Community Power in New York

City?" *Phi Delta Kappan,* 50 (1968), 138.

_____. "Gallup Measures Attitudes Toward Schools by Public Readiness to Pay—With Grim Results," *Phi Delta Kappan,* 51 (1969), 157, 163.

Phillips, E. Lakin, and Daniel N. Wiener. *Short-Term Psychotherapy and Structured Behavior Change.* New York: McGraw-Hill, 1966.

Phillips, J. B. *The New Testament in Modern English.* New York: Macmillan, 1962.

Piaget, Jean. *The Child's Conception of Number.* New York: Norton, 1965.

_____. *The Construction of Reality in the Child.* New York: Basic Books, 1954.

_____. *The Language and Thought of the Child.* New York: Meridian, 1955.

_____. *The Moral Judgment of the Child.* London: Free Press, 1932.

_____. *The Origins of Intelligence in Children.* New York: Norton, 1963.

_____. *Play, Dreams and Imitation in Childhood.* New York: Norton, 1962.

_____. *Six Psychological Studies.* New York: Random House, 1967.

_____. Foreword to Millie Almy, *Young Children's Thinking.* New York: Teachers College, Columbia University, 1966.

Pitcher, Evelyn Goodenough, Miriam G. Lasher, Sylvia Feinburg, and Nancy C. Hammond. *Helping Young Children Learn.* Columbus, Ohio: Merrill, 1966.

Plato, *Republic,* from *Dialogues of Plato.* New York: Pocket, 1951.

Polos, Nicholas C. *The Dynamics of Team Teaching.* Dubuque, Iowa: Brown, 1965.

Postman, Neil, and Charles Weingartner. *Teaching as a Subversive Activity.* New York: Delacorte, 1969.

Rabkin, Leslie Y. and Karen. "Children of the Kibbutz," *Psychology Today,* 3 (1969), 40–46.

The Random House Dictionary of the English Language. New York: Random House, 1966.

Rasmussen, Margaret. *Reading.* Washington, D.C.: Association for Childhood Education International, 1956.

_____ (ed.). *Space Arrangement, Beauty in School.* Washington, D.C.: Association for Childhood Education International, 1958.

_____, and Lucy Prete. *Reading in the Kindergarten?* Washington, D.C.: Association for Childhood Education International, 1962.

_____, et al. *Literature with Children.* Washington, D.C.: Association for Childhood Education International, 1961.

_____, _____. *More About Reading.* Washington, D.C.: Association for Childhood Education International, 1959.

Read, Katherine. *The Nursery School: A Human Relations Laboratory.* Philadelphia: Saunders, 1966.

Redl, Fritz. *When We Deal with Children.* New York: Free Press, 1966.

Revised Standard Version of the Bible. Camden, N. J.: Thomas Nelson, 1953.

Rheingold, H., J. L. Gewirtz, and H. Ross. "Social Conditioning of Vocalizations in the Infant," *Journal of Comparative Physiological Psychology,* 52 (1959), 68–73.

Riessman, Frank. *The Culturally Deprived Child.* New York: Harper & Row, 1962.

Roberts, Wallace. "Can Urban Schools be Reformed?" *Saturday Review,* 52 (1969), 70–72, 87–91.

Robison, Helen F., and Bernard Spodek. *New Directions in the Kindergarten.* New York: Teachers College, Columbia University, 1965.

Roeper, Annemarie, and Irving E. Sigel. "Finding the Clue to Children's Thought Process," in Willard W. Hartup and Nancy L. Smothergill (eds.), *The Young Child: Reviews of Research.* Washington, D.C.: National Association for the Education of

Young Children, 1967.

Roucek, Joseph S. "Milestones in the History of the Negro in the United States," *International Review of Education* 10 (1964), 162–175.

Russell, David H. *Children's Thinking.* Boston: Ginn, 1956.

Sabath, Mildred R. "Children, Parents and Teachers," *Toward Better Kindergartens.* Washington, D.C.: Association for Childhood Education International, 1966.

Salot, Lorraine, and Jerome E. Leavitt. *The Beginning Kindergarten Teacher.* Minneapolis, Minn.: Burgess, 1965.

Schulman, Anne Shaaker. *Absorbed in Living: Children Learn.* Washington, D.C.: National Association for the Education of Young Children, 1967.

Scott, Louise Binder. *Learning Time with Language Experiences for Young Children.* New York: McGraw-Hill, 1968.

————, and J. J. Thompson. *Talking Time.* New York: McGraw-Hill, 1966.

Seidman, Jerome M. *The Child: A Book of Readings.* New York: Holt, Rinehart and Winston, 1969.

Seligman, Martin E. P. "For Helplessness: Can We Immunize the Weak?" *Psychology Today,* 3 (1969), 42–44.

Senesh, Lawrence. *Our Working World: Social Science Units.* Chicago: Science Research Associates, 1964.

Shaftel, Fannie R. and George. *Role Playing for Social Values.* Englewood Cliffs, N.J.: Prentice-Hall, 1967.

Shane, Harold G., Mary E. Reddin, and Margaret C. Gillespie. *Beginning Language Arts Instruction with Children.* Columbus, Ohio: Merrill, 1961.

————, and June Grant Shane. "Forecast for the 70's," *Today's Education,* 58 (1969), 9, 29–32.

————, ————. "Guidance at an Early Age," *Today's Education,* 58 (1969), 37–38.

Shaplin, Judson T., and Henry F. Olds, Jr. *Team Teaching.* New York: Harper & Row, 1964.

Sherer, Lorraine. *How Good Is Our Kindergarten?* Washington, D. C.: Association for Childhood Education International, 1959.

Shumsky, Abraham. *In Search of Teaching Style.* New York: Appleton-Century-Crofts, 1968.

Sigel, Irving E., and Frank H. Hasper. *Logical Thinking in Children: Research Based on Piaget's Theory.* New York: Holt, Rinehart and Winston, 1968.

Skinner, B. F. *Science and Human Behavior.* New York: Free Press, 1953.

————. *The Technology of Teaching.* New York: Appleton-Century-Crofts, 1968.

————. *Walden Two.* New York: Macmillan, 1948.

Smith, Elodie S. *The Continuous Growth Plan at Fairmont School, Richmond, California.* Unpublished M.A. dissertation. San Francisco State College, 1950.

Smith, Nila Banton, and Ruth Strickland. *Some Approaches to Reading.* Washington, D.C.: Association for Childhood Education International, 1969.

Spock, Benjamin. *Dr. Spock Talks With Mothers: Growth and Guidance.* Greenwich, Conn.: Fawcett, 1961.

Spodek, Bernard. "Motivation in Early Education," *Motivation.* Washington, D.C.: National Education Association, 1968.

————, H. Gerthon Morgan, and Harold G. Shane. *Motivation.* Washington, D.C.: National Education Association, 1968.

Spaulding, William E. *How Shall We Judge Them: A Discussion of Materials of Instructions.* Boston: Houghton Mifflin, 1961.

Standing, E. M. *Maria Montessori: Her Life and Work*. New York: New American Library, 1962.

————. *The Montessori Revolution in Education*. New York: Schocken, 1962.

Stone, L. Joseph, and Joseph Church. *Childhood and Adolescence: A Psychology of the Growing Person*. New York: Random House, 1968.

Strang, Ruth. *Reporting to Parents*. New York: Teachers College, Columbia University, 1947.

Strom, Robert D. *The Inner-City Classroom—Teacher Behaviors*. Columbus, Ohio: Merrill, 1966.

————. *Teaching in the Slum School*. Columbus, Ohio: Merrill, 1965.

Stuart, Jesse. *The Thread That Runs So True*. New York: Scribner, 1949.

Sunderlin, Sylvia, and Brooke Wills. *Aides to Teachers and Children*. Washington, D.C.: Association for Childhood Education International, 1967.

Tarnay, Elizabeth Doak. *What Does the Nursery School Teacher Teach?* Washington, D.C.: National Association for the Education of Young Children, 1965.

Tewksbury, John L. *Nongrading in the Elementary School*. Columbus, Ohio: Merrill, 1967.

Time, March 28, 1969, p. 56.

————. November 7, 1969, pp. 77, 80.

Todd, Daniel E., Jr. "For Each Child—His Own Curriculum," *North Carolina Education,* 35 (1969), 22–23, 58–59.

Todd, Vivian Edminston, and Helen Heffernan. *The Years Before School: Guiding Preschool Children*. New York: Macmillan, 1964.

Torrance, E. Paul. *Guiding Creative Talent*. Englewood Cliffs, N.J.: Prentice-Hall, 1962.

Ulich, Robert. *Education in Western Culture*. New York: Harcourt, Brace, Jovanovich, 1965.

————. *Three Thousand Years of Educational Wisdom: Selections from Great Documents*. Cambridge: Harvard University Press, 1948.

————. *History of Educational Thought*. New York: American Books, 1950.

Ullyette, Jean M. *Guidelines for Creative Writing*. Dansville, N.Y.: Owen, 1963.

United States Department of Health, Education, and Welfare. *United States Public School Enrollment in Kindergarten and First Grade*. Washington, D.C.: HEW, Children's Bureau, 1966.

U.S. News and World Report, 67 (1969), 32, 38, 50–52.

Usdan, Michael, and Frederick Bertolaet. *Teachers for the Disadvantaged: The Report of the School-University Teacher-Education Project*. Chicago: Follett, 1966.

Van Allen, Roach. *Attitudes and the Art of Teaching Reading*. Washington, D.C.: National Education Association, 1965.

Wahlquist, John T. *An Introduction to American Education*. New York: Ronald Press, 1947.

Wakin, Edward. "The Return of Montessori." *Montessori in Perspective*. Washington, D.C.: National Association for the Education of Young Children, 1966.

Wann, Kenneth D., Miriam Selchen Dorn, and Elizabeth Ann Liddle. *Fostering Intellectual Development in Young Children*. New York: Teachers College, Columbia University, 1962.

Warner, Dianne. *Beautiful Junk*. Washington, D.C.: Office of Economic Opportunity, 1966.

Warner, Sylvia-Ashton. *Teacher*. New York: Simon and Schuster, 1963.

Weikart, D. P. "Perry Preschool Project Progress Report." Ypsilanti, Mich. Public

Schools. June 1964. Mimeographed.

Wenzel, Evelyn. "Finding Meaning in Teaching," in Alice Miel, *Creativity in Teaching*. Belmont, Calif.: Wadsworth Publishing, 1961.

Wharton, John F. "Toward an Affirmative Morality," *Saturday Review*, 52 (1969), 11–13, 16.

Wilkerson, David. *The Little People*. New York: Pyramid Books, 1966.

Wills, Clarice, and Lucille Lindberg. *Kindergarten for To-day's Children*. Chicago: Follett, 1967.

Wilson, B. O. *On Relaxation*. Martinez, Calif.: Contra Costa County Schools, 1949. Mimeographed.

Woodruff, Asahel D. *Basic Concepts of Teaching: With Brief Readings*. San Francisco: Chandler, 1962.

Wylie, Joanne. *A Creative Guide for Preschool Teachers*. Racine, Wis.: Western Publishing Educational Services, 1966.

Young Children, 24 (1969), 194.

Appendix A
Sources of Information on
Early Childhood Education

Association for Childhood Education International
3615 Wisconsin Avenue, N. W.
Washington, D. C. 20016

Bank Street College of Education
69 Bank Street
New York, New York 10014

Child Study Association of America, Inc.
9 East 89th Street
New York, New York 10028

Children's Bureau
U. S. Department of Health, Education, and Welfare
330 Independence Avenue, S. W.
Washington, D. C. 20201

Information Retrieval Center on the Disadvantaged
Yeshiva University
55 Fifth Avenue
New York, New York 10003

National Association for the Education of Young Children
1834 Connecticut Avenue, N. W.
Washington, D. C. 20009

National Congress of Parents and Teachers
700 North Rush Street
Chicago, Illinois 60611

National Education Association
1201 16th Street, N. W.
Washington, D. C. 20036
(Request publications of the Elementary, Kindergarten, and Nursery Division.)

National Kindergarten Association
8 West 40th Street
New York, New York 10018

Teachers College Press
Columbia University
1234 Amsterdam Avenue
New York, New York 10027

Appendix B
Distributors of
Materials and Equipment

General

Childcraft Equipment Company, Inc.
115 East 23rd Street
New York, New York 10010

Community Playthings
Rifton, New York 12471

Creative Playthings, Inc.
P. O. Box 1100
Princeton, New Jersey 08540
(For catalogs—School Catalog; The Power of Play; The Critical Years; Creative
    Playthings.)

Field Educational Publications, Inc.
609 Mission Street
San Francisco, California 94105

Ideal School Supply Company
8312–46 Birkhoff Avenue
Chicago, Illinois 60620

Instructo Products Company
1635 North 55th Street
Philadelphia, Pennsylvania 19131

Judy Company
310 North 2nd Street
Minneapolis, Minnesota 55401

Learning Center, Inc.
Elementary Department
Princeton, New Jersey 08540

McGraw-Hill Book Company
Educational Games and Aids Division
330 West 42nd Street
New York, New York 10036

Novo Educational Toy and Equipment Corp.
585 Avenue of the Americas
New York, New York 10011

Peabody Language Development Kits (Level, preprimer)
American Guidance Services, Inc.
Publishers Building
Circle Pines, Minnesota 55014

Peripole Products, Inc.
51–17 Rockaway Beach Boulevard
Far Rockaway, L. I., New York 11691

Science Research Associates, Inc.
259 East Erie Street
Chicago, Illinois 60611

Society for Visual Education, Inc.
1345 Diversey Parkway
Chicago, Illinois 60614

Teaching Aids
A. Daigger and Company
159 West Kinzie Street
Chicago, Illinois 60610
(For Learning Aids for Young Children in Accordance with Montessori)

Records

Bowmar Records, Inc.
10515 Burbank Boulevard
North Hollywood, California 91601

Cheviot Corporation, Dept. M-68
Box 34485
Los Angeles, California 90034 (Distributors of Rhythms Productions Records)

Educational Records Sales
157 Chambers Street
New York, New York 10007

Rhythm Record Company
9203 Nichols Road
Oklahoma City, Oklahoma 73120

Stanley Bowmar Company, Inc.
12 Cleveland Street
Valhalla, New York 10595

Young People's Records (Children's Record Guild)
100 Sixth Avenue
New York, New York 10013

Index